LA

AIRFIELDS
IN THE SECOND
WORLD WAR

Aldon P. Ferguson

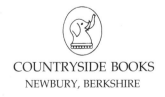

COUNTRYSIDE BOOKS
NEWBURY, BERKSHIRE

COUNTRYSIDE BOOKS
3 Catherine Road
Newbury, Berkshire

To view our complete range of books,
please visit us at
www.countrysidebooks.co.uk

ISBN 1 85306 873 X

The cover illustration shows a USAAF Douglas A20G Havoc
of 646th Bomb Squadron flying over Blackpool
and is reproduced from an original
painting by Colin Doggett

Designed by Mon Mohan

Produced through MRM Associates Ltd., Reading
Typeset by Techniset Typesetters, Merseyside
Printed by Cambridge University Press

CONTENTS

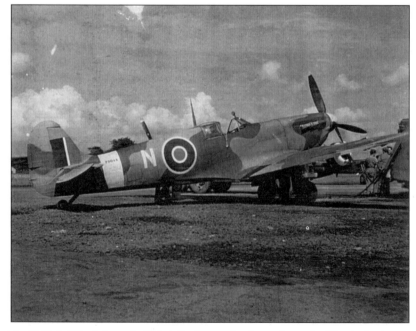

An RAF Spitfire being refuelled at Burtonwood prior to despatch. (Via Author)

LANCASHIRE'S SECOND WORLD WAR AIRFIELDS

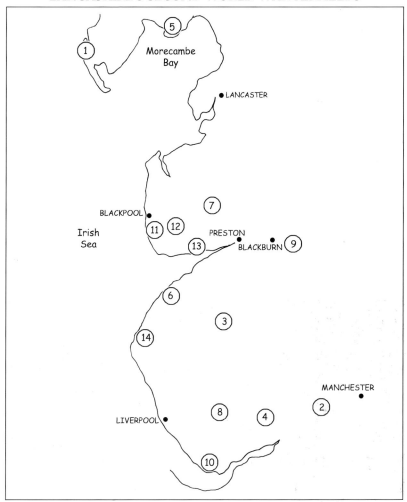

KEY TO MAP

1 Barrow-in-Furness
2 Barton
3 Burscough
4 Burtonwood
5 Cark
6 Hesketh Beach, Southport
7 Inskip

8 Knowsley Park
9 Samlesbury
10 Speke
11 Squires Gate
12 Blackpool (Stanley Park)
13 Warton
14 Woodvale

A view across a busy ramp at Burtonwood, with B-17s filling the foreground. (Via Author)

ABBREVIATIONS

AACU	Anti-Aircraft Co-operation Unit
AEF	Air Experience Flight
AFTS	Advanced Flying Training School
AM	Air Ministry
APC	Armament Practice Camp
ATC	Air Training Corps
Aux AF	Auxiliary Air Force
BAD	Base Air Depot
BADA	Base Air Depot Area
CAACU	Civilian Anti-Aircraft Co-operation Unit
CANS	Civilian Air Navigation School
CL	Chain Low
CLH	Chain Low Home
E&RFTS	Elementary & Reserve Flying Training School
ETO	European Theatre of Operations
FAA	Fleet Air Arm
Fg Off	Flying Officer
FTS	Flying Training School
HF/DF	High Frequency Direction Finding
HMS	His (Her) Majesty's Ship
GCI	Ground Controlled Interception
IFF	Identification – Friend or Foe
MAP	Ministry of Aircraft Production
MT	Motor Transport
MU	Maintenance Unit
NAAFI	Navy Army & Air Force Institute
OTU	Operational Training Unit
(P)AFU	(Pilot) Advanced Flying Unit
Plt Off	Pilot Officer
RAuxAF	Royal Auxiliary Air Force
RFS	Reserve Flying School
RNAS	Royal Navy Air Station
SLG	Satellite Landing Ground
Sqn Ldr	Squadron Leader
UAS	University Air Squadron
USAAC	United States Army Air Corps
USAAF	United States Army Air Force
USAF	United States Air Force
USN	US Navy
USNAS	United States Naval Air Station
VR	Volunteer Reserve
WAAF	Women's Auxiliary Air Force
Wg Cdr	Wing Commander

I
SETTING
THE SCENE

Although much of the UK aviation was pioneered in Lancashire it was the First World War which really made a major impact on the county. Aviation technology advanced at an amazing pace with factories in industrial Lancashire providing aircraft and all sorts of armaments for the war. Lancashire also lost tens of thousands of men in this tragic conflict. However, when the war ended in 1918, Lancashire only had airfields at Southport (Hesketh Park), Alexander Park, Manchester, Aintree, Liverpool and Stanley Park, Blackpool. Nationally, airfield development was on the increase, initially around the major army centres such as Larkhill, Aldershot (Farnborough), Stonehenge, Upavon and Netheravon (Salisbury Plain). Lancashire was considered too far from the active front line and out of enemy aircraft range at this time. This made the county a safe location, ideal for supplying tools of war, although two attacks had taken place in 1916 and 1918.

The inter-war years saw civil aviation develop still further with civil aerodromes opening at Barton, Manchester; Squires Gate, Blackpool and Speke, Liverpool but at the beginning of the Second World War, Lancashire still had no military airfield, for either defence or attack.

By the time of the second war, the German Luftwaffe had the means to reach the north-west of England, however, and in a matter of three years new airfields had been constructed for the RAF at Woodvale, Burtonwood, Warton, Cark and Barrow; for the Fleet Air Arm at Burscough and Inskip and for civilian aircraft contractors at Samlesbury. The RAF requisitioned all airfields at the outbreak of war hence civilian airfields suddenly became RAF Speke or RAF Barton.

The Early Years

But back to the beginning. In the early 20th century, going back to 1911, major aviation development and trials took place in Lancashire, on the beach at Waterloo, Freshfield and Southport. The first flight, piloted by Henry Farman, took place at Squires Gate, Blackpool on 18th October 1909 during the *Daily Mail*-sponsored Blackpool Flying week. Farman was one of six visiting professional pilots who joined with seven British amateurs bringing aviation to Lancashire for the first time. Other pioneers at that meeting included A V Roe, Paulham, Henri Rougier, Leblanc and Hubert Latham. Blackpool led the way by actively encouraging this meeting to the excitement of thousands of locals who flocked to the marked-out flying field and stood on the nearby sand dunes to watch. The longest flight of the week was by Henri Rougier in a Voisin biplane who flew 22 miles and 664 yards (nine laps) in just over 32 minutes.

This week stirred emotions, the desire to fly and to see men flying. It was followed by huge cash prizes offered by newspapers for epic record-making flights. The *Daily Mail* was again in the forefront, offering £10,000 for the first flight between London and Manchester whilst the Sir William Hartley Prize was £1,000 for the first to fly the 35

Henry Melly's original hangars on the beach at Waterloo in 1912. (Via Mike Lewis)

miles between Liverpool and Manchester. Racecourses offered good, open, flat land, with spectator terraces, and made ideal flying grounds for the early aviator. Aintree Racecourse at Liverpool was the venue for the American flying pioneer, Samuel Cody, in November 1909. The Hartley prize was not won and was withdrawn but the £10,000 London to Manchester prize was won by Louis Paulham in a Farman biplane, landing in Didsbury, Manchester on 28th April 1910.

Experimental aircraft were seen all over the county. As a result, safe sites were needed and the beach between Waterloo and Southport was considered ideal for test flying on flat land, with minimum risk of accidents or harm to the public. Bolton, Blackburn and Burnley saw other aviators of the time. A Burnley gentleman, William Cooke, ordered an aeroplane from Howard T Wright in 1909 and the local paper announced the formation of the East Lancashire Aeroplane and Motor Company that was to fly this machine, but it never happened. Samuel Smith developed a machine looking like a venetian blind and showed it at Bolton. Meanwhile, James Shaw built a glider in 1910 but suffered a heart attack before he could try it. Compton Paterson built three hangars at Freshfield in 1910, soon to be joined by others including Henry Greg Melly from Aigburth, Liverpool. Melly left Freshfield to set up the Liverpool Aviation School at Waterloo in early 1911 and built hangars on the beach there. Claude Grahame-White visited Freshfield many times, which became one of the most active flying centres in the country. More development took place further north when Southport beach was used and some hangars were erected just off the foreshore at Hesketh Park, immediately north of Southport.

1914–1918

The First World War stopped private and civilian flying and the Freshfield, Waterloo and Southport hangars were taken over by the military. No further civilian flying took place from Waterloo or Freshfield but Southport grew into an established military airfield (sand) when aircraft constructed at the Vulcan Engineering works at Crossens were taken to the beach at Hesketh Park Sands and flown to their destination.

The war saw a massive increase in the industrial strengths of Lancashire being put to military use. Factories sprang up in Manchester and many other parts of the county, to manufacture aircraft and all forms of military hardware. Liverpool, Birkenhead and Manchester docks imported war and subsistence materials from all over the world, particularly once the USA joined the war. The Lancashire coalfield provided heat and power for industry while huge engineering works in the industrial parts of east Lancashire, Liverpool and Preston turned their hand to the war effort. Two National Aircraft Factories were set up at Heaton Chapel, Manchester (National Aircraft Factory No 2) and Aintree, Liverpool (National Aircraft Factory No 3), with NAF No 1 being at Waddon, Croydon. These units were set up by the Ministry of Munitions for the construction and supply of aircraft and they were flown off adjoining grass landing grounds. In the case of Aintree, they used the adjacent racecourse. Heaton Chapel saw the test flying of almost 400 de Havilland DH9s and a few DH10s.

An area covering 70 acres at Stag Farm at Aintree had been requisitioned prior to the First World War but was never really developed until 1917 when the construction of a factory was started. Located between the racecourse, Ormskirk Road and the Leeds & Liverpool canal, several large workshops were also constructed ultimately employing over 2,630 employees. The factory produced Hispano-Suiza 200 hp engined Bristol F.2B aircraft but work did not commence until March 1918. The target was 40 aircraft per week. The factory became NAF No 3 on 17 October 1918 before any aircraft were built and eventually 126 Bristol F.2Bs were produced. It is possible that an order was received for Sopwith Snipes but was cancelled due to the end of the war. After the war the factory was renamed No 4 Aircraft Salvage Depot taking on responsibility for storage and disposal of up to 2,000 aircraft and 3,000 engines.

A further aircraft factory was constructed at Oldham. Many crated Handley Page 0/400s, delivered from the USA, were put together here. However, the end of the war saw the immediate cessation of aircraft factories and production stopped virtually instantly.

Lancashire had two Aircraft Acceptance Parks (AAP). One was formed in 1918 at Alexander Park, Didsbury, for the acceptance of aircraft from local manufacturers of Avro aircraft into the RAF (just formed from the Royal Flying Corps). It was later named No 15 (Manchester) AAP but disbanded in 1919 when aircraft production virtually ceased. The other AAP was No 11 formed on 15 August 1917 at Southport on Hesketh Park Sands (literally the beach) for the acceptance of new aircraft from the Vulcan Works in Crossens. This unit had two hangars constructed (and very little else) and a ramp for

12

aircraft to taxi onto the sand for take-off. The hangars remained and were taken over again by the RAF in Second World War (see separate chapter on Hesketh Park). The AAP was disbanded on 11 January 1918.

AV Roe had commenced aircraft construction at Miles Platting and Salford, with another aircraft factory established in the Electric Railway and Tramcar Works at Strand Road in Preston (later to become English Electric, British Aerospace and now BAE Systems). English Electric formed when four companies from Preston and Bradford amalgamated. They built two different designs of flying boats and flew them off the Ribble estuary but neither went into production. English Electric later developed to build and assemble thousands of aircraft for the RAF in the Second World War and they still exist as BAE Systems and still build military aircraft.

There were no specific Royal Flying Corps airfields established in Lancashire during the First World War with all flying taking place from manufacturers' airfields or the beach at Southport. Although the north-west was virtually safe from German attacks, there were two successful enemy strikes. The first took place during the evening of Monday 25 September 1916. A German airship L.21, commanded by Oberleutnant Kurt Frankenburg, made landfall at Sutton on Sea, Lincolnshire and flew on to Lancashire via Lincoln and Sheffield. He dropped an incendiary bomb onto Newchurch but it failed to ignite. This was followed by an explosive bomb which also failed to explode. Further bombs, however, did explode causing slight damage to the East Lancashire Railway track and a row of cottages. More bombs fell at Greenmount setting fire to a cottage after which Frankenburg saw the lights of Bolton and headed there dropping several more bombs where he killed thirteen people, seriously injured another nine and destroyed nineteen houses. He dropped seven further bombs before making for home via Whitby.

The north-west was helpless against such attacks, neither fighter defence aircraft nor any anti-aircraft guns were thought to be needed or were available. German airships could wander freely much to the disgust of the local residents, although a blackout was in force which hindered accurate navigation by the enemy. The other attack in the First World War took place on 12th April 1918, when an L.61 targeted Wigan, killing five and injuring nine. It then headed towards Bolton where it dropped two further bombs with no injury and little damage. The airship returned home via Hull, the pilot reporting he had attacked Sheffield! This was the last effective airship raid on England.

13

Between the Wars

The end of the First World War saw the losses of tens of thousands of young men in the trenches of northern France, the run down of orders for war materials and the return to normal peace-time flights. The war had forced huge advances in aviation. Aircraft were now equipped with reliable engines, were stable and safe and very much larger, being able to carry large bomb loads over considerable distances. The Atlantic was crossed for the first time in 1919 by Alcock and Brown in a Vickers Vimy, a converted First World War bomber and eyes were on the development of civilian aviation across the world. Towns were anxious to have their own airports and set up air routes to compete with the railways up and down Britain. Flying boats were perfected and could land in river estuaries, lakes and sheltered water for passenger flying.

RFC had become the Royal Air Force from 1st April 1918 but was shrinking rapidly after the war and had no interest in being established in Lancashire. Aviation development was left firmly in the hands of the civilian companies desperate to stay in existence after the war-time orders were cancelled. The Avro Company started to erect a new purpose-built factory at Newton Heath, Manchester in 1918 but it was not completed until 1920. Part of their work was re-conditioning Avro 504s but was mainly producing car bodies for Crossley Motors. The aircraft flying and testing ground was at Alexandra Park aerodrome but this closed in 1923 and a new site was found at Woodford, Cheshire, to where the flight sheds were removed. At Ten Acres Lane in Newton Heath, Manchester, a new aircraft factory was constructed for Avro. This factory became very important during and after the Second World War and much of it remains standing today.

Civilian flying was booming but only for the rich. Routes were being developed between London and other major cities plus links on routes such as Manchester, Southport and Blackpool. Initially using parks and racecourses, the demand grew for purpose-built landing grounds. Southport had the beach at Hesketh Park and the vacated First World War hangars whilst Squires Gate was remembered and expanded at Blackpool and at Alexander Park, Manchester, shortly to be followed by Barton. Barton opened on 1st January 1930 and was one of the first municipal airports to open in England. The Government of the day encouraged all large towns and cities to earmark sites for aviation. In

1924 civilian flying from Liverpool utilised Aintree Racecourse when Northern Air Lines started a daily air mail service to and from Belfast from Aintree, using DH 50s. The service expanded to carry passengers but the racecourse was not ideal. A search for a more suitable site located a large area at Speke for the development of housing and industry, with provision of a municipal aerodrome in mind. Liverpool opened Speke on 16th July 1930 where, in 1938 the imposing terminal building was constructed. Flying boat services to and from Belfast were operated by Imperial Airways, using a Short Calcutta. These services used a licensed civil aerodrome on the River Mersey itself but otherwise very little use was made of this aerodrome.

The rapid growth of the Nazi Party in Germany and their huge investment in armaments and the military caused much consternation throughout Europe in the mid 1930s. The British military had been decimated after the First World War. Between 1919 and 1920, 256 military airfields were abandoned leaving only 27 military and 17 civil aerodromes by 1924. In Lancashire, Hesketh Park was the only quasi military airfield still in use but as a civilian landing ground only. During the late 1920s and early 1930s many First World War bases were modernized and extended, including Biggin Hill, Kenley and Tangmere (later to become famous Battle of Britain bases). Lancashire languished behind except for civil flying. By 1936 war looked very possible and the RAF started a massive, escalating, expansion programme to match the Nazi threat. A series of Expansion Schemes followed each other. They were Lettered A – M and each involved an increase in size of the RAF in terms of equipment, squadrons and airfields on which to house them. They also included aircraft storage units and maintenance units to supply, maintain, modify and store the new equipment. Flying training school numbers grew, supported by civilian manned elementary schools such as No 17 E&RFTS at Barton.

Lancashire was again ignored in the early expansion schemes but aircraft manufacture was significantly stepped up at Manchester and Preston. Although aircraft research and development was accelerating, the RAF was still operating obsolete bi-plane types and Mitchell and Camm started working on some radical designs which would result in the Spitfire and Hurricane fighters respectively. The aircraft factories in the north-west were again expanded and new airfields were required for test-flying these aircraft plus flying training for RAF crews. In the Manchester area, Avro was producing Ansons and working on new bombers which would become the Manchester and later develop into the Lancaster. English Electric was contracted to assemble Handley

15

Page Hampden bombers and needed an airfield from which to test-fly these new aircraft. Ringway and Woodford, both in Cheshire, were developed for the Manchester factories and Samlesbury was built for English Electric and was also operated by the RAF.

The immediate demand was met by expanding facilities at the civil airfields such as Barton, Speke and Squires Gate which were looked at by the RAF to house training units and possibly fighter units for the defence of the area. German aircraft now had the necessary range to reach this region. In 1937 Barton was used by Fairey Aviation for test-flying Fairey Battle light bombers which were produced at the former First World War aircraft factory at Heaton Chapel and No 17 Elementary and Reserve Flying Training School was formed on 1st October 1937. The school was operated for the RAF by Airwork Ltd and it operated Tiger Moth and Anson aircraft. The purpose was to train as many aircrew as possible to support the rapidly growing number of new RAF squadrons. All E&RFTSs closed at the outbreak of war, including No 17. Some became Elementary Flying Training Schools but No 17 was a totally new unit, not to be formed until January 1941 at North Luffenham in Rutland.

1939–1945

The comparatively calm skies of Lancashire were at last to be changed when it was decided to develop Burtonwood as part of the planned 1938 expansion phase. Burtonwood was to become an RAF Maintenance Unit supplying new aircraft and equipment to the RAF. It also became an Aircraft Assembly Unit. Opened in 1939, as Burtonwood Repair Depot Ltd, it was the first part of this vast base to be finished before the airfield, and initially worked on engine overhaul and components. The Maintenance Unit (MU) and the factory site (BRD Ltd) at Burtonwood were both to share the common airfield. Although the airfield was not ready, the factory was already turning out a mixture of both British and American-built aircraft, assembled or modified here. The 4,000 work force accepted American aircraft like the Martin Maryland and Brewster Buffalo, which were destined for RAF service plus assembling Blenheims. The airfield was finally ready and No 37 MU, plus the now operational airfield, opened on 1st April 1940. At Speke, a huge aircraft factory was constructed immediately adjacent

to the airfield, initially operated by MAP, and later by Rootes
Securities. Squires Gate had a Vickers factory constructed where
2,584 Wellington bombers were built. Barton, Burtonwood, Speke and
Squires Gate also housed regular RAF units for maintenance or training
and in the case of Speke, the only fighter aircraft for local defence.

Whilst no more military airfields were to be opened for at least
another year in Lancashire, the military were not slow in undertaking
an amazing number of other developments in the county. The vast MU
at Heywood on the north-western outskirts of Manchester was
completed and opened as No 35 MU on 1st June 1939, just in time to
work up prior to the commencement of the Second World War. This
base had no runways and was established in No 40 Group as a
Universal Equipment Depot, later to become purely an Aircraft
Equipment Depot. Even though there was no airfield, this huge site
utilized standard aircraft hangars and other brick buildings which were
well dispersed to help protect it against enemy air attack. It also used
many empty cotton mills in the close vicinity. This MU was to remain
active until eventual disbandment in 1967 and the site is now the
Heywood Industrial Park.

Other MUs also used local mill facilities such as No 68 MU at Bolton
which opened in May 1942 as a Ground Equipment Depot in the
former Globe Hosiery Buildings in Lower Bridgewater Street, Bolton,
later also utilizing the Suez Mill, Farnworth until it disbanded in May
1946. In December 1939, 'L' Temporary MU formed at Stanley Street,
Salford as a Clothing Equipment Depot. It was to absorb 'R' Temporary
MU at Worsted Mills, Hadfield, Manchester in July 1940 as a Clothing
and Barrack Equipment Depot with sub sites in Sheffield and Ardwick.
It eventually became No 221 MU in December 1943 with HQ at
Ardwick, and at least 12 other sub sites including Barlow in Yorkshire.
This unit disbanded in May 1946.

RAF basic training also used the seaside resorts and in particular
those away from the potentially threatened area to the east of the
county. Blackpool and Morecambe promenades saw thousands of
newly-recruited airmen and women being billeted in boarding houses
and drilled and introduced into military life by cruel drill sergeants on
the wind-swept promenades in all types of weather. Many war-time
airmen joined up and were kitted out only to be sent to these resorts for
six weeks' basic training prior to moving on to trade training.
Recruitment was refined with purpose-built centres opening at
Wilmslow and West Kirby in Cheshire; Bridgnorth in Shropshire,
and Padgate near Warrington in Lancashire. Here, thousands of airmen

joined up and the bases continued until the demise of National Service in 1962.

Padgate was opened in the Second World War and was a vast hutted camp with hangars for drill and basic training. Thousands of conscripts arrived at Padgate station to be met by RAF drill sergeants who showed no mercy in getting their civilian recruits straight into the rudiments of service life and grinding them down only to rebuild them as smart, efficient men. Most hated their time there. On arrival they gave up their civilian clothing and donned military uniform. Their civvies were wrapped up and sent home and for the first six weeks they had to stay in uniform and live, eat, breathe and sleep the RAF, five and a half days a week. Their lives followed the relentless pattern of drill, sport, drill, RAF history, drill, military leadership, drill, personal hygiene, drill, polishing, drill, cleaning, drill and more. There is no trace of RAF Padgate now, the entire site having been swallowed up into the expanded Warrington, but the local roads bear the names of famous RAF aircraft.

US troops waiting on the platform at Warrington Central Station for a night out in Manchester.

18

After basic training, the recruit advanced to technical training, much of which was undertaken in Lancashire. A Polish Technical Training School was set up at Blackpool, in July 1942 only to move on to Halton in Buckinghamshire later the same month. Before that Nos 8, 9, 10 and 21 Schools of Technical Training had opened at Weeton, Morecambe, Kirkham and Burtonwood respectively between November 1939 and July 1941. No 9 at Morecambe had the shortest life being set up in November 1939 to train Flight Mechanics and Flight Riggers but closed down in May 1942. No 21 at Burtonwood used the BRD Site and specialized in training RAF ground crews on US manufactured, but RAF operated, aircraft such as the Havoc, Flying Fortress, Mitchell which were delivered under the Lend-Lease arrangements. A mixture of RAF and civilian instructors taught the different aspects, including airframes, engines and electrics. This unit worked very closely with the Americans at Burtonwood and was the only RAF unit to remain active after the American occupation of the base, finally disbanding in May 1946.

Numbers 8 and 10 Schools of Technical Training were located a few miles apart; No 8 at Weeton in the centre of The Flyde and No 10 at Kirkham on the main A66 Preston to Blackpool road. Both taught Flight Mechanics and Flight Riggers courses and were substantial timber-hutted camps with several T2 type hangars for instructional airframes and training equipment. Both were destined to survive well beyond the Second World War, training RAF tradesmen in many subjects, including engines, sheet metal, undercarriages and even the RAF Driving School at Weeton. Kirkham disbanded in November 1958 and was redeveloped into a prison. Weeton continued until September 1965 when the school disbanded and the site was handed over to the Army. To this day it remains an army camp, albeit with more modern accommodation.

Military development was not restricted to the RAF as the Royal Navy and Army were also very active in Lancashire. The Army had several regiments stationed and training in the county, including the South Lancs Regiment at Peninsular Barracks in Warrington, The King's Own Regiment in Liverpool, the Lancashire Fusiliers at Fulwood Barracks in Preston and further barracks in Manchester and Lancaster. To cater for the huge expansion in the Army, even greater than the RAF, further barracks were constructed such as Harrington Barracks at Formby. This huge hutted camp built between the pinewoods and the Southport to Liverpool railway remained in use until the late 1950s before closure and demolition. It is remembered by the naming of Harrington Road which runs through the middle of what was once the barracks. Peninsular and Fulwood barracks remain in army use as do many TA depots in all major centres.

Defence Posts

The Army had been responsible for the defence of the Mersey estuary by the establishment of forts at Seaforth on the Lancashire (north) side and Fort Perch Rock on the Cheshire (south) side at New Brighton. These stone-built coastal defences originated in Napoleonic times, with Perch Rock opening in 1826. It had stone walls rising 32 feet on the land facing side, to 40 feet high facing the river. The forts were initially armed with sixteen 32 pounder guns, later to be re-equipped with 64 pounders with greater range. With the centre of the river well in the range of each fort, they could engage any ship attempting to slip into the Mersey. Six-inch guns arrived in both forts in 1897 and remained throughout the First and Second World Wars, supplemented by machine guns, searchlight towers and an observation tower. Radar was added in 1941 making them much more effective. The forts were obviously a success with no known enemy shipping attempting to get into the Mersey in either war. Both forts were decommissioned in 1954. Fort Seaforth was demolished when the Gladstone Dock complex was extended, at the extreme west end of the Liverpool Docks, in the 1950s to accommodate container and other larger ships. Fort Perch Rock remains.

Fort Crosby was built at Hightown around the same time, camouflaged amongst the sand hills. This fort survived the same period of time and looked out across the channel approaching the Mersey. Various guns were sited here and although it virtually closed between the wars it was fully operational during the Second World War acting as a look-out and forward gunnery position before ships got within the range of Fort Seaforth and Fort Perch Rock. Fort Crosby was decommissioned in 1954 having been used as a prisoner of war camp for many years at the end of the war. The remains were finally demolished in the late 1960s. Although these three forts protected the river against surface shipping, there was a risk of both enemy submarines and aircraft attacking shipping or mine laying. In fact, several mines were laid and the ship *Ullapool* detonated a mine

Coastal gun defence towers in position in the Mersey estuary 1945. (Via Chris Foulds)

Fort Crosby at Hightown as it was in 1958. (Chris Foulds)

whilst lying off the Princess landing-stage in March 1941, sinking immediately. The *Tacoma City* suffered a similar fate and the tanker *Dosinia* hit another at the Bar Lightship in 1940 also sinking rapidly but all her 57 crew were rescued.

Mines damaged other ships including the *Westmorland* and *Dorcasia* and efforts were needed to try and prevent minelaying by aircraft. The answer was a series of three anti-aircraft forts erected in the sea and carrying Bofors guns to engage any enemy aircraft. Manufactured at Bromborough on the Wirral, these structures were like modern oil or gas platforms. Sitting on concrete stilts they were towed out and sunk to the seabed and then linked by gangplank type walkways. Each of the three groups comprised six separate structures, some housing guns and radar whilst others housed the men and equipment. They were known as 'Formby', 'Queens' and 'Burbo' named after the sand banks on which they were sited. There is no recorded evidence of them going into action but the deterrent obviously worked. One was badly damaged by a storm and soon after the war another was struck by a ship. They were all demolished by 1950.

Coastal defence did not stop here. The flat sand between Fort Seaforth and Southport could have made an ideal assault beach for the

Line of coastal defence towers being built at Bromborough before being towed out and sunk onto the sea bed in the Mersey estuary. (Via Chris Foulds)

Germans either by ship or aircraft. Anti-invasion posts were erected along the entire length, positioned to stop enemy aircraft or gliders landing on the beach. On the sand hills at Formby, observation posts were also erected and behind that, defensive gun positions. They had good sight of the beach from which an enemy attack could be repulsed. Fortunately they were never needed. The posts were a terrible eye-sore and great danger to swimmers after the war ended and they were all removed in the early 1950s. The coastal defences remained for many years, most being demolished by the coastal erosion that has constantly affected the area and today nothing remains. Behind the beaches was a labyrinth of further defences in the form of pillboxes. These structures stretched across the whole country and were positioned at railway and road junctions, bridges, and anywhere that could be used as a bottleneck to stop and destroy an invading army. Many of these remain across Lancashire to this day. Similar hard, utility-type structures were air-raid shelters. Thousands sprang up in the early days of war and more during and after the Liverpool Blitz. Many were long brick structures without windows and with a blast wall protecting the

23

HMS Queen Charlotte, *the RN Gunnery School in 1945 at what is now Ainsdale Lido, Ainsdale, Southport. (Author)*

entrances at each end. The flat roofs were reinforced concrete to resist incendiary bombs or blast. These were positioned for ease of access and where it was thought they would be needed, on school grounds, for example, and one remained adjacent to Freshfield railway station for many years. Several still remain.

Target Practice

Often the coast had restricted access to the public and the Lancashire coastline was heavily used for artillery ranges. Virtually the whole of Morecambe Bay was a gunnery range both for ground-to-ground and ground-to-air. Several Lancashire airfields housed co-operation squadrons which towed targets behind for anti-aircraft practice. Targets were laid out on the marshes of the bay for air-to-ground gunnery. The lido at Ainsdale beach was requisitioned by the Royal Navy, together with the few hotels which had sprung up in an effort to make it an extension of the resort at Southport. Collectively they became HMS *Queen Charlotte* which was a gunnery school for navy gunners. Aircraft from Woodvale trailed targets parallel to the coast for live gunnery practice. The lido remains, having been refurbished, some of the hotels became a nightclub and Pontins Holiday Village was built later behind the site. Different sites were allocated numbers and No 9 Light Anti-Aircraft Practice Camp was located at Flookburgh, on the edge of the Lake District. It was provided with targets by No 1614 AA Co-operation Flight at RAF Cark from 1942 until the end of the war.

Yet another range was established even before the First World War at Altcar, between Formby and Hightown. This army-owned rifle range utilized the sand hills and beach as a safe area for rifle firing and the range remains active to this day. This complex has several ranges of different distances with a butts system for marking, scoring and changing targets. Mostly used by the Army and TA, it is available to cadet units and other services and remains one of the largest of its type in the north-west of England. When first constructed it had its own railway station on the Southport to Liverpool railway adjacent to the Power House (the original source of electric power to the railway) just south of Formby and a narrow gauge railway linked this station with the centre of the range.

26

The Royal Navy

Except for Liverpool Docks there were no permanent Royal Navy bases for ships on the Lancashire coastline but a large training base was established at Croft, near Warrington known as HMS *Gosling*; HMS *Queen Charlotte* occupied Ainsdale Lido near Southport as a gunnery school and two Fleet Air Arm airfields were built at Inskip and Burscough (see separate chapters).

At the Liverpool Docks a facility was made available at Wallasey for trawlers from Fleetwood to be based for mine sweeping operations and a much larger facility was made available at Gladstone Dock for a small group of destroyers. Gladstone Dock was large enough at accommodate any ship of the day and the Navy brought such famous ships as *Rodney*, *Illustrious*, *Hood*, *Furious*, *Ark Royal*, *Ramillies*, *Indomitable*, *Eagle*, *King George V* and *Duke of York* in for repair or modification. A destroyer flotilla was established to protect the convoys using the docks.

The Mersey Docks were the most important in Britain after London but much less susceptible to bombing attack. The escort force based at Liverpool was commanded by Captain Frederick John Walker DSO and two bars, who distinguished himself leading the convoy defence against submarines. No fewer than 1,285 convoys arrived at Liverpool during the war. They varied in size and had to endure the constant menace of U-boats on their perilous journey across the Atlantic. Capt Walker and his escort force would go out to meet the convoys with great success against the U-boats. Early in 1944 his force sank six enemy submarines on one patrol, being obliged to borrow some additional depth charges from the convoy itself to maintain the constant attacks. He was a hero and recognised as such by the First Lord of the Admiralty and the C-in-C of the Navy. Unfortunately he worked himself to death and died in July 1944. His body was borne down the river and he was buried at sea.

The western side of the Atlantic, now known as the 'Western Approaches', required careful control and protection to safeguard the numerous convoys sailing both ways across the Atlantic to and from North America. Initially Canada and later the US provided much of our daily requirements in terms of food, war materials, aircraft and men. To protect them against enemy aircraft and submarines a complex defence strategy was constantly evolving with new scientific developments and increased numbers of ships and aircraft. A complex under Derby House by Exchange Flags, in the centre of Liverpool, managed the control of the whole area. Constructed in great secrecy during the early part of the Second World War and manned by both Royal Navy and RAF personnel, this complex was totally unknown except to those who worked there. It was built under massive concrete reinforcement. The Germans would have been even more aggressive in their bombing of Liverpool had they known of its existence. A warren of offices, cipher rooms, rest rooms and a large control room, the complex was closed down after the war and abandoned. It was only in the 1970s that it was rediscovered and the story of its war-time existence told. It is now open to the public on a daily basis.

Enemy Attacks

The first air raid warning in Lancashire was sounded on 25th June 1940 but the first bombs arrived on the night 28th–29th July, when three were dropped near a searchlight post at Altcar near Formby. The first casualty was on 9th August when bombs were dropped on Prenton, Birkenhead followed by another stick of seven high explosives on Wallasey the next night. The first on Liverpool were dropped on the night 17th–18th August followed by another minor attack ten days later. This was bad enough but a prelude to what was on its way. In September there were 20 light raids on Merseyside, 15 in October and nine in November; averaging one every alternate night. Of the 20 raids in September Liverpool was hit 16 times, 14 times in October and 16 times in November. Whilst many were small and some ineffective, the cumulative impact was severe. On 6th September a Children's Convalescent Home was hit without fatal results, Central Station, Liverpool was hit on 21st–22nd September. The first major attack was on 28th November when a 2½ hour attack killed 200 people.

There were a total of 68 bombing raids between September 1940 and May 1941. The 'May Blitz' was the worst and 3,966 people lost their lives and 3,812 were seriously injured. There were 10,000 homes destroyed and a further 184,000 damaged. Manchester suffered in a similar manner with the Trafford Park area representing a target due to the major manufacturing resources there. Where was the defence?

Anti-aircraft guns surrounded Liverpool but with primitive range-

28

finding equipment and no radar. Barrage balloons were also in place but fighter defence was restricted to Squires Gate, Speke and Cranage in Cheshire, none of which had proper night-fighter capability. Lancashire had been caught napping and like Coventry, London, Birmingham, Southampton and Portsmouth, Manchester and Liverpool had to get better air protection. The airfields in the area in early 1940 were the requisitioned Speke Airport with virtually no fighters, Hooton Park at Ellesmere Port, literally across the river from Speke, but it was a training station and Sealand on the England/Wales border at Queensferry. Sealand was one of the few First World War airfields that remained open between the wars and was a training station. Hawarden was another MU and training station but had a fighter flight of three Spitfires in constant readiness. This flight scored success in August 1940 when an He111 was brought down after attacking nearby RAF Sealand. RAF Cranage, near Northwich, also in Cheshire was opened too late to help the May Blitz on Merseyside but Defiants of No 96 Squadron based here did have some success in destroying enemy bombers at night. RAF Squires Gate had no fighters in 1940 until a detachment from No 96 Squadron at Cranage was sent there to help protect this industrial region. All this was far too late and the few aircraft at Speke could not gain sufficient height in time to be effective against enemy bombers. As a direct result of this shortcoming, RAF Woodvale was planned and constructed specifically for the protection of Merseyside but did not open until December 1941, again too late to effectively protect Merseyside but this was not known at the time.

Radar Intelligence

Radar was very much in its infancy but its secret development pre-war allowed a chain of radar stations to be positioned around the coast to give advance warning of approaching enemy aircraft, and eventually to locate allied aircraft by use of IFF (Identification – Friend or Foe) and guide them back to a safe airfield. Developed from 1935 by scientists at Orfordness and later Bawdsey Research Centre, Chain Home radar was being constantly refined throughout the war period. Two main types of Chain Home installations were developed, East Coast and West Coast stations. East Coast were stations built on the pattern of the experimental establishment set up at Bawdsey in 1936, mostly large towers 240 feet and 350 feet high with all support buildings being protected against enemy air attack. West Coast operated from unprotected buildings with transmitter aerials mounted on 325 feet guyed steel masts. These high masts were very conspicuous and many Chain Home stations on the east and south coasts were attacked during the Battle of Britain. Technology advanced and Chain Home stations were supplemented by Chain Home Low; originally designed for plotting ships it could also be used to track low flying aircraft and used much smaller gantries and aerial arrays. Coastal Defence/Chain Home Low was a chain set up to provide radar plotting of both shipping and aircraft and operated on the same 1.5 m wavelength as the Chain Home Low stations. These stations were originally manned by the Army, or jointly by all three services but eventually the RAF took overall control of them. The timber gantry supporting the aerial array was mounted on top of the building and not on the ground.

Many sites were purpose-built but the coverage on the west coast was nothing like as comprehensive as on the east because the perceived threat was always from the east and south. However enemy ships, submarines and aircraft did, of course, operate in the Irish Sea and our shores had to be protected. No 9 Group Fighter Command was established at Barton Hall, Preston and had responsibility for the defence of the area, later to become the Woodvale Sector. Sites were sought for Chain Home Low stations and the coast at Formby and Blackpool were perfect, plus north Wales and the Isle of Man. At Formby a small promenade had been constructed by the Formby Land and Building Company between 1876 and 1888 but only a few houses had been built. At that time sand was being naturally deposited at Formby (unlike the erosion now prevalent) and the 'Promenade' was soon overwhelmed by sand. One building constructed was a large square house with a flat roof and was named *Stella Maris*. It had been occupied by a male-only religious group but was requisitioned by the RAF in late October 1940 as a station to defend Liverpool Bay with a similar one sited at Blackpool. Construction started at Formby together with the provision of a generator so it could be self-sufficient. The aerial array was situated on the roof and the plots received from both stations were sent to the No 9 Group Sector Control Station. Originally this was established in a temporary room at Aughton Springs, Halsall until 12th January 1943 when the purpose-built Operations Block was opened at Broad Lane, Formby, a dispersed site of RAF Woodvale.

From here all air defence was co-coordinated until August 1944 when the Sector was amalgamated into the Church Fenton Sector. All shipping information was fed to HQ Western Approaches located under Derby House in central Liverpool. This was the control centre for all shipping, especially convoys, in the Irish Sea and the approaches to Britain well beyond Ireland. Kept secret for many years this control centre is now open to the public. The Formby CHL station was numbered 64A and the planned one at Blackpool was station number 64, it is not certain that this station ever functioned satisfactorily. The Formby station opened in January 1941 and in August 1941 its performance was upgraded to a 'Common Working Aerial' when the whole aerial switched between transmit and receive functions and the power was increased fourfold. The radar display was also greatly improved by the introduction of a Plan Position Indicator (PPI) tube in addition to the range display. After the D-Day landings the threat to the western shores had diminished sufficiently to allow the station to close and release the manpower. The Royal Navy took the house over after the RAF vacated and it became No 277 Radio Installation Unit with the permanent staff located at HMS *Ringtail*, Burscough. The building has now been demolished.

Barrage Balloons

Barrage balloons were another deterrent against low-flying enemy aircraft and became a feature of many industrial and other vital potential targets. Balloons were manned by RAF units with a headquarters and many dispersed satellite sites. The balloons were hydrogen filled requiring huge numbers of gas bottles to be transported to each balloon. The balloons were tethered to a mobile winch, which could be positioned anywhere but normally was immediately adjacent to a target or in a massed group near to a city, and on the side where an attack might be expected. The winch had a cable allowing the balloon to rise up to 3,000 feet or more. This made it very dangerous for aircraft to fly in the barrage area in case they hit either the balloon or cable. Sometimes balloons were also a danger to Allied aircraft and pilots had to keep a good look out for them. Charts were marked where balloons were positioned. Another problem was a runaway balloon, which escaped from its tether. Often RAF aircraft were called in to shoot them down before they became a hazard to navigation.

The HQ at Liverpool was RAF Fazakerley to the north of the city and in Manchester it was at Bowlee where substantial sheds were built to house balloons and to test inflate them, repair and modify them as necessary. Gas was distributed from here to dispersed sites by truck. Administration and records were managed from here together with the support for mobile inflation parties, winches and their drivers. Maintenance of vehicles was also carried out at this site. RAF Fazakerley remained an active RAF station until the early 1960s when it closed. Its post war role included support of 3611 Squadron RAuxAF which was a ground-based Auxiliary fighter interception unit and HQ Merseyside Wing ATC. RAF Bowlee acted in a similar way for 3613 Squadron. Nothing remains of RAF Fazakerley today. The balloon units were commanded by No 31 (Barrage Balloon) Group at Birmingham under which there were six balloon centres. No 88 was at Fazakerley, No 9 at Warrington and No 10 at Bowlee, Manchester. Fazakerley controlled 919 (at Birkenhead) and 921 (at Fazakerley) Squadrons with 52 and 48 balloons respectively; Warrington controlled 922 (at Cuerdley), 923 (at Runcorn) and 949 (at Crewe) Squadrons with 32 balloons each whilst Bowlee controlled 925 (at Manchester and Bowlee) and 926 (at Bowlee) Squadrons with 40 balloons each.

Transportation

The huge numbers of items that had to be moved around for the military were often accommodated on the railways. Many pre-war airfields had their own railway station or direct siding. Liverpool and Manchester docks, plus the smaller ports at Preston, Garston, Widnes, Heysham and Lancaster, all had substantial railway systems and direct railway links to the national network. RAF Burtonwood was to develop a substantial railway link to the Warrington to Liverpool line and had many sidings allowing materials to come straight from the docks to the depot. Similarly out-going goods could be transported the same way. Burtonwood was eventually to manage the maintenance of RAF locomotives as the RAF had its own fleet for this very purpose. Warton was served by a complex of sidings on the opposite side of the

Preston to Blackpool road. Other airfields were located adjacent to railway lines. For instance Woodvale was served by both the Liverpool to Southport electric line and the Cheshire Lines, which had a station at Woodvale itself. Troops and materials could be delivered to the doorstep.

As more and more sites developed, however, so the railway system became overloaded. Wagons and carriages were in full use and new production could not keep pace. Enemy action also disrupted the railway system, especially in the south. To support the railways a vast number of new vehicles were requisitioned by the military and others were manufactured for them. MT Companies were set up, such as No 5 in Sefton Park, Liverpool. This unit had hundreds of vehicles used for any war related business including ferrying fighter aircraft from Liverpool and other ports to Speke, Burtonwood and Warton for erection, testing and flying to their operational units. It was also used to ferry equipment and food brought in by ships from the USA, bombs and ammunition from factory to air base, or to replenish the ships in Manchester and Liverpool docks. Sefton Park was a central location, which could use the trees for camouflage and large open spaces were available for parking and maintenance. Little was provided in the way of accommodation so working on the vehicles in winter was only marginally better than working on an aircraft on an open airfield. At the end of the Second World War, No 5 MT Company transferred to Woodvale as it had shrunk dramatically and it had superior accommodation, hangars and hardstandings, as well as better security.

Using the Docks

The docks played a most important role in the Second World War and with both Liverpool and Manchester docks, Lancashire was the major gateway for goods, materials and men both inward from the USA, Canada and the Empire and later outward, supporting the invasions of Europe in both northern and southern France. Facing the USA made Lancashire an obvious place for inbound convoys together with its comparatively large distance from occupied Europe and the enemy aircraft based there. As we have seen it did not deter the Luftwaffe from making many attacks and causing substantial damage and disruption. Had this continued there is no doubt the war would have been extended substantially. Fortunately Hitler turned his attention eastward well before he had managed to destroy the RAF or inflict sufficient damage on our ports and manufacturing base.

Liverpool docks cover a narrow strip of land no more than half a mile long at its widest point. Flanking the river for seven miles, it contains nearly 500 acres of docks and 29 miles of quays. Liverpool also

P-47s at Pier Head, Liverpool after being unloaded after their transatlantic voyage. (Mersey Docks & Harbour Board)

P-51 Mustangs on the deck of an aircraft carrier in Liverpool docks, 1945. (Mersey Docks & Harbour Board)

had the Princess Floating Landing Stage (part of which is still operational today) capable of berthing any size ship regardless of the state of the tide and also housing the famous Mersey Ferries. Troop ships from around the world moored here. Together with the Birkenhead and Wallasey docks (182 acres), Garston, Widnes and Manchester it was vitally important to Britain and a great target for the Luftwaffe. With such a small strip of land it was inevitable that many bombs would fall into the surrounding residential and industrial areas with devastating consequences.

During the 68 months of war, Germany did everything to disrupt and destroy the docks by placing mines at the river entrance and bombing the ships and port facilities. Undeterred, Liverpool dealt with 120 million tons of ocean-going shipping which may be translated into an armada of 12,000 ships of 10,000 tons, to be docked, unloaded, perhaps repaired, fitted out, loaded and sent out again, all with the utmost speed and urgency. It coped with night-time blackout and a

35

P-47s on the Princess Landing Stage, 1944. (Mersey Docks & Harbour Board)

shortage of everything. In addition to this, 23 million tons of coastwise shipping was handled. Along with the ships she harboured, Liverpool dealt with the enormous total of 75,150,100 tons of cargo, of which 56,494,800 tons were the imports Britain needed in order to live and carry on the war. 18,655,300 tons were sent out of the port, mostly in the form of war stores to our battlefronts all over the world. No fewer than 73,782 aircraft and gliders were landed at the port and over 4,700,000 troops passed through, of which 1,200,000 were Americans!

By 1943 import figures reached over 190,000 tons per week when the USA started to send war equipment over in huge quantities. This was to continue until the end of the war. Fighters and small aircraft could not be flown from the US as they simply did not have the required

range. The four-engined bombers and larger transport aircraft followed a route taking them up the Canadian coast as far as possible, then hopping across to Greenland, Iceland and Scotland. It was a hazardous journey in winter with few hours of daylight and certain death in the event of a ditching into the sea. Many aircraft and crews were lost this way, but fortunately most made it through. For the smaller aircraft, they were prepared for the voyage by having wingtips and tails removed together with propellers. These parts were crated and formed normal cargo. The aircraft fuselages were then covered with Cosmoline, a form of rubberized cocoon to protect them from salt spray, which would cause corrosion. Initially these aircraft were shipped over as deck cargo on freighters and later on specially adapted

A converted vehicle ferry acting as a tender unloading P-51 Mustangs from convoy ships. (Mersey Docks & Harbour Board)

tankers. The Birkenhead goods ferry steamer *Oxton*, one of the fleet used extensively in taking vehicles across the river before the opening of the Mersey road tunnel, was fitted with a Scotch derrick type of crane and sent to unload the planes from the vessels in mid-river. The idea proved so successful that a second derrick was added and two other ferry steamers were similarly fitted. Over 11,000 planes were landed in this way – lifted from the decks and brought ashore by these highly manoeuvrable craft, which also took off tanks, crated planes and other unwieldy loads. Several aircraft carriers brought a full load of aircraft across the Atlantic on their decks, and these had to be discharged in dock by float cranes.

The aircraft were unloaded onto the Princess Landing Stage where they were placed onto specially adapted trucks for transport to the respective airfield. Generally they went to Speke where the Lockheed facility would remove the Cosmoline, replace the wingtips, tails and propellers, test fly them and deliver them, normally to either Burton-wood or Warton. As explained in the individual chapters on these bases, Burtonwood mainly specialized in radial engines and therefore took delivery of fighters like the P-38 Lightning and P-47 Thunderbolt. The P-51 Mustang with its in-line engines would go to Warton. Transporting such an unwieldy load by road had its problems and a specific route to Speke was established with all obstructions removed. The aircraft was balanced across the road vehicle with the tail hanging out, counter balanced by the weight of the engine. The convoys had a police escort to stop all other traffic. Crated aircraft could be transported more easily and the thousands of gliders that were imported were often taken straight to specific airfields for erection, normally in the south of the country. These would be transported by road by either RAF or USAAF trucks.

Armament Factories

Another major potential target for Luftwaffe bombers was armament factories, which opened in the north-west of England. Huge areas were taken over for manufacturing, case filling and storing of all types of ammunition. Lancashire was home to the Ordnance factories at Chorley, Lostock, Kirkby and Risley. These areas were closely guarded and had extremely strict safety regulations, specifically against smoking, sparks or anything that might ignite the volatile materials stored. The area was covered with curved roofed storage igloos, normally covered in earth and grass to absorb an incendiary attack and also act as camouflage. Normally the units would have railway lines running to all areas, which were difficult to camouflage against enemy aircraft. The factory at Chorley was closed and sold for redevelopment in 2003 but the Kirkby site became the Kirkby Industrial Estate immediately after the Second World War and remains so today with a few original buildings to be seen. Initially the labyrinth of railway lines remained but these are now all gone. For some reason the Luftwaffe never bombed either site. Another similar site was located just outside the county at Risley to the south of Warrington.

Military Bases

Speke had seen the establishment of 611 (West Lancashire) Squadron, Royal Auxiliary Air Force, in 1936, one of ultimately 21 similar squadrons formed across the country. This unit was initially equipped with Hawker Hart and Hind bi-planes plus a few Avro Tutors for flying training and was established as a fighter squadron. The personnel were all volunteers drawn from the local area (hence the name West Lancashire) and operated at weekends and for a continuous training period during the summer. The CO, Adjutant and a few specialist engineers were regulars but the majority operated on a part time basis. The principle was to supplement the RAF with a fully trained, but cheap to maintain, force in the event of war. Initially working like a mix between an RAF squadron and a civil flying club these units soon became very efficient fighter (and sometimes bomber) units. In 1939, 611 Squadron re-equipped with the Supermarine Spitfire

P-51 Mustangs being towed from the Pier Head to Speke passing the bottom of Water Street, Liverpool, 1944. (Mersey Docks & Harbour Board)

I but travelled to RAF Duxford in Cambridgeshire for summer camp later that year only to be called-up on the outbreak of war and never return to Speke. Lancashire's own fighter squadron was very active in the Battle of Britain elsewhere in the country. Before its move, 611 operated out of temporary timber huts and a canvas Bessoneau hangar at Speke. Soon more accommodation was provided and several hangars plus dispersed hardstandings were added around the periphery of the base.

As war started so the building of military bases accelerated. Burtonwood was still the only permanent airfield to be constructed in Lancashire, all the others being converted or adapted civilian airfields or temporary bases designed to last the period of hostilities and then revert to their former use. Burtonwood was unusual in having two units (one civilian and one military) sharing the same airfield. A decision was made in 1936 to construct Aircraft Repair Depots with Engine Repair Depots in addition to a planned 24 Aircraft Storage Units (ASU). Initially these units were to be civilian-manned and bases were designed and planned at Tern Hill, Kemble, Aston Down, Hullavington and Shawbury. These designs were subsequently accepted as the standard design for all ASUs. Burtonwood was selected to be both an Aircraft Repair Depot and an Aircraft Storage Unit and was one of six so designed. Two civilian-manned units were planned at Kidbrook and Ruislip and three service-manned units at Henlow, St Athan and Sealand. The ASU formed part of the 1938 expansion programme involving ten new stations at Kirkbride, Silloth, Wroughton, Aldergrove, Wigtown, Lyneham, Llandow, High Ercall and Colerne, together with Burtonwood. Earlier expansion bases had buildings designed by the Commission of Fine Arts with beautiful neo-Georgian brick constructed buildings, messes and substantial brick 'C' type hangars. Each expansion plan reduced the quality of the buildings to save both cost and time. Burtonwood had brick buildings with pitched roofs in many cases, but the hangars were more utility being known as *protected* 'C' type having concrete walls instead of brick, and gabled roofs covered in tiles and not slate. The base also had a shadow factory located to the east of the airfield, which opened in 1939 before the airfield was open. RAF Burtonwood opened as No 37 MU in April 1940, just in time to supply Spitfires for the Battle of Britain.

Civilian Airfields

The next developments all revolved around the civil airfields which were requisitioned immediately on the outbreak of war. Squires Gate housed an Elementary and Reserve Flying Training School. It quickly expanded to become a Coastal Command training base with No 3 School of General Reconnaissance forming in 1940. On the declaration of war it had been used as a scatter airfield for Battles and Wellingtons from Nos 63 and 215 Squadrons respectively. Barton already housed training units; Speke had lost its resident fighter squadron but received Hampdens of Nos 61 and 144 Squadrons under the scatter scheme immediately after war was declared. This scattered RAF squadrons as widely as possible in case of immediate Luftwaffe attack. Fortunately this did not happen. Eventually Speke received fighter squadrons prior to Woodvale being available plus an RN co-operation squadron and eventually the Merchant Ship Fighter Unit. Samlesbury had quietly come on line just about at the time war was declared, assembling bombers made by English Electric in nearby Preston. Samlesbury never received any front line RAF units but did have several support units, specifically related to HQ No 9 Group at nearby Barton Hall, Preston.

Southport Hesketh Park was in use by civilians until the war when it was taken into military control initially as a satellite to civil repair by Martin Hearn at Hooton Park in Cheshire, before becoming an aircraft packing depot. The search was on for more military bases using the flat coastal plain of Lancashire but no new airfields would be ready for another 15 months. In the meantime the Satellite Landing Ground at Knowsley Park was officially available for use by Burtonwood in late 1941 but was waterlogged and not useable until the following spring. This landing ground was one of many around the country providing aircraft storage MUs with additional dispersed parking space for aircraft in case of Luftwaffe attack. As long as an open space for a runway was available, many parks and wooded areas were requisitioned because they provided natural camouflage. Unusually no buildings were erected except for stores and guards as little work was done except for daily prop swinging to keep oil circulating. Knowsley Park was not open to the public so ensured even greater security and each SLG was normally able to accommodate up to 100 aircraft.

RAF Bases

The building programme was now showing results and RAF Woodvale opened in December 1941 together with RAF Barrow on the same site that the Royal Navy airship operated from during the First World War. Both stations were *temporary utility* standard with three hard runways, three hangars each, plus blister hangars around the periphery and single brick thick walled hutting with asbestos roofs. Both had a number of dispersed living sites, spread to allow as much as possible to survive enemy air attack, including communal sites for messes for RAF and WAAF. It is interesting to note that both airfields are still active and both original control towers are in use today.

Warton was next to become active as a relief landing ground for Squires Gate in 1941 before being very dramatically expanded into Base Air Depot for the USAAF in 1943. Positioned alongside the River Ribble this base became the second largest US maintenance depot after Burtonwood and the two bases between them were responsible for supplying over 26,000 aircraft to the 8th, 9th, 10th and 15th US Air Forces during the Second World War with over 35,000 US personnel based on Lancashire soil.

RAF Cark was next to open in March 1942 being a similar design and size to Woodvale and Barrow, all having accommodation for approximately 1,200 personnel. Cark was designed as a fighter base but became a training base upon opening. It was the Staff Pilot Training Unit training pilots who were to become instructors at Air Observer Schools, a role it maintained until closure at the end of 1945.

Naval Bases

Cark was the last RAF airfield to open but was followed by two Royal Naval Air Stations at Inskip and Burscough. The FAA needed bases to train crews, work up new types of aircraft and it was rapidly expanding with new aircraft and more carriers. Eyes were eventually on the Far East where it was anticipated they would have to operate from carriers in the eventual defeat of Japan. The Navy also needed airfields for use by carrier-borne ships when coming into port. Aircraft cannot fly on or off ships when they are in port so have to be flown to a shore base. With many carriers coming in to Liverpool, Burscough was available for this purpose. It was the last airfield to open in the county, in September 1943, just after Inskip, which opened in May. All FAA bases were known as *'Stone Frigates'*. They had formal Navy names and these two were commissioned as HMS *Nightjar* and *Ringtail*. Navy airfields had four runways, each only 100 feet wide, instead of the 150 feet used on RAF runways. This narrower strip better represented the small carrier deck and it is assumed they had four runways because when on board a carrier they would always land and take off directly into wind. Four runways gave them a better chance of achieving this than three would. Accommodation at these bases was again *temporary* with brick and nissen type hutting. Both bases were very well dispersed with many navy 'S' type hangars built scattered all around them and with living and mess sites also well away from the airfield itself.

These bases were to see less than three years' operation life. However the achievements of the Second World War for Naval aviation were immense. Even with a loss of five fleet carriers, four escort carriers and 2000 aircraft, the FAA established the aircraft carrier rather than the battleship as the Fleet's capital ship. From being instruments to slow down the enemy fleet prior to destruction by big guns, naval aircraft, taking off from their carriers, were strike weapons in their own right. The essential support of the front-line squadrons had also expanded out of all recognition. It now provided communications flights, target towing, radar calibration and all the various training tasks, which included operational training units and the Naval School of Airborne Radar at Burscough.

Decoys

So all the Lancashire airfields were now complete. Due to the threat of enemy bombing, especially after the May Blitz in 1940, the RAF was understandably deeply concerned about enemy air attack. In an effort to frustrate the Luftwaffe a series of decoys were developed to prevent their accurate navigation and hopefully leading to their dropping bombs on open countryside rather than important targets. These were in the form of dummy airfields and flare paths. Daytime decoys were known as 'K' sites mainly for satellite airfields and night decoys became known as 'Q' sites, representing both permanent and satellite airfields. The 'K' sites comprised tents and dummy aircraft, often made of timber and canvas. These were virtually given up in 1941 with the emphasis moving onto 'Q' sites which had electric lighting systems laid out to simulate airfield flarepaths, albeit in open countryside. These were developed into 'QF' sites where mock fires were lit to try and mislead enemy bombers into thinking there were burning towns and cities. The first of this type were used to protect airfields with the night urban decoys becoming 'QL' sites. Following the May Blitz many major towns were provided with decoys with the codename 'Special Fires', 'SF', or 'Starfish'.

Lancashire had many decoys for various purposes. Starfish sites for Manchester were located at Chat Moss, Tatton Park, Park Moor, Chunal Moor, Mossley, Carrington Moss, Ludworth Moor, Reddish and Elkstone whilst those for Liverpool were at Hale, Ince, Formby and Little Crosby. There were also Heswall, Moreton, Gayton and Burton Marsh, Brimstage and Wallasey all on the Wirral, and Llandegla and Llansas in Wales. Warrington had three at Hatton, Appleton and Arley; Preston had four at Farington, Clifton Marsh, Hoghton and Brinscall; Accrington had five at Haslingden, Accrington, Burnley, Worsthorne and Mameldon Hill. Barrow docks had four naval decoys at Whicham Valley, Lowsy Point, Westfield Point and Snab Point/Wylock Marsh. The Army had decoys for their units at Chorley and Blackburn. There's more! Liverpool had civil QF decoys at 14 locations across south Lancashire and the Wirral; Manchester had three and Chorley, Warrington and Blackburn had one each. Two of Lancashire's airfields had decoys. Woodvale's was at Great Altcar and Burtonwood had one at Bold Heath. The other bases were built so late that it was probably decided they did not require a decoy.

Due to their nature of being temporary and having virtually no buildings, little remains today of these decoy sites except the odd generator building or control shelter. Some remains of the Woodvale decoy remain at Altcar.

POW Camps

War always results in prisoners being taken and the Second World War was no exception. German and Italian prisoners had to be contained in camps, which were spread right across the British Isles. Numbers grew so large that many were taken across the Atlantic to Canada and to other Empire locations to take the pressure off Britain and decrease the chances of escape. Fortress Britain made it very difficult for prisoners to escape and it is a credit to the system that only one prisoner actually escaped and made it back to Germany, and this was from Canada. This was Francis von Werra, a Luftwaffe pilot shot down over England. He returned to active duty only to be killed later in the war. The Isle of Man was used as a holding point for many civilian aliens who were detained as being of possible help to the enemy. They travelled from Liverpool to the Isle for the duration of their internment.

Prisoner of war camps were required almost immediately. German aircrews were being shot down over Britain and Navy personnel brought to shore after Naval engagements. All prisoners were interrogated to assess and classify them in accordance with their political view – grey, black or white. Whilst many were transported to Canada, many thousands remained in specially constructed camps. Lancashire had eleven camps, not all purpose-built but using whatever suitable buildings were available. They included Glen Mill, Wellyhole Street, Oldham where the large cotton mill and associated sheds were utilized as a base camp. Another camp was set up at Warth Mills, Bury. Other locations included Ormskirk; Garswood Park, Ashton-in-Makerfield; Bank Hall, Bretherton, Preston; Melland Camp, Sandfold Lane, Gorton, Manchester (formally a Heavy Anti-Aircraft battery); Newton Camp, Newton-with-Scales, Kirkham; Brookmill Camp, Woodlands Hall, Kirkham; Penketh Hostel, South Lane Farm, South Lane, Barrow's Green, near Warrington and Fort Crosby (coastal defence site) at Sniggery Farm, Hightown (as mentioned above). It is interesting to note that two were at Kirkham very close to two large Schools of Technical Training and one near the massive American base at Burtonwood.

Low-risk prisoners were often billeted on farms and helped in the fields. In many cases they (illegally) fraternized with the local girls and many married them and stayed in Britain after the Second World War. When the war ended many were released from the camps but not allowed home and again worked on local farms and other duties. Many Italian prisoners worked at Burtonwood in 1946. One of their jobs was to recover and repair thousands of bicycles left by the Americans on their departure. Under Lease Lend and other agreements between the UK and USA it was agreed that war surplus would not be allowed to flow into the local economy as it would stifle post-war industry. Hence when the Americans vacated Burtonwood and Warton they either took back their material with them or destroyed it! There are many tales of whole aircraft buried in 1946 but they remain to be found. At Burtonwood leather jackets were slashed and burned, furniture and equipment from the messes was either burned or piled up and soaked with water to make them rust. Bicycles were piled high and tracked vehicles ran over them to destroy them. These were discovered by the British when they retook control of the base and needed the bicycles to get to far parts of the base – hence this work for Italian prisoners.

Lancashire's Contribution

Lancashire played a huge part in supporting the war effort during the 1939–45 conflict, and winning it. No bomber ever took off from a Lancashire airfield and bombed Germany and no fighter took off from Lancashire to attack aircraft or targets over occupied Europe. However its relatively safe distance away to the west allowed it to train, sustain, support, repair and provide the war material and men for the conflict. Of the 13 Lancashire airfields open in the Second World War, six remain open at Barrow, Barton, Speke (albeit on an adjacent site), Squires Gate, Warton and Woodvale. Of these only Woodvale lingers on as a military airfield operating Tutor trainers for the University Air Squadrons of Manchester & Salford and Liverpool, together with providing air experience for Air Cadets. All the others are civilian-operated. Speke is now John Lennon International Airport. Warton is very active being the manufacturing and test flying centre for BAE Systems having built the Canberra, Lightning, Tornado, Hawk and now the Typhoon. The erection shops remain the original Second World War hangars used by BAD#2. Of the others Burscough still has some of its runways, its control tower and many of its hangars and airfield buildings. Inskip remains a RN signals base with the airfield covered in high masts. Knowsley Park is a safari park and open to the public; Samlesbury is still used by BAE Systems but for manufacturing and no flying is possible except for Air Cadet gliding which continues each weekend. Hesketh Park is back to a natural shore, the buildings have gone but some pleasure flying still continues from Birkdale Sands in the summer time.

Each airfield played an enormous part in the Second World War. They had a massive impact on the men and women who served there and the amazing achievements by those personnel are too numerous to mention. Many came across the Atlantic to become Allies and work with the British to destroy Nazi tyranny. BAE Systems continues to be at the forefront of military aviation research and development at Warton and Samlesbury. Let us not forget these people and their achievements and the remains of the airfields they have left behind.

2
BARROW-IN-FURNESS (WALNEY ISLAND)

1 mile NW of Barrow-in-Furness on Walney Island
SD 175713

Looking at Barrow airfield today, isolated on Walney Island on the edge of the English Lake District, it is very difficult to imagine it in its heyday as an Air Gunnery School with over 1,500 personnel based

Aerial view looking south, taken after the war but showing how close several runways are to the sea. Barrow in the background. (Via Peter Yuile)

there. Overlooking the Irish Sea and very exposed to incoming weather systems from the west, mountains to the north-east and the large industrial town of Barrow-in-Furness immediately adjacent, it is an unlikely place for an airfield. The flat land of the island made it easy to lay out the runways but two have very short over-runs before reaching the sea and two others slightly longer runs before meeting the same wet ending!

Flying first came to Barrow in 1908 when the Admiralty approached the engineering firm Vickers, after seeing the success of the German Zeppelin company who had been successfully building airships for a number of years. The British had nothing to compare. Vickers at Barrow was given a specification and the first airship, later named 'Mayfly' was begun in 1910. There was virtually no expertise in this type of design and construction, hence a major defence manufacturing company being approached, well away from prying eyes in the south of the country. The specification called for a cruising speed of 40 knots, a ceiling of 1,500 ft and a carrying load of three tons. It was officially His Majesty's Airship No 1 and Captain Murray Sueter was to co-ordinate the design and construction. He was no stranger to innovation having been involved in the concept of the tank and torpedo bomber. There were many problems to overcome; land was found on Walney Island for the construction of a shed in which to build the Mayfly but eventually a floating shed was built! Finally emerging from the shed in May 1911 the Mayfly endured a storm, was badly damaged and never actually flew as she broke her back on the ground. No further airships were built until 1913 when R9 was ordered. Eventually several more were built at Barrow right through the First World War. The last one was R80 on which work began in April 1918. Although well advanced at the time of the Armistice, work on this airship was stopped. Reluctantly permission was given to complete her and she did fly, but was scrapped in 1924.

No more flying took place at Barrow until the RAF surveyors homed in on the land at Walney Island again, remembering the First World War activities there. Locations near the coast were sought for gunnery schools and the airfield was designed. Construction started as a temporary war-time airfield with the traditional three runways and temporary buildings. A total mixture of temporary brick, Magnet, Nissen and asbestos Quonset type huts. The airfield had three runways, No 1 24/06, No 2 18/36 and No 3 12/30 were 1,100, 1,100 and 1,300 yards long respectively. They were all 50 yards wide and finished with a tarmac wearing surface. The main site was to the south-east of the airfield with three steel Callendar Hamilton type hangars There were also temporary brick buildings comprising the control tower (to design 518/40), a large instructional centre for the students, a free gunnery trainer, offices and stores. The dispersals were all to the north comprising nine Extra Over Blister hangars and open dispersal bays

To the south of the airfield lay the nine dispersed living sites. There was the communal site with officers' and sergeants' messes, gymnasium, barber's shop, education block and other buildings. Then five airmen's living sites, two WAAF sites, located immediately adjacent to the village of North Scale, and a sick quarters site. To accommodate the large number of permanent staff needed to operate the aircraft and school, as well as the students, there were 60 barrack huts, 66 Nissen huts, 18 officers' huts and 17 for sergeants. In total these were capable of accommodating 1,273 airmen, 53 corporals, 128 sgts, 88 officers and 352 WAAFs. RAF Barrow was a big establishment.

Although, construction commenced in early 1941, the base was not ready to accept aircraft until October when No 3 Air Gunnery School started to form. The official establishment was based on existing schools and was to be 58 officers, 104 SNCOs and 887 corporals and airmen plus 180 pupils. The first recorded activity was on 4th October when the small indent party arrived to take over the airfield as the contractors completed. The Communal Site (No 3) was handed over on 7th October; with SHQ on the 8th, Ration Store on the 11th; fuel compound on the 13th, Dining Hall and No 6 Site on the 15th, Main Stores on the 16th, No 8 Site on the 17th, NAAFI on the 23rd and the Sergeants' Mess on the 25th. During the first week, when few personnel were on site, there were no cooks so five gunners were volunteered and part of the Sergeants' Mess was used by all ranks. However numbers were soon to rise dramatically. Wing Commander C J Giles arrived as CO on 11th October. A week later four Lysanders arrived with no warning and in terrible weather, these were followed by two more the next day and two more on 20th. The School officially opened on 20th October with an initial strength of ten Lysanders and two Defiants. The role was to teach air gunners and air engineers, a combined role in the early days of the war when aircraft were comparatively simple and there was nothing larger in the RAF's inventory than twin-engined trainers and bombers. The first instructors, two sergeant air gunners, did not arrive until 14th November and by that time there was sufficient barrack space for 100 officers, 140 sergeants and 1,200 airmen. Although far from operational and suffering the exposed location and winter weather, the unit was visited by Marshal of the RAF Sir Edward Ellington on 24th November and a guard of honour was provided. No sooner had the unit started to resemble some formal order, than discussions took place about moving No 3 AGS to Castle Kennedy and replacing it with No 10 AGS, which was already established at Castle Kennedy.

The swap over took place on 1st December 1941. In reality it took several days for the units to complete the change but Wing Commander Giles remained as CO. Formed on 1st August 1941, No 10 AGS was fully up to strength and training. On 5th December, 41 pupils arrived from Castle Kennedy for No 6 Air Gunners course. Training and flying recommenced on 8th December with No 5 Course arriving from Castle Kennedy on 15th December and immediately continuing their training. Courses averaged 40 pupils made up of all ranks from LAC to sergeant. The work started in the classroom with theory and in the turret trainer, where they could master the basics whilst still on the ground. Eventually they were put into Defiants to shoot from the rear-powered turret at targets both on the sea and drogues towed by the Lysanders. Aircraft numbers rose with 12 Defiants arriving on 13th followed by five more on 14th plus one Lysander and one Master.

Inevitably, accidents soon started to happen. This was not surprising given the level of intensive training, using battle weary aircraft maintained in primitive conditions by mechanics with minimal expertise. The first recorded incident was to Defiant T 3989 on 8th January, which was damaged beyond repair. This was followed by slight damage to Defiant T4046 the next day and to V1173 the day after. No-one was hurt. By the middle of January 16 Defiants and nine Lysanders were available but all flying ceased on 19th January when the airfield lay under 16 inches of snow! The snow plan was immediately put into action to clear the runways and taxiways but no flying was possible until 25th January. Time had to be made up to keep the courses on schedule. By the end of January No 7 Flight Engineers/Air Gunners course passed out and No 8 commenced with another 40 pupils.

With the demand for aircrew, courses were flowing very fast with No 9 starting on 8th February followed by No 10 on 22nd. Both had 40 pupils and No 8 passed out on 27th with 36 successful pupils. Courses lasted six weeks with five in progress at any time, each with 40 pupils. It was difficult to keep pace with demand especially in the winter months with short daylight hours for flying time and the inevitable cross-shore winds. Unit records show the wind usually southwesterly but always gusting between 5 to 25 mph. The first fatal accident took place on 8th March when Sgt T Krol, a Polish pilot, and his student, Sgt C Lambert, died when Defiant H1811 crashed at Biggar Village. Lambert's course (No 9) passed out on 21st March with 35 successful, four suspended and Lambert killed. The 19th March was a bad day for accidents with a Gypsy Moth overturning on landing, Defiant T4046 force landing two miles from Ulverston and Defiant N1700 also force landing. No-one was badly injured.

Courses continued unabated, with an initial average of 35 out of 40 passing out. As the instructors and pilots became more experienced so the average increased until Courses Nos 21 and 22 saw all 40 pass out successfully.

Unfortunately, a serious accident happened to an Anson from Wigtown, which hit a balloon cable from the balloon barrage protecting Barrow. All four crewmembers were killed when it crashed into Cavendish Dock, Barrow. The bodies were brought to the station sick quarters for identification and dispatch back to their parent unit. It was a very unpleasant job but one which was to become more frequent in the next few years.

After surviving the cold and windy winter the station staff couldn't believe it in June when it got so hot the runways started to melt in the sun! The top coat of tar got so wet that all flying had to stop and 100 men were involved in applying 160 tons of chippings to the runways to make them serviceable again. Only two days of flying were lost. With Barrow being so close it was still a potential target and a red alert sounded on 20th and 21st July with the balloons raised to a height of 4,500 feet and all flying at 10 AGS grounded until the 'all clear' was given. No enemy aircraft appeared.

Defiants were not proving to be efficient because each aircraft could only carry one student at a time. As a result, Avro Ansons were brought in from early 1943. These twin-engined, all metal, low wing aircraft had a turret mounted at the rear top of the fuselage and could carry three students plus the pilot and an instructor. Hence each flight was longer and simultaneously allowed three students to experience flying and target shooting in one sortie. This was a major advance.

The first course named 'Wireless Operator/Air Gunner (WO/AG) commenced as No 31(A) course alongside No 30 on 23rd August 1942 with 60 and 40 students respectively. On 19th September, 59 of the 60 WO/AGs passed out. At this point in their careers the students would go to an Operational Training Unit (OTU) to convert onto types such as

'A' Flight of 10 AGS in front of Anson LF777 '13' of 10 AGS, 1944. (Peter Yuile)

No 25 Course, Flight Engineers June/July 1942. Cpl R Marsden, 7th from left on back row took part in the Dams Raid as part of Fg Off W Ottley's crew in Lancaster ED910, 16/17 May 1943. (Peter Yuile)

Wellington, Hudson, Blenheim etc and also join up with the rest of the new crew. They would then finish their training as a complete crew prior to joining a front line squadron. In September the Station Sports Day took place at Vickerstown Sports Ground in Barrow with teams drawn from RAF Walney Island plus local army, navy and police units. The station cup was won by the team from SHQ and all prizes were presented by the CO's wife, Mrs Giles. On 20th September a special church service was held in No 2 Dining Hall in observance of the deliverance and national thanksgiving for the Battle of Britain, two years earlier. In early October the Group Demonstration Flight of the RAF Regiment came to the station and gave seven demonstrations, which was recorded as 'very instructive'.

Considering the number of aircraft movements accidents were rare. Two Defiants are recorded as having wheels fall off on 27th October 1942 but there were no injuries. An incoming Defiant crashed near Preston on 24th October killing the sole occupant, pilot Sgt Goulter. There were also several forced landings due to engine failure and landing accidents with undercarriages collapsing. The two streams of courses, now with 60 students on each, continued at the end of the year by which time the strength had grown to 67 officers, 144 SNCOs, 818 corporals and airmen plus the WAAF contingent of five officers, 10 SNCOs and 371 airwomen. More red alerts disrupted flying on 26th and 31st October when No 970 (Balloon) Squadron again raised its balloons to defend Barrow but again no enemy raiders were seen. Wing

Commander Giles passed command to Group Captain M L Heath with effect from 1st January 1943 as the station faced another cold and blustery winter.

The first Anson to suffer an accident was N9739 on 18th March 1943 when it struck a starter trolley whilst taxiing. Minor accidents continued but with very few injuries. Course numbers were now reaching 50 with No 54 starting on 3rd April. On 9th April, 58 students out of 60 on No 55 Course passed out and No 58 Course (again with 60 students) commenced on 4th April. All flying ceased for the afternoon of 3rd April to help celebrate a Wings for Victory week in Barrow with a march-past by both the RAF and WAAF, a band from RAF Jurby on the Isle of Man and the salute taken by Marshal of the RAF Sir Edward Ellington. Flying was again disrupted on 11th April by a full scale station defence exercise with the 'enemy' being the 11th Argyll and Sutherland Highlanders.

A serious accident happened on 31st May 1943 when Anson LT778 collided with Martinet tug HP303. The Martinet managed to land but the Anson crashed on the beach ½ mile west of the station killing the pilot Sgt Anderton, instructor Fg Off Creed and three students LACs Hudson, Lenagham and Wilson all WOPs under training. Another Anson was lost when its port engine failed whilst flying over the sea near Blackpool. The pilot, Sgt Prince, successfully force landed on the sea allowing all occupants to get out safely and be picked up after the aircraft sank. On 9th September No 69 WOP/AG Course passed out, No 70 followed one week later and No 71 a week after that whilst No 74 Course started on 18th September.

The station theatre opened on 12th November with a performance attended by AOC No 29 Group, Air Commodore L G LeB Croke CBE. Another distinguished visitor was Prince Bernhard of the Netherlands who arrived by air from RAF Hendon, on 22nd November, to visit Vickers Armstrong at Barrow-in-Furness; he departed the next day.

The station records proudly state that in November 1943 several days saw a 100% flying programme completed with no engine failures and no details lost. The previous two years of intense operations and experience with engineering and operations was finally making itself felt. No 80 Course arrived on 5th December. Over 5,000 air gunners and engineers had already been trained by this one unit, a record of which to be proud. But the war was still on and the invasion of Europe was still six months off. At the end of 1943 and starting with Course No 76, it was decided to award a silver cup to the best all-round student to try and increase competition and make all students work even harder.

It proved to be a great success. Also starting with Course No 80 additional cine film training commenced with the 75 feet of film previously allowed being extended to 100 feet. During December the average number of live rounds fired per student was 3,300.

A Christmas party for local children was held on the unit at the end of 1943, with the chief instructor, Sqn Ldr Mills DFC, acting as Father Christmas. There was no flying on Christmas Day but 56 of the 60 members of No 78 Course passed out on this day with another 60 to form No 82 Course arriving on 29th December when the station concert party gave a performance of a musical *Shavings* in the station theatre. Unfortunately, two days before, on the 27th, there was a fatality. Flt Sgt Ciurkot (Polish) and his tower target operator LAC Collins died when their Martinet JN493 crashed 1½ miles south at Biggar Village after engine failure. Martinets were now replacing Lysanders as target tugs but had been experiencing numerous hydraulic problems with many accidents due to undercarriage failure. All Martinets were subsequently grounded on 2nd January 1944 for a few days for special checks.

End-of-year festivities continued with the RAF Cark concert party giving an excellent show entitled *Happy Landings* in the station theatre and the station dramatic society gave a performance of *The Wind and the Rain* on 14th January, no doubt inspired by the local weather conditions. RAF Millom provided a pantomine at the station on 31st January when *Cinderella* was performed. On 30th March the concert party performed *Musical Bumps* at the station theatre, this

ATC Cadets parade in the rain on the runway in 1943. (Peter Yuile)

58

Staff of Flying Control sitting on top of the control tower, 1944. Back row L-R Jones, Sgt J Thornton & Sgt Dransfield. Front W/O Gleed, W/O Harry Kilsby, Fg Off David Roach FCO, Anne ? (RT operator), Sgt Gibbs & Cpl ? FCA. (Peter Yuile)

was attended by Air Vice Marshal E D Davis OBE, AOC No 36 Group who presented the station badge to the CO during the interval.

Starting from Course No 85, which convened on 13th February 1944, all courses at 10 AGS became specialist air gunners courses, removing wireless operating and air engineer training from the syllabus. Courses remained at 60 each with four running concurrently giving a student population of 240 at any time. Work took priority but there was some time for play. On 18th April the Sergeants' Mess beat the Officers' Mess at indoor sports and recovered the cup back to their mess after it was captured by the officers on the previous occasion. An ENSA party arrived on 28th and presented *The Merchant of Venice* in the station theatre. The next day saw the start of the Barrow 'Salute the Soldier Week' with another RAF and WAAF march-past. On 30th April the station concert party presented *Shavings* in His Majesty's Theatre in Barrow. This was followed the next night by the station dramatic society presenting *In the Wind and the Rain* in Barrow Town Hall, followed by an encore two nights later.

D-Day came and went with no comment and no let up in training with No 91 Course passing out on 10th June with 61 students and No 95 convening the same day with another 60. The average number of details per day was well over 100 with 143 on 21st July. ATC cadets started coming to Barrow for their summer camp and Marshal of the RAF Sir John Salmond GCB visited to see the cadets and make sure they were being well looked after. On 14th August Gp Cpt Heath relinquished command to Gp Cpt L R S Freestone OBE. Pressure to complete the courses was so intense that all leave was stopped for a while and RAF and WAAF Rest Camps were set up on the base to allow personnel to relax off duty but preventing them from leaving the station. This situation lasted until the end of 1944 when the camps were closed down. Even if the airmen and airwomen did want to go on leave it was quite an effort. Whilst there was a good train service from Barrow to Kendal, which then connected to the north–south LMS line, it still took a long time to get anywhere.

Earlier that year, in February 1944, the CO had visited the Italian prisoner of war camp at Milnthorpe to see if it would be possible to employ sympathetic prisoners to cultivate the land on the airfield. War-time austerity required every spare piece of land to be utilized for growing food. With the workload at Barrow so high and with constantly changing student courses, it was impossible for the station personnel to find time. The principle was agreed but it took until 16th September before the first 26 Italians arrived for duty. There is no record of what they did or where they lived but it can be assumed they cultivated land on and around the airfield and lived in a controlled area, probably one of the living sites.

At the end of 1944 the allies were pushing across Europe but there was a long way to go and the war in the Pacific was still fiercely raging on. Demand for gunners continued unabated with course No 100 passing out with 61 out of 63 pupils on 21st October and the main operating aircraft were Ansons, with Masters and Martinets acting as tugs. The tugs would take off with a drogue in tow at least half a mile behind to protect the tug and its crew. There is no record of a tug ever being hit by a stray bullet at Barrow. The students would take off in an Anson and normally would rendezvous over the sea to the west, safely away from land and in a danger area where shipping was not allowed to stray. The students dipped the nose of their bullets in different coloured paint and after the sortie the drogue would be dropped onto the airfield and the tug landed. The students would then land and check the drogue to see how many hits they had, if any. Each

Wellington of 'A' Flight 10 AGS, 1945. LACWs Marion Jackson and Elsie Rhodes sitting on the nose, another Wellington behind. (Peter Yuile)

individual bullet hole would have a tell-tale colour to prove who the gunner was. At one stage the trainee gunners suffered a form of rash on their hands and the type of paint had to be changed to prevent this happening. All student gunnery was carried out in the Anson Mk I whilst the Masters and Martinets acted as drogue tugs. The drogues were like a windsock trailed on a steel cable behind the tug, brightly painted to present a relatively easy target. This was a far cry from operational flying in combat conditions. Cold, tired and in the dark, this was when this training proved its effectiveness.

Accidents were still relatively few but New Year's Day 1945 was an exception. Flt Sgt A J Wood had taken off in Anson LT741, with instructor air gunner W/O T W Johnson and two trainee gunners, Sgt J L Turner and Sgt K Jenkins. They had not been airborne long when they crashed into high ground and all were lost. On 6th January, 90 details were flown but snow again disrupted flying from 28th to 30th January. The snow plan was once again put into action, to allow aircraft to land and take off in case of emergency. With so many transit flights up and down the country, Barrow together with near neighbours Cark and Millom in Cumberland, received many transit aircraft either for fuel, for overnight stays or simply because they had lost their way.

Wreck of Wellington LP981 of 10 AGS crashed 13th April, 1945 off Fleetwood killing five of the seven on board. (Peter Yuile)

February 1945 saw 129 details on the 9th and 119 on the 19th and also the arrival of the first Wellington bombers. Wellingtons had turrets on the nose and tail and were substantially larger than the Ansons. The Wellington had long been relegated from front line service so many war weary examples were available for training. More students could be carried, thus increasing efficiency. The first two, Mk X's, arrived from No 48 MU at RAF Hawarden, near Chester, on 10th February followed by another the next day and four more on the 20th with the establishment rapidly rising. The incessant use of the runway resulted in emergency repairs being undertaken in February, especially as Wellingtons were substantially heavier than Ansons, hence more wear and tear on each landing. As the Wellingtons arrived, so the Ansons were disposed of. The Wellingtons were supplemented by both Hurricanes and Spitfires to give the gunners more practice aiming camera guns at real fighters. Again the Spitfires were old examples, mostly Mk IIAs which were now obsolete for front line work.

May and June 1945 saw an average of 75 details per day but the number of students on each course began to dip slightly as the war was known to be coming to an end. VE-Day, 8th May, was celebrated with all flying cancelled. There was great jubilation around the camp and an all-ranks dance in the evening. The next day just 21 details were flown.

The ageing Wellington stood up well to the high workload with the inevitable accidents, mostly taxiing accidents, crash landings and an unusual one on 8th September. Whilst in flight, a student ejected a belt of ammunition from the front turret which splintered the propeller forcing the pilot, W/O D R Jones to make a swift emergency landing. He made a textbook landing and was awarded with a Green Endorsement in his logbook for exceptional airmanship.

Although the war in the Pacific continued, the number and sizes of courses was reducing radically. Average details in June and July were down to 60 and several Martinets were being ferried away as surplus to requirements. Personnel numbers on 1st August 1945 reflected this with 57 RAF officers, 112 SNCOs, only 380 airmen plus four WAAF officers, eight SNCOs and 179 airwomen. However the school was earmarked to continue after the war when so many other units were disbanding. Although in a reduced state, a new CO arrived on 29th August when Group Captain M H Garnons-Williams from No 2 Flying Instructors School took over. VJ-Day is hardly mentioned in station records with 8 details on 13th August and 25 on 18th but there was a Victory Day holiday. An 'At Home' Day was staged for 15th September as the beginning of the annual RAF Battle of Britain open days, now sadly reduced to almost nothing in 2004. Back in 1945 the stations displayed a Typhoon, Mosquito, Lancaster and an Anson from the Staff Pilot Training Unit at Cark, to remind everyone of the vast numbers that had flown so recently from Barrow. It was meant to raise money for the RAF Benevolent Fund but although 10,000 people turned up little was available in terms of refreshment and only £52.10s was made. However the crowd was entertained by formation flypast by Wellingtons, Spitfires and Martinets plus mock attacks on Wellingtons by Spitfires and low flying attacks.

Mr James Paul was a civilian clerk at Barrow who ended up in charge of the Orderly Room and in the middle of all the administration. He has vivid memories of the students who came from all over the world with a sprinkling of Poles, Czechs and Canadians, as well as some from Greece, Cyprus and Malta. He remembers, 'The dances in the Sergeants' Mess were really hectic and, in fact, got out of hand. The Canadians were quite "wild" and I used to go to the mess to make out monthly bills and find it half wrecked. The CO finally stepped in after one wild night when a local dance band had several instruments damaged. Fights were common but 90 per cent of the reason was the sudden baptism in strong liquor which the young ones received and which they couldn't handle. I remember there was a mixture of aircraft,

Lysander for drogue towing, plus Boulton Paul Defiants, the odd Hurricane, Wellingtons and the perpetual Ansons. There were crashes and losses. In the sea, overshooting, stalling and hitting the hills around Millom.'

He continues, 'One of the events at 10 AGS was the placing of the redundant Balloon operators from the various disbanded units, later in the war. We got our quota and a scruffy, undisciplined crowd they were. The Station Warrant Officer Watkins was in his element knocking them into shape! ... I do remember seeing one fellow being shot! One day I saw a very truculent airman being marched back to the guard room by an NCO (corporal) and another LAC. Suddenly the prisoner broke away and started running and the corporal raised his revolver and shot. The airman fell and we thought it was the finish of him. However, he had been nicked in the shoulder and he was quickly up and taken away to the medical quarters. The corporal got a severe lecture from the CO who quite rightly said it was impossible for the prisoner to get away. Shortly after the corporal was posted to avoid repercussions.

'I remember with pleasure the Education Officer, Flt Lt Richards, aided by a man called Kelly who had an established music shop in Barrow and also used to conduct a local orchestra. Kelly provided many records. There were notabilities on the camp, no doubt more than I knew. Many in the sporting line, a Plt Off Ferrier who played league soccer, a Fenner who played for Motherswell and a third, possibly Smith, who played for Birmingham City; another was a Sgt Phillipson who played cricket for Lancashire, he also played hockey and RAF Walney always won when he played.

'There is no doubt *the* most popular CO was Group Captain Freestone. He was no red tape man – he enjoyed life – a real extrovert! At camp concerts he used to dress up and play a banjo with a few more types. Concerts became a huge success. He was a real public relations man and he instigated the throwing open of the station to the public once in a while.'

The last CO, Group Captain Garnons-Williams, wanted Mr Paul to go to Valley with the unit but it never happened and he returned to civilian life in Barrow.

Just after the end of the war, a detachment of No 577 Squadron arrived from Woodvale on 11th October 1945 with three Vultee Vengeance TT.IVs and two Spitfires. This squadron's HQ was at Castle Bromwich. It played a co-operation role with ground-based artillery units, such as the Coastal School of Artillery at Llandudno plus work in the Lancaster area and Altcar ranges on the Lancashire coast. The Fleet Air Arm were about to pull out of Woodvale so the detachment received orders to move to Barrow making the move over three days from 9th to 11th October. The CO, Flt Lt Wroe, moved across on the 4th, followed by the road transport on the 9th, the advance party on the 10th and all aircraft except Vengeance 424 which was unserviceable but which finally arrived at Barrow on the 17th.

With the war over and bases closing all the time there was little work for this unit. It deployed wherever it was asked, to provide targets for either radar calibration or drogues for the numerous ranges on the Lancashire coastline. For this a detachment was kept at Barrow. In November they were advised they would have to vacate Barrow to make room for more Wellingtons but this did not happen. In the middle of December they were warned that they would need to send a flight to Sealand due to an increase in commitment there but again it did not happen. By January 1946 the Barrow flight operated Spitfire XVIs SM391 and SM394 plus one Vengeance IV, which was unserviceable whilst the main unit had a mixture of Spitfires, Beaufighters, Hurricanes and Oxfords. With Barrow likely to start running down during the year, the detachment returned to its HQ at Castle Bromwich on 11th February 1946.

At the end of 1945, No 10 AGS was still extremely active having 130 cadets under training and averaging 40 details a day during the shortest days of the year. Although the war-time pressure was off the training continued. The Mountain Rescue Unit from Cark arrived on 9th January 1946 when Cark closed. This unit had rescued many aircrew from accidents across the Lake District and continued its good work from Barrow. Its first task from its new home occurred in February when a Dakota went missing in the Skiddaw area. A second 'At Home' took place on 12th May with the airfield open to the public who flocked to see a Halifax, Lancaster, Warwick, Wellington, Sea Otter, Mosquito, Argus, Seafire and Spitfire on display plus a very spirited display by Vickers Armstrong's famous test pilot, Geoffrey Quill. This time they raised £347 for charity. The Air Ministry then decided that 10 AGS should relocate to RAF Valley, Anglesey so after a rapid run down it moved as a working school. It was fully operational at Valley by the end of 1946. The air was strangely quiet with no powered aircraft remaining on the airfield.

The last unit to operate from Barrow in military colours was No 188 Gliding School run for air cadets. This school had formed at Cark by February 1944 and was established at Barrow by May 1947 flying

65

Aerial view looking west showing hangars and main site after the airfield had closed down, August 1947. (Peter Yuile)

Cadet Mk I and II gliders. It was only active for a short time and closed in October 1947 but reopened on 1st May 1948 still flying Cadet gliders now with the Mk III and the Sedbergh TX.1. The school had the run of the entire airfield each weekend until 1st September 1955 when it finally closed for good.

No sooner had the RAF vacated the numerous buildings, than squatters immediately occupied them. Most had been made homeless by the bombing of Barrow and these buildings offered larger accommodation for their families. They remained occupied this way until the families were re-housed in council accommodation. Once the old RAF buildings were vacated, they were immediately demolished to stop other families taking occupation.

Local pressure was applied to Barrow-in-Furness council to try and turn the airfield into a civil airport and visits were made to Blackpool Squires Gate to see how they had transformed their ex-RAF base into an airport. Nothing came of it and eventually Vickers took over the airfield for their executive aircraft and they also allowed other general aviation aircraft to use the facility. One of the problems Vickers considered before taking it over was a long bank of slag from the days when there were steel mills in Barrow. The slag had been dumped in a row aligned north to south along the east side of the airfield up to a height of 162 feet above sea level, causing quite an obstruction. It is still there, but is now greatly reduced having been used for hardcore and is not a hazard for the current runways. Today two runways are in use, 06/24 and 17/35, being 3,524 ft and 3,327 ft long respectively with a civilian gliding club still operating. Good approach and runway lighting is available but only one hangar remains. The airfield is in good condition and is operated by BAE Systems and although all the administrative and living areas and dispersed blister hangars are long gone there is still considerable civilian life left in the 'temporary' RAF Second World War airfield.

3
BARTON

2 miles WSW of Eccles, on A57
SJ 745970

Now threatened by development to the east and just to the north of the Manchester Ship Canal, Barton just lies within the original boundary of Lancashire. Early flying in Manchester was centred on Trafford Park, and later Alexandra Park, where several record-breaking pioneer flights took place. The site was used by A V Roe & Co Ltd for assembly and test flying of the aircraft they produced in Manchester until the airfield closed in 1924.

In the late 1920s the Government was asking councils of larger towns and cities around Britain to nominate a piece of land suitable for a municipal airport. Initially Manchester developed an area at Wythenshawe but this was to be temporary pending the construction of the new permanent airport at Barton Moss. Wythenshawe opened in April 1929 and claimed to be the first municipal airport in the UK to be licensed.

The site at Barton was outside the city boundary, being in Eccles, but had been used for many decades by the city council as a refuse and cinder dump. It therefore remained an open piece of land and part of it was made available for aviation in late 1928. Early maps show a light railway crossing the site from the south-west and this was used to transport the spoil for tipping onto the site. Cinders made a very good, firm yet well-drained surface and three grass runways were constructed running NE–SW 600 yards, E–W 500 yards and SE–NW 500 yards.

One large hangar was constructed and some existing farm buildings were pressed into use. The airfield was formally opened on 1st January 1930 as a civilian airport named Manchester Municipal Airport, managed by Northern Airlines (Manchester) Ltd.

Early routes included a 1930 summer service from London (Croydon) to Liverpool via Castle Bromwich and Barton run by Imperial Airways. Operators grew from 1934 to include Railway Air Services Ltd and routes were extended to include Blackpool, the Isle of Man and Glasgow. Early passenger aviation was for the rich, however, and it took some years for the companies to establish financially worthwhile routing with more efficient and economic aircraft types.

The 1931 edition of *Air Pilot* details Barton. It shows a location map and layout plan and advises that it is available for public use and that customs arrangements could be provided on demand. It says it is 'located six miles west of the Manchester city centre and 70 feet (21 metres) above sea level. The runways were cinder-covered, fairly well drained and generally hard but soft spots may occur after heavy rain.' It continues that 'the airfield is intended to be extended to the south and southwest but this area is currently unsuitable for landings due to hedges, ditches, the light railway and a deep depression containing a stream. The name "Manchester" is painted twice in white letters on the hangar roof. The hangar is constructed of brick and steel and is 100 feet wide by 200 feet deep with a door height of 30 feet and 100 feet wide. Aviation fuel, oil and water were available as well as refuelling pumps. There were no night landing facilities, nor was there any radio.' Barton's unique control tower was erected in 1933 with a dominating aerial array on its roof for direction finding, now removed. Two large transmitting towers were erected ½ mile north of the airfield.

Types of aircraft were initially Armstrong Whitworth Argosy and Handley Page W8 and W10 in 1930. From 1934, de Havilland DH 84 Dragon, and 1934 DH 89 Dragon Rapides were available. A number of locally re-built Avro 504s were used for charter and pleasure flying. Aviation was a growing industry and Airwork Ltd took over the management contract of Barton in 1933 subsequently operating No 17 Elementary & Reserve Flying Training School. F Hills & Sons Ltd, a woodworking business based at Trafford Park, test-flew some early aircraft at Barton, subsequently assembling over 700 Proctors here. Fairey Aviation Ltd took over the buildings of the National Aircraft Factory No 2 at Heaton Chapel in late 1934 and needed a base to assemble and test-fly Hendon bombers and took a short lease on the Municipal hangar in 1936, later assembling Fairey Battles before moving to Ringway in June 1937.

The first RAF unit at Barton was No 17 Elementary & Reserve Flying Training School which opened at Barton on 1st October 1937 to provide ab initio flying training to local civilians in the RAF reserve. The school was entirely civilian-manned and operated by Airwork Services Ltd flying Moths and later Tiger Moths and Avro Anson aircraft. The more advanced flying was to be done in the Ansons from Ringway. Flying was similar to a civil flying school but to the more exacting standards required by the RAF. Barton was one of 32 similar schools set up around the country but on the outbreak of war they were all disbanded and replaced by twenty Elementary Flying Training Schools. Unfortunately one was not established at Barton and the school disbanded the day before war broke out. Military flying was not to return to Barton until after the war but several thousands of RAF and Royal Navy aircraft were built at, or flew from, Barton during the conflict. On 1st March 1940, No 6 Anti-Aircraft Co-Operation Unit formed at nearby Ringway, Cheshire, and was due to have a detachment at Barton but this was not to be.

On the opening of the Second World War the Ministry of Aircraft Production requisitioned the airfield and, later, land to the west as suggested in the *Air Pilot* back in 1931. Several civilian companies received contracts to build, erect or repair military aircraft. The huge manufacturing complex at Trafford Park was close by, as were the factories of Avro and Fairey. There were also the smaller companies such as David Rosenfield Ltd from Cheetham in Manchester who repaired Fairey Battles in one of the new west-side Bellman hangars. This contract started in 1942 and by the end of the war they had overhauled in excess of 300 aircraft comprising Fairey Fulmars, Fairey Barracudas, Fairey Swordfish, Chance Vought Corsairs and Hurricanes. In the summer of 1945, the firm scrapped many elderly Swordfish.

Air Taxis Ltd had relocated north from Croydon on the outbreak of war and made Army Co-Operation flights from Barton. They won a contract from MAP to repair civil Dragon Rapide aircraft and RAF Dominies. The company also later repaired and undertook major modifications to Ansons. This role continued until the end of the war and they repaired or modified over 500 Ansons for the RAF. This work had utilised the original 1930 hangar.

F Hills & Sons Ltd obtained rights to build a Czechoslovakian-designed aircraft from Prague and they named it the Hillson Praga following the local spelling of Prague, although the original name was the 'Praga' Air Baby!

Approximately 35 of these Pragas were assembled in a newly built hangar next to the main hangar. They were flown from Barton and the experience was sufficient for Hills to obtain a contract from MAP to

70

Barton-built Fairey Gordon bomber and Dominie behind outside the tower at Barton late 1936. (R A Scholefield)

build Percival Proctors. These were the military version of the Vega Gull light sports aircraft which first flew in 1935. The aircraft was a single-engined low wing monoplane powered by a de Havilland Gypsy Queen II engine. The Mk I was used as a three seat communications aircraft and 25 of the total of 245 were built by Hills. The Mk II was a radio trainer and all were built by Percival but the Mk III was also a radio trainer and all 437 were built by F Hills. The Mk IV was built as a radio trainer with a deeper fuselage for carrying four plus additional radio equipment. Many Mk IVs were used as communication aircraft with dual control and 250 of the 256 received by the RAF were built at Barton by Hills in a west-side hangar.

Mr A P Pease of Whitefield was an engineer at F Hills & Sons Ltd and recalls, 'During the war the airfield was known as "Barton Airport" and used by Messrs F Hills & Son of Trafford Park to flight test the Proctor aeroplane. This single-engined craft was built in the factory complete at Trafford Park and towed complete to Barton airfield, wings of course fitted at the airfield, and then tested at the airport. Then flown and delivered by their test pilot (forgotten his name) to the RAF stations as required. I was in charge of the tooling of the Proctor. 75% of the tools for the making of parts for the Proctor was subcontracted of course and spread all over the north to smaller tool makers and AID approved companies. I remember Waring & Gillows prepared centre sections and Wilsons of Coventry made the petrol

Proctor III HM463 built by Hills at Barton seen as 'N' with Middle East Communications Squadron, Heliopolis in 1944. (Harry Holmes via R A Scholefield)

tanks, quite well-known companies. Barton was very close to the various factories producing parts of the Proctor and it was, to my knowledge, the only aircraft that was assembled completely at Barton – from factory to flying.'

Some civil passenger flying returned during the early part of the war when West Coast Air Services Ltd and Aer Lingus flew de Havilland 86B Express airliners and a Douglas DC-3 to and from Dublin until the service reverted to Speke. Hard runways were never built and Barton still operates on grass. However many larger RAF aircraft did land and take off including the Bristol Bombay, Douglas Havoc, Whitleys and Wellingtons. The largest visitor was Lancaster ND920 of 115 Squadron, which visited on 25th April 1944 from Waterbeach and managed the take off with no problem. It was piloted by Flt Sgt Crawford. Many USAAF C-47's visited from 1943 onwards.

Several new buildings were erected to accommodate the war-time expansion with three hangars including two Bellmans on the south-west MAP area which was linked by just a narrow taxiway. Hills had a hangar erected in 1937, immediately adjacent to the Municipal hangar and two blister hangars were put on the technical site.

With the large number of landings and take off it is surprising that the RAF opened a gliding school for air cadets. Many were formed around the country to give boys too young to join the RAF experience in flying to encourage them towards the military when they were old enough. Schools were set up at Stanley Park, Blackpool, Samlesbury, Warton, Wilmslow, Speke, Woodvale, Manchester and Stretton locally and all over the country. In March 1944, No 185 was formed at Barton with a Cadet Mk I basic glider. The school did not last for long and disbanded in December 1947 following prohibition of gliding at Barton by the Ministry of Civil Aviation in June 1947.

Post-war aircraft production stopped almost overnight and Ringway was now the undisputed airport for Manchester with its hard runways and permanent buildings. Scheduled services did not continue from Barton but it was used for maintenance and charter flights by Sivewright Airways Ltd's Miles Aerovan, Dragon Rapides and Ansons. Other small short-lived charter operators also used Barton until 1952. Lancashire Aero Club moved to Barton from Woodford in 1946 and still operates light aircraft. Many private planes and helicopters are now based here. The RAF returned in March 1946 when Manchester University Air Squadron moved to Barton after being formed at Ringway in April 1941. This unit trained university undergraduates up to the primary flying badge, standing them in good stead if they joined the RAF or, if not, giving future 'Captains of

Tiger Moths of Manchester University Air Squadron at Barton in 1948. (M Fadil via R A Scholefield)

73

Aerial photo, 1938, with the Tiger Moths of MUAS visible bottom centre. (Photair via R A Scholefield)

Industry' a good insight into service life. Equipped with three and later five Tiger Moths they flew weekends or whenever the students could be available.

At the same time as MUAS, No 2 Reserve Flying School formed in October 1948 with six Tiger Moths. The RAF had 21 Auxiliary Squadrons, mostly flying fighters, plus a huge number of recently demobilised air crews such as pilots, navigators and signallers who were held in reserve in case of national emergency. In order to keep these aircrews up to speed, 25 Schools were set up around the country mostly centred on the larger cities in the UK. Hooton Park, Cheshire, was home to No 19, which later moved to Woodvale in July 1951. Reid & Sigrist Ltd (who also maintained the aircraft of MUAS) operated No 2 at Barton. They also employed ex-RAF aircrew to fly the 15 Tigers, which were later partially replaced by Chipmunks, all of which flew in military markings. The contract was transferred to Short Bros & Harland in October 1952 but the schools disbanded in March 1953 because of defence cuts.

Barton was proving to be unsuitable for consistent MUAS training

A 1948 aerial view of the control tower and main hangars. (R A Scholefield)

because of its boggy surface, poor weather conditions and proximity to Ringway airport. Flying was not possible for days on end. Night flying had been carried out at Woodvale and the MUAS therefore transferred its Chipmunks there on 15th March 1953 to join with Liverpool University Air Squadron, which was already located there.

Today Barton is home to the oldest flying club in Britain, The Lancashire Aero Club and is also home to over 80 light aircraft. Most of the war-time expansion area has been redeveloped but the west-side 'temporary' hangars survive, and several original buildings are now demolished. With the encroachment of buildings and inevitable complaints about noise, Barton has been threatened with closure many times but has a fascinating history and hopefully will continue for many years to come.

4

BURSCOUGH

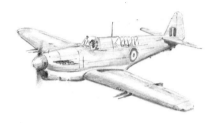

2 miles north of Ormskirk, on A59
SD 425110

Royal Naval Air Station Burscough was the last airfield to be built in Lancashire during the Second World War. Located two miles north of Ormskirk, to the west of the A59 and north of the B5242 and immediately south of Burscough Bridge, the base sits on flat, high-quality agricultural land. Covering an area of approximately 650 acres it was considered ideal for an airfield but it is thought it may originally have been earmarked for the RAF. However it was constructed to the normal Navy plan with four runways instead of three, all of which were only 30 yards wide instead of the RAF standard 50 yards. The extra runway allowed the aircraft to land and take off as close as possible into the wind, with eight different directions to choose from. The narrower landing strips also simulated take off and landing on aircraft carriers.

During 1942 the Fleet Air Arm planned to increase its number of operational aircraft from 2,665 to 6,350. This was a huge increase which would require many new airfields to provide bases as well as train and support the new crews. This land was acquired on 12th December 1942 and Burscough was built as a temporary base for the duration of the war. Consequently, there was no fine architecture or planning. It was designed to accommodate up to 80 aircraft and the runways were all similar in length being 1,000, 1,005, 1,025 and 1,240 yards. The longest was orientated 08/26 with 26 being on a bearing of 260° or SSW, directly into the prevailing wind. An Admiralty style, three-storey brick control tower was built on the east side with an excellent view

76

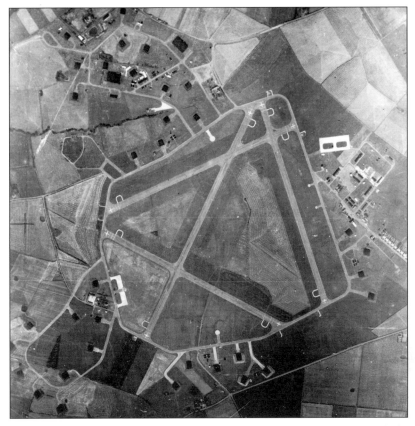

Vertical showing dispersed sites and four runways, 1944. (Via Author)

across the base and of all approaches. There were 32 Mainhill type hangars constructed, 18 for squadron use and 14 for storage, with two Callender type for major servicing. Four dispersal areas were formed to allow four units to operate from the base simultaneously plus dispersed fuel and ammunition storage and two living sites, both immediately east of the A59 between the road and the railway.

The administration and living buildings were mostly Nissen huts, which were quick and cheap to build but cold, damp and difficult to keep warm in the winter. It was unusual for a base of this size to only have two dispersed living sites but it is assumed that the threat of air attack by this stage of the war was sufficient to remove the need for wide dispersal. It also speeded up time to and from work and to the

Oblique aerial view looking north-east, taken on 23rd October 1943. (Fleet Air Arm Museum)

messes. The living site could accommodate 189 officers and 1,204 sailors plus 15 Wren officers and 355 Wrens. The HF/DF site was at Throstles Nest Farm, Pippen Road. Burscough also used part of Fletcher's Farm, Liverpool Road as a temporary school and occupied 4,444 sq yards of land at Moorfield House Farm for GCI sets. The base also housed the staff that took over the CLH base at *Stella Maris* at Formby when it became No 277 Radio Installation Unit in 1944 (see Setting the Scene).

Like all FAA bases, Burscough was named after a bird. It was formally commissioned as HMS *Ringtail* on 1st September 1943. Its role was to accommodate day and night fighter, torpedo fighter, Fleet Requirement units and a radar school. It was to be a very busy station with 40 units ultimately being based there, some for a very short time.

The first to arrive was No 808 Squadron from the carrier HMS *Hunter*, having been involved in the Mediterranean at the battle of Salerno whilst embarked on HMS *Battler*. The nine Seafires arrived at Burscough on 6th October 1943 with Lt Cdr A C Wallace as CO who was replaced by Lt Cdr J F Rankin on November. Whilst at Burscough they continued training in close support. On 21st January they re-embarked on HMS *Hunter* for exercises then moved to Lee-on-Solent in Hampshire from where they supported the Normandy landings in June before departing for the East Indies. Next to arrive on the following day (7th October) was No 886 Squadron from Machrihanish, Argyll. They too had Seafires. They worked up until 29th December when they left for HMS *Attacker*. The third squadron, No 807, arrived on 9th October disembarking from HMS *Hunter*. This squadron had 12 Seafires and had supported the North Africa landings in November 1942, shooting down two French fighters. Their role was tactical reconnaissance and fighter cover which they undertook in the western Mediterranean for two months. They came back to the UK via HMS *Indomitable* (damaged by a torpedo on 16th July), Gibraltar, HMS *Battler* from which they supported the Salerno landings in September, HMS *Hunter* and Burscough. Their CO was Lt A B Fraser-Harris and whilst at Burscough they increased their aircraft strength to 20 Seafires. They re-embarked on HMS *Hunter* for exercises and training from late January to late February and again in March, finally leaving Burscough on 30th April for HMS *Hunter*, via Andover, Hampshire, when she sailed back to the Mediterranean.

The fourth squadron to arrive was No 897, which came in the very next day again with nine Seafires. This unit came from HMS *Unicorn* and stayed just over two months before flying onto HMS *Stalker* on 29th December. Together Nos 808, 807, 886 and 897 formed the 3rd Naval Fighter Wing.

On 19th December, No 879 Squadron arrived from Andover immediately taking the place of 897 Squadron. Another Seafire unit, this squadron had also been in the Mediterranean and supported the Salerno landings from HMS *Attacker*, flying 75 patrols with two aircraft actually landing at Paestrum airstrip for a while. They returned to the UK via Gibraltar ultimately flying off to Andover before flying north to Burscough. The CO was Lt Grose who was replaced by Lt Cdr D G Carlisle in October. Whilst at Burscough they also increased their size to 20 Seafires joining HMS *Attacker* for practice deck-landing and other training in March and moving on to Long Kesh, Northern Ireland on 24th March 1944 and HMS *Attacker* on the 30th.

The station was now holding four Seafire squadrons simultaneously with one immediately replacing another. As one departed its dispersal was filled virtually the same day. All these units had seen action in the Mediterranean, coming home for more aircraft and crews before returning to the same area. Deck-landing practice was also available at Burscough where a dummy deck had been painted onto a runway and cables positioned so aircraft could land and actually pick up a cable exactly as they would on board. This way, new pilots could experience some of the sensation of landing on a carrier. Nothing could actually train them adequately, however, without practice on the real thing.

Next to arrive was 809 Squadron which had formed at Stretton, Cheshire in April 1943, provided fighter cover for Salerno and returned to Burscough on 19th December with ten Seafires under the command of Major A J Wright RM. They only stayed ten days before joining HMS *Stalker* in the Clyde, working up and spending some time at RNAS Dale, Pembroke, before returning to the Mediterranean.

The constant flow continued with No 894 Squadron arriving on 8th January 1944 from Henstridge, Somerset where it had re-equipped with Seafire IIs. This unit was another veteran of the Salerno landings but only stayed one month before departing to Ballyhalbert, Co Down, on 5th February with Lt Cdr Walker as CO. In August this squadron provided cover for the attack on the Tirpitz. One day later No 823 Squadron flew in from Fearn with Barracudas again only staying until 26th February when they embarked on HMS *Atheling*. They were joined the following day by 1836 Squadron which had formed in Brunswick, Canada under Lt Cdr C C Tomkinson, with 10 Corsairs, which they brought to Burscough on HMS *Atheling*. At Burscough their establishment was increased to 14 aircraft and after a short work up they left for HMS *Victorious* on 8th March. Cover for the Tirpitz attack on 2nd to 4th April was also provided by 1836 Squadron, before moving on to Ceylon in June.

As they moved out, 1837 Squadron arrived from HMS *Begum* also with Corsairs. They continued training for eleven days before moving to RNAS Stretton on 12th February. The next successively numbered squadron, No 1838, arrived simultaneously but from Machrihanish and also with Corsairs. Again, after a short work up this squadron moved on to HMS *Atheling* on 26th February.

Two more Seafire units arrived on 6th and 7th February when 879, with 20 Seafires, and 886 returned from exercises on HMS *Attacker*.

The first squadron to form at Burscough was 1840 when it was commissioned on 1st March 1944 with ten Curtiss Hellcat aircraft. Under the command of Lt Cdr Richardson this unit worked up quickly on its new aircraft and moved to Eglinton on 14th April where it received another ten aircraft before embarking on HMS *Indefatigable* in June.

On 3rd March, 1771 Squadron arrived from Yeovilton, Somerset with twelve Firefly aircraft (later to increase to 20) and was destined to remain here more than the few weeks that all the preceding squadrons had managed. This unit had formed under Lt Cdr Henry M Ellis DFC, DSC, RN at Yeovilton and continued its work up here before moving to Machrihanish in August.

Ex Chief Petty Officer Tom Hicks of Paisley, Scotland remembers his time with 1771: 'I have fond memories of Burscough. The position of the Bull & Dog could not have been planned better! Many nights were spent at this watering hole, only a stone's throw away from Site II. On two occasions we visited Southport, a very pleasant seaside resort. Our accommodation at Burscough was very basic but waterproof. The station appeared to have several spells of foggy days, which upset our working up. Most days the crew were put through their paces working up to 29th June, when we flew to HMS *Trumpeter*.' Tom Hicks returned to Burscough in August 1945 with 1791 Squadron but the decision was made to disband that squadron on 23rd September 1945 and he moved on to Yeovilton, Somerset.

In March, 735 Squadron moved in from Inskip on the 18th with a mixture of aircraft not seen here before including Swordfish, Anson, Hellcat and Barracuda. This was a training squadron, in fact all training units were in the 700 series of numbers whilst front line units all started with an '8'. The unit trained observers and radar operators.

The flow of front line units continued on 20th April with the arrival of the Avengers and Wildcats of 846 Squadron from Machrihanish but they only stayed eight days before departing for HMS *Tracker*. Commanded by Lt R D Head this squadron had served on HMS *Tracker* in the Mediterranean having attacked six U-boats in the period 28th March to 4th April and another two later in April. After their short stay at Burscough whilst their ship was being replenished they re-embarked and flew patrols for enemy shipping south-west of Ireland. As 846 departed Nos 881 and 896 Squadrons arrived from HMS *Pursuer* with ten Wildcat aircraft each. They had been operating in the south-west Pacific and were involved with the attacks on the Tirpitz before returning to the UK for the ship to benefit from a month's replenishment, repair and re-equipping. The squadrons re-embarked on 2nd June when they went onto fighter protection and convoy escort duty.

Squadron 1772 formed here on 1st May 1944 with twelve Firefly Mk1 aircraft and 30 aircrew. The Firefly was a tandem two-seat fighter-bomber which could fire unguided rockets and also had four 20 mm cannon, two in each wing. Fireflies were ideal for low-level fighter sweeps and that was the operation role of 1771 Squadron when they were sent to the British Pacific Fleet to attack many targets on mainland Japan in July and August 1945. They worked up with deck landing practice on HMS *Empress* in the Irish Sea during November. The original aircraft were then replaced with ones fitted with long-range

Pilots of 1772 Squadron on a Firefly outside their HQ, 1944. (Via Ray Jones)

tanks and they embarked on HMS *Ruler* in Belfast in January 1945. Under command of Lt Cdr A M D Gough they sailed for Australia and in July and August took part in strikes against the Japanese mainland right up to the end of the war.

Meanwhile, 1772 Squadron, known as 'The Friendly Squadron', suffered a gem of a taxiing accident on 25th October, when all three aircraft were on the ground at the time of impact! The exercise was organized to fill in a bad day, when visibility was down to 200 yards. Lt Cdr Gough planned a carrier deck-ranging exercise in which aircraft tucked themselves in closely at the end of the runway, as is usual on the more restricted area of a flight deck. In fact a dummy flight deck was marked out on the runway. The idea was that, on a signal, each aircraft would move into a position on the 'centre line', open up, roar off at take-off revs and then throttle back. Subsequent planes would follow on in the same manner. The long nose of the Firefly is not as inhibiting to vision as with a Seafire, but nevertheless, the nose is long, and in a tail down position, the vision was not good. Thus the scene was set for what was called 'a monumental cockup'. Firefly 4Z failed to throttle back, overtook 4M, hitting it with the port wing tip. 4M ground

Firefly of 1772 Squadron with Croos Parry and observer Knocker White, 1944. (Via Ray Jones)

looped. The process was repeated on 4J. They all ground looped, and they all lost their undercarriages. The exercise was abandoned and fortunately no-one was hurt, just very embarrassed. The new CO, Lt Cdr Les C Wort, arrived on 1st November!

The records of 1772 Squadron show many accidents, the first only five days after formation, when on 6th May, Firefly Z1979 landed with its undercarriage retracted. The pilot, Sub Lt S H Jobbins, was unhurt. Similar accidents with no undercarriage, landing short of the runway, ground looping, tyre bursts etc occurred too often with 24 recorded, two being fatal. The first fatality was on 26th June. Sub Lt Harry Garbutt, pilot, with Midshipman Ken Neuschild as observer failed to pull out of a loop off Blackpool pier and crashed into the sea. The other was on 29th July 1944 when the CO Lt Cdr Gough and Lt Wright, the Senior Pilot, collided in mid-air. The CO had planned a particular type of formation. There were two such formation trips and Squadron Pilot Teddy Key had recorded in his log book after the first one – 'Shambles'. Undeterred, the same formation was attempted the following day, with disastrous consequences. An eye witness described: 'Having scrambled some of the Squadron I watched two planes, chasing each other, then to

Pilots of 1772 Squadron celebrating a birthday at the Bull & Dog pub at Burscough – on a non-flying day, of course. (Via Ray Jones)

my horror they collided and went down out of sight. Holding my breath, I waited but all too soon, a plume of black smoke could be seen rising up, indicating the worst had happened.' The pilots survived but Lt Jimmy Sloan RN, flying with Wright, and Lt Monty Baker RNVR, with the CO, died.

The Barracudas of Nos 829 and 831 Squadrons were next to arrive on 20th May, whilst HMS *Victorious* was in port. They continued their training here departing six days later to re-embark on *Victorious*. On 11th May 829 had taken part in a fly-past for HM The King and went on leave whilst at Burscough. One aircraft, piloted by Lt (A) George Grindrod RNVR, crashed en route from Burscough to HMS *Illustrious*. Grindrod was unhurt but his observer, Leading Airman Alan Sim, was killed.

On 10th June 1944, 888 Squadron reformed here as a single seat Photographic Reconnaissance Unit, with six of the impressive Curtiss Hellcat II (PR) aircraft. The squadron had previously flown Wildcats off HMS *Formidable* in the Indian Ocean. It had returned to the Mediterranean to support the Italian landings at Sicily and Salerno and

Fairey Firefly I Z1977 'S' of 1772 Squadron Burscough taken by Jack Knight, test pilot from BAD#2 Warton, over Ribble Estuary on 17th June 1944. (Harry Holmes)

then disbanded. Like many squadrons working up, there were never enough spare parts to go round and demands to stores took forever to arrive or were hijacked by other units. On one occasion 888 were short of Hellcat spares and the American liaison officer arranged a trip to the American base at Burtonwood where they specialised not only in radial engines but in American radial engines such as the Pratt & Whitney Double Wasp which powered the Hellcat. A case of whisky ensured a truckload of unofficially donated spares including an entire engine, and the comment from the storekeeper, 'One thing's for sure, Mac, these spares sure ain't gonna win the war sitting in here!' The squadron went to Glasgow to embark its increased establishment of eight Hellcats on HMS *Rajah* for passage to Belfast and then Ceylon where they undertook photographic reconnaissance training sorties. At the end of the year it joined HMS *Indefatigable* for operations early in 1945 over Sumatra in Operation 'Lentil'.

The Swordfish of 835 Squadron were next to arrive on 4th July from HMS *Nairana*. Swordfish were slow bi-plane torpedo bombers and the

First photo of 1772 Squadron, 1944, showing the size of a mobile RN squadron. (Via Ray Jones)

squadron had been undertaking Atlantic anti-submarine and convoy patrols, losing two aircraft. Its remaining nine aircraft were increased by three whilst at Burscough and they returned to HMS *Nairana* on 13th August. In July, 1770 Squadron flew in from Donibristle with Fireflies for three days and another training unit arrived on 6th August. This was 'Y' Flight of 787 Squadron operating Seafires for fighter affiliation and they remained here until November when they departed for Speke.

The only FAA Helldiver unit arrived in August, when 1820 Squadron arrived from the USA, with Lt Cdr Ian Swayne RFC, RN as CO. They had reformed in the USA in April. The Helldiver was the first purpose-built dive bomber directed to front line duties with the FAA since the Skua of the late thirties. The pilots were trained by the US Navy and had completed the severe dive bombing course at USNAS Vero Beach, Florida. They then expected to join an FAA

Helldiver squadron but as the US Navy was re-equipping with them it was some time before aircraft were available to form the unit. Most pilots joined the unit at Brunswick, Maine before moving to Boston USNAS around May 1944 spending the next two months working up with, finally, deck landings on a USN carrier in Chesapeake Bay. The squadron then embarked on HMS *Arbiter* for Liverpool.

The arrival, via Speke, was enjoyed by the pilots and Ewan Jones, now of Tauranga, New Zealand, continues the story. 'Burscough, from a flying point of view, was rather good, easy to get in and out from in all sorts of weather. Aircrew accommodation comprised two Nissen huts, one each for pilots and observers. Heating was from the standard pot belly stove and condensation was something that had to be put up with! A wardroom and dining area were also part of the establishment. On the airfield itself the facilities were very good and that was, of course, the important part. While the scenery was nothing to write

A Helldiver of 1820 Squadron at Burscough, 1944; the only unit to operate this type. (Via Ray Jones)

home about, the pub across the road from the main gate and those delightful Wrens, all helped to make Burscough not too bad at all. We made our recreation and I enjoyed being a playing member of the Ringtail rugby team.

'So far we had only one casualty, in the States, when Sub Lt Dawson and his observer were killed. On 19th August 1944 on a low cross country over Westmorland, my aircraft suddenly lost power at 300 feet and I had no option but to force land with the undercarriage retracted in a fairly tight area at Home Farm, Sedburgh. I don't think I frightened my observer, Alf Coombes, too much and a test on the engine showed supercharger failure.' Around early October the squadron flew a dive bombing exercise on the Morecambe Bay bombing range. The aircraft flown by Sub Lt Neville had Steward F T Turner, a squadron steward, as passenger instead of the observer. Pilot Jones describes what happened next. 'I was diving two behind Neville, dropped the bombs to pull out at about 600 ft and looked back to see with some surprise, a blazing ring of fire where the target used to be!' This was a not uncommon occurrence in the dive bombing course, where pilots during the dive drifted off target fractionally and then tried everything to get back on station with fatal results. Neville and Turner are buried at Burscough parish church.

Jones also recalls: 'The squadron was getting better and better, showing off its skills doing a mock bombing attack on one of the smaller carriers in the Irish Sea. Whilst on leave in London I received a telegram recalling me to the Squadron, which was on its way to Hatston, Orkney, to prepare for carrier duty. When I got to the Orkneys I found the aircrews had already checked out on carrier landings and were ready to go. On an exercise following John Fenwick I did a "chase me Charlie" run and as both aircraft were pulling out of a dive I saw John's starboard elevator disintegrate and hoped that the port one would not follow suit. He managed to get back to the airfield whereupon all aircraft were grounded. Inspection showed elevator faults in all planes. Suspicion arose as to whether something similar had happened in the crashes of Dawson and Neville. Eventually we were ordered to return to Burscough on 4th December, John was promoted to acting CO and I got to be Senior Pilot. But by mid month the Squadron was disbanded, it was a waste of skilled aircrews and ground staff and we have often wondered why modifications were not made to the elevators.' Burscough was to house the only two Helldiver units in the UK, in unhappy circumstances.

In the meantime 812 Squadron, with Barracudas, arrived from Crail, Scotland in September for a month. In November 813 Squadron arrived for ten days from Machrihanish with Wildcats and Swordfish prior to embarking on HMS *Campania*. On 30 November 810 Squadron arrived at Burscough to be sent on leave. The squadron had an illustrious career helping in the sinking of the Bismarck in May 1941 then moving out to the Indian Ocean on HMS *Illustrious* in 1942, initially with Swordfish and then converting to Barracudas. 1944 saw them in Ceylon where they disbanded and returned to the UK without aircraft. On return the squadron found a new CO, Lt Cdr A C Heath, and twelve new Barracudas which it worked up on until February 1945 when they moved to Thorney Island, Hampshire for anti-shipping patrols in the English Channel.

New Year's Day 1945 dawned bright and cold with another new night fighter unit forming. Under the command of Lt J H Neale, No 1790 Squadron initially had six Firefly NF.1s, increasing to 12 during March. The role was primarily night fighting with the secondary role of day reconnaissance. The Fireflies were equipped with the very latest radar, an American AN/APS.4 (ASH) air-to-surface homing. The unit looked like a bomb slung under the engine and was used for Airborne Interception (AI) but ASV (Search) was useful for mapping coastlines and could spot a convoy at 45 miles and a small motor vessel at 20 miles. This unit spent a comparatively long period at Burscough working up from March to June with 15 crews who flew for 1,456 hours of which 658 were at night. Half the flying was devoted to Ground Controller Interception by day and night. On 25th May nine Fireflies embarked on HMS *Puncher* and the squadron completed its work up with deck landing and take-offs and carrier drill. Two night interceptions were carried out in co-operation with the Fighter Direction Ship *Palomares*. The squadron completed 475 deck landings, with 131 at night. They suffered two accidents in day landings and six during night landings, none serious. Once it was fully worked up, 1790 Squadron embarked on HMS *Vindex* and set sail to Australia. It was joined by No 707 Squadron which formed from 'B' Flight of 735 Squadron on 20th February to act as the Naval School of Airborne Radar and radar trials with a mixture of Swordfish, Barracuda, Avenger and Anson aircraft. This unit had two functions as the control authority in this specialised subject and to train flying personnel in its use. Aircraft would use ships and ground features as targets and would range far and wide across northern England. Another training unit, 737 Squadron from Arbroath, Scotland, joined 707 in April. This unit was the Naval Anti-Submarine Squadron with Swordfish and Anson aircraft training up new aircrews in this specialist role. The war was going well in Europe with the Allies making deep advances into the German occupied area so Burscough was now seeing more training units rather than front line units. However the war in the Pacific was far from won and 707 moved to Gosport, Hampshire in August whilst 737 Squadron stayed until mid November before disbanding.

Although heavily involved with training, there were so many aircraft at Burscough that it looked for expansion space with which to work up squadrons for the Far East. Looking west, RAF Woodvale was now becoming surplus as a fighter station for the defence of the north-west and provided an ideal satellite base. Accordingly the Fleet Air Arm took Woodvale over from the RAF and navalised the base, then opened it as a 'tender', HMS *Ringtail II*, on 7th April 1945. It was able to immediately bring the HQ of 776 Squadron from Speke to Woodvale and also saw the forming of 889 Squadron on 1st June with Hellcats, immediately followed by B Flight of No 736 Squadron, which was a

A Helldiver of 1820 Squadron at HMS Ringtail, *1944. (D J Smith)*

fighter affiliation unit. They arrived from Hal Far in Malta with
Seafires, Beaufighters and a Dominie.

The massive flow of units at Burscough continued with No 1791
Flight moving in from Drem, Scotland in August with 16 Fireflies
under command of Lt Cdr H J Hunter RCN but only to be disbanded in
September. The dropping of the two atomic bombs on Japan brought a
sudden and dramatic end to the Second World War and Woodvale was
rapidly closed with two squadrons, 822 and 776 moving across to
Burscough when the FAA handed Woodvale back to the RAF. The
former had operated in India and then back to the south coast for anti-
shipping patrols on the south coast. It moved from Maydown to
Woodvale to re-arm with Fireflies under Lt Cdr D A Davis moving
over to Burscough and then up north to Machrihanish in December.
The fleet requirements squadron, 776, saw its role instantly diminish
and was disbanded in October. This left room for the final four
squadrons. The first, 825, arrived in November followed by 824, both
flying Fireflies. In February 1946, 825 moved to Lee-on-Solent,
Hampshire but 824 disbanded at Burscough in January.

Phil Blakey, now living in New Zealand, remembers his time at
Burscough when he was detached to 825 Squadron to convert the
pilots to Fireflies. He remembers the CO was Lt Cdr D W Tattershall,
a pre-war RN(A) pilot. He was a Canadian and many of his pilots had
been transferred from the RCAF. He writes: 'On a day when visibility

was not good and the cloud base quite low, I was asked why we were not flying and I explained the standard circuit was 1,000 ft. Lt Cdr Tattershall said he was going to fly his men and two Fireflies manned by regular RCN sub-lieutenants took off. One went directly up through the overcast, when he wanted to return he could find no gaps and had no aids to get himself back. He baled out and his Firefly came down in Bootle, where sadly it killed a postman. The other chap must have found Southport pier as it was known that lined up on that, flying east brought you to the airfield circuit at Burscough. Tattershall went over to Canada with 825, but was killed later in an aircraft accident'.

Jim Williams of Margate also remembers 825. He was a leading air fitter with the station armourers' training ground crews in maintenance and working with all the ordnance they would come into contact with. One of his jobs was to fly to Ronaldsway on the Isle of Man to test-fire rockets on the firing range at Jurby to the north of the island. He made modifications to the Firefly cannon and recalls 825's 16 Firefly FR1s with four cannon each giving him 64 cannon to look after. 'Not a lot of time off in that period!' He recalls 825 embarking on HMCS *Warrior* on 23rd March when six of the Fireflies either crashed or were damaged on deck landing. He also recalls site III was used as a school for the training squadrons. Air cadets would come out to the base at weekends for experience. Several ground crew were state prisoners, offered a pardon if they would take part in the war; and armourers would do a town patrol in Burscough Bridge and Ormskirk to stop fights and other trouble. Once he got lost in dense fog on the base taking four hours to get back to the tower. He remembers two other incidents. Just after the base was commissioned and many aircraft were taking off and landing someone in the tower suddenly spotted a lady pushing a pram down the side of the runway in use! How she got past the guards remained a mystery. The other was when an RAF Mosquito was given permission to land but parked north of the tower and the pilot did not report in but disappeared. His aircraft was checked by the aircraft handling crew only to find it was fully loaded with rockets and bombs. Mr Williams was called to make the aircraft safe. The pilot was found at a wedding in Ormskirk and was escorted back to Burscough by Navy guards and civilian police. Other visiting aircraft included many B-17 Flying Fortresses of the USAAF; these are specifically remembered as having several boxes of cigarettes on board which were distributed around the station. A Gloster Meteor landed with a technical problem. An armed guard was placed round the aircraft with fixed bayonets because it was still secret at the time. It was moved to a remote hardstanding, repaired by some 'boffins' and flew out two days later. Another incident involved two USAAF P-38 Lightnings that landed on the perimeter track due to fog on the airfield

Another fleet requirements unit, No 772 Squadron, arrived from Ayr in January 1946 to become the last unit to fly from Burscough. Its Seafires and Fireflies soldiered on, providing support to RN ships in the north-west until May 1946 when Burscough was declared surplus. All flying stopped and HMS *Ringtail* was 'paid off' on 15th June 1946. Burscough was part of the inevitable rapid run down of the FAA after the Second World War which saw 59 front line squadrons disbanded within a year of VJ-Day and a comparable number of second line squadrons.

The control tower was closed. Big crosses were painted on the runways to show they were not being maintained, cleaned or cleared of obstruction. The living quarters were closed down and all equipment was shipped away for disposal. Suddenly Burscough town and Ormskirk were strangely quiet with no sailors wandering their streets and frequenting the pubs. The facility was, however, to remain in Navy hands for some time. HMS *Blackcap* at RNAS Stretton, just south of Warrington, remained a very active FAA airfield and they took over

Aerial view of Maintenance area, taken 4th June 1976. (APF)

Control tower as viewed on 18th June 1976 and now demolished. (APF)

the site of Burscough for storage with the Naval Engine Holding Unit. Stretton succumbed to the defence cuts of Defence Minister Duncan Sandys in 1957 when the auxiliary units of the RAF and FAA were disbanded and Stretton closed. Burscough was no longer needed, the buildings were beginning to deteriorate and the base was given up in 1957. Most of the hangars remain but the large brick control tower was finally pulled down in August 2004. The majority of other buildings have gone but large sections of the runways are still there and were used for a while by a parachute club and crop spraying aircraft. The ROC had a bunker for monitoring, and until 1982 an aerial array stood near the tower as an air traffic radio beacon known as 'Ormskirk'. The site is now agricultural with the technical area forming an industrial estate with the appropriately named 'Ringtail Road'

The Fleet Air Arm left five of its members in Burscough Parish Church graveyard. Neville and Turner, as described above, plus Sub Lt P G Sutherland RNVR and Sub Lt M W Williams who both died on 25th August 1944 and Sub Lt R A Colbeck RNZNVR on 11th November 1943. Their graves are tended by the Commonwealth War Graves Commission who look after all Commonwealth forces graves across the world.

A memorial to the men and women of HMS *Ringtail* was unveiled in October 2004 to keep the memory of this once very active Fleet Air Arm base alive.

5
BURTONWOOD

2 miles NW of Warrington
SJ 565905

Burtonwood was the biggest airbase in Europe during the Second World War. In fact, there are not enough superlatives to do it justice. Burtonwood was open the longest and was the last to close. It had the most US personnel, the highest production, the most aircraft, the longest runway and even the most marriages. Located just north-west of Warrington on the north–south and east–west railway lines, Burtonwood was almost out of range from the Luftwaffe. It was also close to a huge pool of labour, as well as the ports of Liverpool and Manchester. The air base lies on flat, well-drained land with the village of Burtonwood to the north and Great Sankey to the south. As part of the pre-war expansion of the RAF, a decision was made in 1936 to construct Aircraft Repair Depots (ARDs) with Engine Repair Depots, in addition to the planned 24 Aircraft Storage Units (ASUs).

The majority of ASUs were to share airfield facilities with Flying Training Schools such as Tern Hill, Shropshire and Hullavington, Wiltshire. It was more economical to have joint HQs and other buildings as well as certain accommodation. Initially these units were to be civilian-manned. Design and other contracts were prepared in respect of building requirements at Tern Hill, Aston Down, Hullavington and Shawbury. These drawings were adopted as the standard design of all ASUs subsequently erected. Burtonwood was to be both and was one of six designed to accommodate shared facilities. Two civilian-manned units were planned at Kidbrook and Ruislip and three service units were planned at Henlow, St Athan and Sealand. All were controlled by the Ministry of Aircraft Production (MAP). The ASU formed part of the 1938 expansion programme involving ten new stations at Kirkbride, Silloth, Wroughton, Aldergrove (Northern

Ireland), Wigtown, Lyneham, Llandow, High Ercall and Colerne, together with Burtonwood, all located on the west side of the country.

The role of the ASU was the acceptance of new aircraft from the manufacturer. The unit would then update operational equipment, including the fitting of radio equipment and armament, together with the storage, painting and other modifications required by the RAF. Once ready the aircraft was placed in storage ready for delivery. With the fall of France, however, and the turn of the war against Britain, aircraft never stayed in store for long.

The standard design of an ASU was a two runway configuration with an HQ site for administration. This was where dismantling and erection of aircraft was also undertaken. Up to six sub sites were designed for storage, most sites having two or three D, E, L or Lamella type hangars. All had similar floor plates but different construction. Burtonwood also had a J and a K type hangar at its HQ (later known as Tech Site), a second working site (A Site) with two K type hangars and two sub sites (E & G) with three L types on each. Additionally Mary Ann Site was developed for Burtonwood Repair Depot and constructed to Main Site specifications with three hipped C type hangars. This site was later embodied into the main base. To prevent possible damage from an enemy air attack, the sites were spread right around the airfield. Further storage sites comprising fields were also requisitioned for the open storage of aircraft. Some cover was provided by 20 Robin hangars for airmen working on aircraft so far away from the main sites. Robin hangars could accommodate two or three single-engined fighters. As some were located almost a mile from Tech Site they were linked by semi-prepared cinder tracks.

Burtonwood Repair Depot (BRD) was a separate stand-alone factory built at the same time, to the south of the airfield. Work was completed just as war broke out. The unit opened before the airfield could accept aircraft. BRD operated as a 'shadow factory' and Fairey Aviation was appointed as parent company in September 1940. This unit was totally civilian-manned and was part of the policy to spread aircraft production as widely as possibly to make it difficult to the Nazis to attack. Shadow factories, like Samlesbury, were assembly points for components made elsewhere and brought together at an airfield, from which the completed aircraft could be test-flown and delivered. BRD employed 4,000 personnel, initially working on components such as wiring looms for aircraft, assembling Bristol Bisleys, modifying Martin Maryland bombers and engine overhaul. Control of BRD changed regularly at first. The first Controller was a First World War pilot,

Major C H Chichester-Smith DSC, FRAeS, who was quite a character and was often seen riding his horse around the site! Lord Nuffield of Morris Motors made plans to take control but these failed to materialise. Later Rolls Royce and Rootes had interests in the site. Once the airfield was available the completed aircraft could be towed to or from the airfield via Mary Ann Site, where final modifications were made. Fairey took on an increasing volume of work modifying American-built aircraft acquired under the Lend-Lease scheme. These included Brewster Buffalo fighters, Douglas Boston bombers, Curtiss Mohawk fighters and eventually the first B-17 Flying Fortresses for the RAF which arrived on 14th April 1942.

Meanwhile the RAF arrived just as the building work was nearly completed. RAF Burtonwood really came alive when No 37 Main-tenance Unit (MU) formed there on 1st April 1940 with Squadron Leader Stibbs acting as CO. There were very few completed buildings, however, and it would be October before all the hangars were handed over by the contractors. The Robin hangars were not all ready until 1941. The first aircraft movement to be logged was on 19th April, when an Oxford undertook a forced landing after becoming lost. He must have scared the contractors who were still working on the runways. One thousand gallons of camouflage paint arrived on 20th May, together with 30 men to paint the runways. Airfield defence was also provided with over 100 men being assigned to try and protect the perimeter of this vast base.

The first scheduled aircraft arrived on 26th May, which comprised four new Handley Page Hampdens from English Electric at Preston (from Samlesbury airfield). These were quickly dispersed on G Site with an armed guard to protect them. They were followed by a slow trickle of aircraft at the rate of about one a day. Virtually no living accommodation was provided so the airmen were billeted in local houses much to the consternation of the local families. There are stories of airmen arriving at Warrington Central and Bank Quay stations asking where RAF Burtonwood was. In many cases no-one knew or they kept the secret and so they were guided to Sankey police station. Here they were given the name and address of a house in which they were to live. They were also given some rations, including eggs, to soften the blow to their unwilling hosts. Once established many long standing relationships developed but many lived in great discomfort. In one house, an airmen and a flight sergeant were expected to share a double bed!

By June 1940 the MU was holding seven Beauforts, thirteen

An RAF Spitfire, with cannon and rocket pods under the wings. (Via Author)

Hampdens, nine Magisters and seventeen Oxfords but no aircraft had been delivered. The first production Hampden was ready on 13th July, No 1 Hangar on Tech Site was taken over and the airfield was almost fully open. Initially the airfield had two short concrete runways 04/22 and 13/31, each being 3,150 ft long.

Aircraft numbers rapidly grew with 82 aircraft delivered in July 1940 including Beaufort, Buffalo, Hampden, Lysander, Magister, Oxford and Spitfires. Another 72 were issued in August, including 19 Spitfires for use in the Battle of Britain which was then at its height. The first accident occurred on 7th August when Hampden P2073 crashed on landing but the pilot, Plt Off Baynham, escaped without injury. The first fatal crash was on 6th November 1941 when Sgt Sim from SLD Uxbridge, together with a civilian official from the Royal Aircraft Establishment, died during the test-flight of an unspecified aircraft from BRD. Another occurred the following day when First Officer I Pareded, an ATA pilot, died when Hampden P5396 crashed. It was also being test-flown. By this time all building work for the RAF had been finished. Limited accommodation was made available on the base itself and the first of three control towers was built in front of Mary Ann Site. This was a small tower on a square base building but was adequate for the volume of take offs and landings at that time. In their leisure time many airmen walked to the Limerick pub on Cow Lane, (now Burtonwood Road), close to the current M62 interchange. A Burtonwood Brewery pub, it was unfortunately pulled down to make way for the extended and new runways.

BRD was converting Douglas Boston twin-engined bombers into Turbinlite Havocs, which was an idea to provide a very powerful searchlight in the nose of the aircraft. They would fly at night, accompanied by a fighter, in the area of expected Luftwaffe bomber streams. Using the primitive AI radar of the time, the Havoc would attempt to locate and illuminate the bombers with the searchlight and the fighter would shoot it down. Many were converted at Burtonwood and Havoc flights formed for this purpose but they were not successful and the idea was dropped. The first of several base magazines was named Havoc after this project. The Boston was American-built and BRD started to specialise on US-manufactured aircraft. BRD was now controlled by a Board of Directors and Fairey Aviation and Bristol

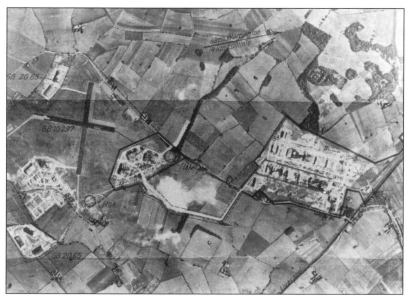

Vertical taken in 1941 by Luftwaffe of whole base, note only two runways at this time. The BRD Site is to the right.

Aeroplane Co. It was split into two divisions, Aircraft and Engines. Engines Division had specialists from Rover Car Co, Rollason, Sunbeam and BOAC. Types specifically assigned and parented by Burtonwood (BRD) were the Autogyro, Martin Baltimore, Bermuda, Boston, Buffalo, Harvard, Havoc Turbinlite, Havoc Pandora and Havoc Intruder, Maryland, Stinson and Vengeance. The larger aircraft sometimes flew across the Atlantic but most were transported as deck cargo on convoys and assembled in England at either Speke or Burtonwood. Burtonwood's location near Liverpool was now showing benefits.

In late 1941 representatives from the American engine manufacturers Allison Engines, Curtiss Wright and Douglas Aircraft arrived to co-ordinate engine maintenance. The RAF side was similarly growing rapidly. In February 1941, A Site was fully operational and production had increased to 90 aircraft in the four weeks ending 13th March. Space on the airfield and in its dispersals was becoming full so a search was started for a satellite landing ground (SLG) to which aircraft could be moved for longer term storage. A site was developed in the grounds of Knowsley Hall, the home of Lord Derby, and this became No 49 SLG Knowsley Park (see separate chapter). This was a landing strip, a few temporary buildings, possibly a couple of Robin or blister hangars and hides created under the cover of trees. Water logging was a problem but it opened at the end of April 1942 with space for 50 aircraft. Simultaneously another SLG was taken over in October – No 21 at Ollerton in Shropshire, but this site never received any aircraft from Burtonwood being transferred to No 27 MU at Shawbury. It was immediately replaced by No 29 SLG at Hodnet, Shropshire with the first three aircraft arriving here on 30th April. A reconnaissance flight overhead proved the camouflage to be excellent although not all the hides had been completed. On 5th May the SLG received 25 aircraft and dispatched six.

The huge bombing raids on Liverpool and Manchester in 1940 and 1941 had little effect on Burtonwood. Vertical reconnaissance photographs had been taken by the Luftwaffe which clearly idenfitied each site. Calculations showed the floor area, length of each runway and location of flak guns. Reconnaissance flights continued until well into 1943 and were often chased by fighters from RAF Woodvale on the Lancashire coast (see separate chapter). It is very strange that the Luftwaffe made no determined attempt to bomb Burtonwood. A concentrated attack could have wrought havoc, especially if BRD Site had been hit. As it was it was only attacked twice and then not very significantly. On 6th September 1940 two Ju88s attacked in daylight flying low over the airfield and dropping incendiary bombs near the runways close to G Site. No damage was inflicted to either runways or aircraft. Equally, the defensive machine gun posts fired at the intruders but no hits were scored. On other occasions bombs dropped into open fields close by were usually stray bombs from attacks on local towns or Liverpool.

Yet another RAF unit opened on 7th July 1942. Number 21 School of Technical Training (SofTT) operated from BRD Site with RAF instructors training RAF ground crews on US-manufactured aircraft in service with the RAF. These included B-17, B-24, Boston, Maryland and Hudson. Training was on engines, airframes and armament with courses lasting approximately three weeks. The school had several sectionalised engines on which to train plus some war-weary aircraft. It is interesting to note that this school already had several advisers from the American manufacturers. The school operated from two 80 ft by 20 ft buildings and the first three courses were American Engines (general), Hydraulics and Electrics. They soon became more specialized. On 4th April 1942 new courses started extending subjects to Wasp, Cyclone and Twin Wasp engines, Mustang airframes and Mustang electrics. The hutted accommodation for 200 students was too small and it was enlarged by 100 per cent in May. Further accommodation was also made available for 30 officers. Courses grew even more to accommodate B-17, B-24, B-26, P-47 and P-51 together with their associated equipment including gun turrets, engines, handling etc. The school remained open until 16 April 1946 when it disbanded.

Following the attack on Pearl Harbor, the Americans were soon looking to England for air bases and Burtonwood was the obvious choice for a support and maintenance base. As early as March 1942 a report was prepared by a Mr Devereux for HQ United States Army Air Forces in the British Isles. This was accompanied by a document entitled 'Plan for the early acquisition Burtonwood (and Mary Ann) Repair and Maintenance Depot'. This plan envisaged the US forces taking over the whole base. The intention was to improve on repairing and modifying US aircraft, arrange to bring over 200 to 500 Air Corps mechanics for repair and maintenance work, and to use Burtonwood to train mobile teams of mechanics to work through the UK. They would also replace the civilian management with military personnel, expand the engine maintenance, make provision for new equipment and machine tools and expand the living accommodation. At this time BRD employed 4,740 UK employees and engine production was averaging 40 per week and 60 propellers per week.

The RAF and BRD were not too happy about handing everything over to the Americans but the Americans moved very quickly and received permission from the British to take the base over. The first Americans arrived on 11th June 1942, barely three months after the first American inspection. It was agreed that No 37 MU would disband and move their aircraft (they were holding 102 at this time, comprising various marks of Beaufort, Halifax, Hampden, Lysander, Magister, Oxford, Spitfire and Wellington) to other MUs as quickly as possible. No 21 SofTT and BRD would remain, but under control of the American military. The first three USAAF units comprised eight officers and 153 enlisted men with a further 45 officers and 692 enlisted men arriving the following day. BRD saw a big influx of American Civil Service technicians, mostly from San Antonio AFB in Texas. The first group of 497 men were dispatched from Duncan Field, San Antonio on 13th August and arrived at their permanent accommodation at Bruche Hall on 8th September. The impact on Warrington was immediate, civilian Americans had never been seen except on the cinema screen and here they were with their ten gallon hats, cowboy boots and loud manners. They became affectionally known as 'Feather Merchants' because they were not under the same hard military discipline as the enlisted men and not in uniform. Their first job was on engine production. They formed two shifts, with the first one reporting for work on 13th September.

A massive expansion scheme commenced immediately to accommodate the anticipated American personnel. The A type hangar on BRD site was pressed into service as living accommodation, with bunks three tiers high installed to make space for hundreds of men. Sites 4 and 5 were started, Site 3 doubled in size and Site 2 expanded to include a 200 bed hospital, Officers' Club and officers' accommodation. On Mary Ann Site two huge warehouses were constructed and churches, theatres, mess halls and hundreds of Nissen huts sprang up. Even though accommodation on base rapidly provided 10,000 bed spaces it was still far too small so two British Army bases were taken over known as Canada Hall at Padgate and Bruche Hall further into Warrington. Buses and trucks were used to transport the men back and forth all day. Two further sites at Risley and Marbury Hall, near Nantwich in Cheshire were also requisitioned for living accommodation. Hangar No 32, on BRD Site, was now known as Site 9 and could accommodate 1,000 men, albeit in very substandard conditions. When the WACs arrived in 1944 they were accommodated at Canada Hall (now Padgate College of Further Education) and were also bussed to and from the base by truck.

The American requirements were urgent. Burtonwood was to be the principal supply and maintenance base for the 8th US Air Force which was UK-based and tasked to bomb Nazi occupied Europe, provide fighter cover and all logistical cover such as provision of bombs and ammunition, food and clothing, trucks and jeeps, spoons and typewriters. The 8th AF was sending bomber groups over to the UK as fast as they could and Burtonwood had to be ready to supply them. The civilian workers on BRD Site were not getting on too well with their new American neighbours. Both had different work ethics. The British were still deeply unionized and worked on projects with a strict demarcation between jobs. Job sharing was not acceptable. The Americans had the benefit of knowledge of production line techniques developed by the large car manufacturers like Ford and General Motors and they had no time for old fashioned work ideals. They found a brand new screw machine still in its original wrappers and discovered that the British had refused to use it because they thought it would put men out of their jobs. The Americans had it working in days. Another bone of contention was that the Americans were paid substantially more than their British neighbours, had better clothing and ate better in their messes leading to understandable differences of opinion. It soon became obvious that the two groups were not going to work together so the majority of the British were moved out to other manufacturing jobs in the north-west of England leaving the Americans in charge. Some British did remain and found they enjoyed the new work ethic. The final transfer of British employees was announced on 10th September 1943 and the base was officially handed over to the 8th Air Force on 21st October when General Harry Miller watched the Stars and Stripes being raised over Burtonwood. Colonel (later Brigadier General) Isaac W Ott, Commander 1st Base Air Depot delivered the formal address for the occasion. As with all RAF bases, they retained their RAF title but were 'loaned' to the US for the duration of the war at no rent. US bases were given numbers so, for secrecy, the name was not used as it would give away the location. Burtonwood became Army Air Force No 590 (AAF 590).

Back in June, the first Americans to arrive were No 5 Air Depot Group. They were billeted at Canada Hall whilst they waited for their new accommodation on base to be completed. They had been assembled very quickly to be sent overseas to join the new war effort.

P-47s inside hangar on Mary Ann Site c 1944. (Mason Hise)

One member, Glen Lundquist recollected: 'I had been working as an aircraft mechanic in sub depots in the States. Seven of us volunteered from Chamite Field, Illinois. We trained at Kelly Field, San Antonio, Texas. We shipped out in the Queen Elizabeth, landing near Glasgow. We were taken by train to Burtonwood. I was first at Site 4, then to Site 1. I was assigned to armament inspection on A Site. I was now doing a job after about three months in the Air Force. We inspected B-17, B-24, P-51 and P-38 aircraft working three shifts. When we arrived at Burtonwood we were put into an empty hut. We put up beds and ate rations. We had no cooks and they asked for volunteers to learn to cook. I had enough of volunteering and sat that one out. I did however volunteer for Officers' Mess orderly, it paid extra money. Waiting to get assigned to hangar work was very rough, things were not organised very well at first.' That soon changed!

Soon No 5 ADG was joined by No 21 ADG, also travelling across the Atlantic on the Queen Elizabeth and arriving in Scotland on 24th November 1942. They were taken by train to Burtonwood and had to endure the winter in cold, drafty, badly heated huts – a far cry from the Texas temperatures. Many other groups also arrived including the 2nd ADG, signals specialists, security, armament, medical, administrators, a weather unit, postal unit, a band, an air traffic control unit, many truck battalions and even a railway company.

BRD site was connected directly to the British Railways network on the Warrington to Liverpool line with sidings running along the main production building. There was a specially built loading/unloading dock and lines running the entire length of the site. Burtonwood had to get material to and from bases and docks all around the country and trains were the main method of transport. It was clear that this system would not cope with the extra demand from the huge numbers of Americans coming in so truck battalions were formed to drive left-hand-drive American trucks around our English country lanes. Most airfields and all ammunition dumps were established in the open countryside and many a driver told tales of getting lost, stuck and exasperated by our narrow roads.

The numerous smaller units and the larger ADGs were all amalgamated into one large unit named Base Air Depot No 1 from September 1942 and then formed into Aircraft and Engine Divisions. Aircraft mainly occupied the airfield whilst Engines occupied BRD Site and in particular Building 100, which became an engine repair base on an assembly line basis. BAD No 1 was the first to be formed but it became apparent that Burtonwood alone could not cope so two more

P-47 Thunderbolts under modification in a hangar on Mary Ann Site. (Via Author)

BADs were planned, to be controlled by Base Air Depot Area (BADA) which formed at the Sunnyside Hotel in Southport. BAD No 2 was to be at Warton, near Lytham St Annes (see separate chapter) and No 3 at Langford Lodge in Northern Ireland. It was going to take some time to get Nos 2 and 3 up and running so all the initial emphasis was on Burtonwood. Having BADA at Southport did not work so the HQ moved to Burtonwood during early 1944 bringing command of all Air Depots to Burtonwood. Small units known as Strategic Air Depots were set up in eastern England and are often mistaken as being bigger and more important than the Base Air Depots but, in fact, they were dramatically smaller and operated under the control of Brigadier General I 'Ike' W Ott at Burtonwood.

Production mushroomed. When the base was officially handed over in October 1943 it was substantially bigger than the site which had been made available six months earlier. There were now eight 1,000-man living sites in addition to the production facilities at BRD Site, Tech Site, Mary Ann Site and A, E and G Sites. There were 17 hangars plus the massive factory at BRD Site, as well as 20 further Robin hangars at the dispersals. The airfield had also undergone massive expansion. The two short runways would never have coped with the increased work load in either construction or length. One runway was totally rebuilt

P47s, C-47 and B-17 Mary Ann Site c 1944. (Mason Hise)

and lengthened, on a slightly different alignment, runway 15/33 was lengthened from 3,150 ft to 4,248 ft and a totally new runway, 09/27, was constructed and was 5,280 ft long (exactly one mile). It was this runway that necessitated the demolition of the Limerick pub. Work did not stop there. The western end of the new runway could not be seen from the control tower so a new tower was built in front of Tech Site, further out onto the airfield in order to give a panoramic view across the entire base. New messes were built and each of the five living sites on base was doubled in size. In June 1943 the American personnel numbered 2,550 but by December this had grown to 13,180. By July 1944 it stood at 16,063 and by January 1945 the figure was 18,063.

The impact on Warrington was now alarming. The Americans were working shifts and had time off in town. Many frequented the local pubs and cinemas, while others took the train to Manchester and Liverpool where the choice was bigger, and there were more girls. The streets swarmed with men in USAAF uniforms. Special Services (set up to provide entertainment and recreational facilities for the men and women) began to offer whatever facilities they could. Dayrooms were installed on each living site with pool tables, table tennis and radios. Film projectors were acquired and regular shows presented. Soon there were movie theatres on each site. Two or three times a month USO – Camp Shows Inc, American Red Cross or RAF – provided stage shows

A P-47 crunches into a jeep while taxiing at Burtonwood. (Via Author)

and toured the sites playing in recreation halls, mess halls or wherever a building was available. USAAF bands such as Eddie Kistlers Swing Tips arrived and played on base and at community halls, Parr Hall and other venues in Warrington and on other nearby military bases. The gym at Burrough's Hall was acquired together with the swimming pool and the sports ground at Crosfields Soap Company. Warrington Council met to decide whether to allow cinemas to open on Sundays in order to try and get Americans off the streets.

Two American Red Cross Clubs were set up in Warrington where the servicemen and women could relax in an American environment. They could drink soft drinks, use the library, write home or just talk about home and get away from the war. Such clubs were set up in all large towns near American bases and more were established in Liverpool and Warrington. After the Sunnyside Hotel, in Southport, was vacated by HQ BADA, it also became a Red Cross Club with accommodation where the guys and girls could stay over night. Similar ones opened in London and they were always packed out. American and British civilians manned the clubs and British girls would often act as hostesses. As a result many romances blossomed.

Accurate records of aircraft production have not survived for the period up to early 1943 but thereafter the numbers illustrate the size

B-24 in hangar on Mary Ann Site being converted for clandestine dropping of agents and supplies into occupied Europe as part of the 'Carpetbagger' project, 1944. (Walter W Ott)

and rapid expansion of work. On 5th November 1943 there were 151 aircraft on the base with 68 ready for delivery to units. During the previous 24 hours 49 aircraft had been received comprising 25 P-47D, 21 B-17 and three B-24. A further 27 aircraft, excluding transit aircraft, were received in the same period comprising 25 P-47D and two B-17. The following day the first work on a 9th Air Force plane, a B-17, started and at this date BAD1 had three C-47 Dakotas for the ferrying division. Ferrying Squadrons were set up specifically to deliver aircraft to and from Burtonwood and the base had its own Flight Test section with many pilots and ground crew. Their job was to receive aircraft from Maintenance Division, check them out on the ground and then test-fly them to ensure all snags had been removed and they were fully airworthy and suitable for delivery. Test flights (known as 'hops') took place all day every day whenever the weather was good enough.

All single-seater fighters arrived by ship, normally with the propeller and tail removed to stop damage. Many thousand aircraft arrived in the Mersey at Liverpool docks and were lifted off the ships onto specially modified trucks. Most were taken to Speke where they were re-assembled and then flown, initially to Burtonwood, although later the P-51s went to Warton. Here they were fully checked, modified as necessary, test-flown and issued. Most bombers were transported on their own wheels and when Speke got too congested, many aircraft made their way directly to Burtonwood. This caused a headache for the Liverpool police who had to escort convoys of aircraft from the docks, down pre-designated routes, to Speke or Burtonwood.

All sorts of special projects were designed and built at Burtonwood. 'Carpetbaggers' were converted B-24 aircraft, specially designated for dropping agents into enemy-held Europe. The work included removing the nose turret and fairing it over and then painting the entire aircraft an overall black finish, which proved to be effective against searchlights. A CG-4A Waco glider was fitted with two engines and test-flown around the base before the project was scrapped. Special Plexiglas (transparent perspex) nose and tail cone assemblies were manufactured for Martin B-26 Marauders. Self-sealing tanks were installed in P-47s, barometric release units made, armour plate fitted to protect the crew in B-17s and P-47s and extra radio equipment installed. Another special project, code named 'Aphrodite', involved stripping all non-essential items from B-17s and packing them full of explosives and fitting them with a remote, radio-controlled, automatic pilot. Their purpose was to fly into the gates of U-boat pens because normal bombs could not penetrate the concrete protection. The aircraft

CG-4A Waco glider which was converted into a powered aircraft and test-flown successfully three times. (Carl Winkleman)

would take off with just a pilot on board. Once flying at a pre-set altitude and under the control of a 'mother' aircraft, the pilot would bale out. The 'mother' aircraft (another B-17) would then guide the flying bomb to the U-boat pens. With radio control in its infancy this was not an easy task and many problems had to be overcome and many lives were lost. Joseph Patrick Kennedy, brother of John F Kennedy, was lost in one of these conversions.

Warton and Langford Lodge were now coming onto line with the momentum of the US 8th Air Force growing all the time. The USAAF 9th Air Force was designated as the occupying Air Force of Europe once the Allies invaded and had a foothold on continental Europe again. BADA and Burtonwood were tasked to support this air force and later the 12th and 15th Air Forces as well. Burtonwood could not cope with the pressures and had to find additional units and bases to spread the load. By 1945 BAD1 had sub-bases at the following locations: Honington, Suffolk (Advance Depot and Strategic Air Depot); Little Straughton, Beds (Advance Depot); Kirkby, Lancs (Warehouse Site); Poynton, Cheshire (AAF 571, Warehouse and Distribution Site); Bures, Suffolk (AAF 526, Ordnance Depot); Taunton, Somerset (AAF 446 Supply Depot); Marchington, Staffs (AAF 193 Supply Depot); Stansted, Essex (AAF 169 Supplies Division);

Baverstock, Hants (AAF 802 Supply Depot); Haydock Park, Lancs (AAF 530 Supply Depot); Smethwick, Worcs (Supply Depot); Sudbury, Suffolk (AAF 158 Maintenance Depot); Liverpool Docks (AAF 513 Port Detachment); Cardiff Docks (Supply Depot); Barry Docks (Supply Depot); Glasgow Docks (AAF 571 Supply Depot); St Mawgan, Cornwall (Supply Depot); St Mellons, Glamorgan (AAF 516 Port Intransit Depot); Barnham, Suffolk (AAF 587 Ordnance Supply); Braybrook, Northants (AAF 521 Ordnance Depot); Cinderford (Chemical Ordnance); Groveley Wood, Wilts (AAF 592 Ordnance Depot); Earsham, Norfolk (AAF 545 Ordnance Depot); Riseley, Beds (AAF 541 Chemical Warfare Est); Sharnbrook, Beds (AAF 583 Ordnance Depot); Wortley, Yorks (AAF 581 Ordnance Depot) and Aintree, Lancs (Warehouse Site).

Engine production on BRD Site ran at approximately 40 per week prior to the American occupation. Now run on dramatically different lines Burtonwood specialised in radial engines for aircraft like the B-17, P-38 and P-47 whilst Warton specialised in in-line engines such as those which powered the P-51 and P-38s. By February 1944 engine production reached 714 for the month. This involved stripping the engine down, checking each component part and checking for damage, wear or deteoriation. The engines were then reassembled and test-run for at least three hours on the special test rigs at the back of BRD sites. The noise was incredibly high with unsilenced engines running 24 hours a day, seven days a week and could be heard across the whole of Warrington. Numbers continued to grow. By November the number reached 1,590 engines and by January 1945 it was 2,128 engines. The absolute record was achieved in February 1945 at 2,155 engines.

Numbers of aircraft produced now became mind boggling. In March 1944, 508 aircraft of all types were made ready for delivery. In April there were 579 aircraft deliveries into Burtonwood comprising 39 B-17, 254 P-47, 57 P-38, 12 aircraft to go back to the States, 106 B-24 and 111 miscellaneous. In one month, 481 were put through the production hangars, 454 were made ready for delivery and 443 were actually delivered! In addition to this work BAD1 made modifying kits for the external hydro-oil line for R-1820 engines, overhauled 1,052 machine guns, made Plexiglas tail turret canopies for B-24s and reconditioned 112,120 spark plugs. Burtonwood's rail link was also shipping vast quantities of goods. In April alone 5,607 railway trucks carried a total tonnage of 6,752.

The big push was for D-Day although no-one knew just when it would happen. Huge demands went out for black and white paint and

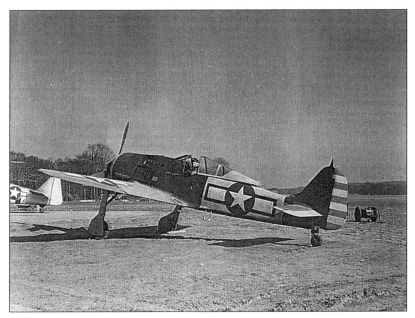

A captured German FW 1980 fighter in US markings at Burtonwood, in 1944. (Via Author)

hundreds of aircraft flew in to be painted in invasion stripes. Hundreds of men went out to forward bases to paint the aircraft there. Generals Eisenhower and Patton visited Burtonwood to tour the workshops and hangars to encourage the men to achieve maximum production. They met with Brig Gen Ott, commander of BADA and over 38,000 men, and also with Col Billy Arnold, Chief of Maintenance, who before the Second World War had been a very successful racing car driver who won the Indianapolis 500. Prior to D-Day, a seven day week was established with all men working continuously for almost a month before they were allowed one day a week off. Production increased dramatically.

D-Day required a massive logistical effort and Burtonwood had to rise to the occasion, fulfilling every demand. One example was the large quantities of consumable photographic films and processing chemicals that were collected and forwarded to advanced areas, relieving shortages that arose as a result of greatly expanded photographic reconnaissance. The build up to D-Day was extraordinarily successful with Burtonwood having fewer aircraft on the ground

115

P-47 with invasion stripes, 1944. (Ray Bronziensky)

for some time with only 115 during the third week of the month, excluding 61 B-17s in storage. However that week had seen a total of 138 aircraft made ready for delivery and test-flown, including 62 B-17, 4 C-3, 18 P-47 and 23 P-38, plus 31 miscellaneous types. Burtonwood didn't stay quiet. Arrangements were in hand for 130 P-47s from the 9th Air Force to come in for conversion to paddle-type propeller blades at the rate of twelve a day. Simultaneously four USAAF Mosquitoes arrived for installation of American-type radio equipment including Gee, VHF and IFF. The first week in July saw many new projects start with ten F-5s and 29 C-47s arriving from the States for radio installation. The first six P-61s were assembled and the arrival of C-5s and C-47s continued to increase with 307 aircraft on the field at the end of the week. Special modifications were made to C-47s for

116

Commanding Generals who had moved over to Europe after the invasion. These aircraft were fitted out for VIP operations with a bed, office, special seats and one with a jeep slung underneath. Similar modifications were made to some B-17s into which seven airline-type seats were installed, as well as cooking and toilet facilities. The tail cone was plated over and the rear turret and armour plate removed. Soundproofing was installed and the interior covered with leather. One was modified here for General Eisenhower.

In August 1,019 aircraft were modified, assembled or repaired, with 726 delivered in October and 671 in November. The base could now supply more than the demand for the first time. The 'Carpetbagger' project was stopped and then restarted, because the attrition rate was so low. An excess of B-17s was being accumulated since the requirements of the operational groups had been fulfilled but in order not to demotivate the engineers they were flown away to be stored at Stansted, instead of languishing at Burtonwood.

All work and no play makes an engineer a dull boy! So to keep the boys happy a continual flow of entertainers came to Burtonwood, and other USAAF bases to entertain the troops. The most popular were Bob Hope and Bing Crosby who had to give three or more performances at Burtonwood because of the numbers and also because of the shift work. Stages were made of aero engine boxes, unusually with the engine in them! Bing Crosby commented that he was using the most valuable stage he had ever sung on. Due to inclement weather, concerts were often in storage warehouses or hangars with special lights and sound systems set up. Bob Hope brought Frances Langford with him, Bing crooned to the delighted audience. Shortly before he mysteriously disappeared en route to France, Glenn Miller gave a concert, with the famous British bandleader Joe Loss and the forces darling Vera Lynn. James Cagney visited and christened an aircraft after himself, followed by numerous British and American stars. Shows were also put on in Warrington and WAAFs and WRENs were brought in for dances and parties from local bases such as RAF Padgate and HMS *Blackcap* at Stretton.

Four unwelcome visitors arrived on a Saturday night in December 1944. A military policeman, Private 1st class Arthur Seher, was guarding dispersed B-26 Marauder bombers on a dispersal when he saw a flicker of a light coming from inside. He challenged the light and was shocked when four escaped German prisoners of war emerged from the aircraft with their hands held high. He pulled his gun and ordered them out. One of the prisoners told Seher that they were trying

Bob Hope relaxing with base commander Brigadier General Ike Ott and co-star sitting on his knee, 1945. (Walter W Ott)

to get home for Christmas but they did not offer any resistance and were handed over to the British authorities. They had escaped from a prisoner of war camp near Northwich, Cheshire and passed through Warrington in the dark eventually finding Burtonwood. They had not eaten for two days. Seher had four swastikas painted onto his hut door to commemorate their arrest.

Post D-day work continued as usual with pressure to support the push across Europe to win the war. January 1945 suffered from bad weather and the customary shorter daylight hours but Flight Test worked through 112 B-17s and 139 P-47s making the bulk of 449 aircraft delivered out. The approximate daily total of aircraft on the airfield was 450 with 100 undergoing work, 200 in Flight Test and 50 ready for delivery. On 2nd January alone 130 aircraft were delivered out, by the end of the month 482 had been received and 503 delivered out. The 2,128 engines passing test in January had a combined horsepower of 2,442,000! February saw 1,041 aircraft delivered.

HQ BADA at Burtonwood commanded all servicing and storage facilities for Air Service Command in the UK totalling 32 separate locations, plus having its own personnel at 14 other locations outside

Joe Loss, Vera Lynn and Glenn Miller. (Via Wally Baldwin)

its command. The total personnel commanded by BADA as at 8th April 1945 was 38,281 including BAD No 2 at Warton, 1,227 at the now reduced BAD No 3 at Langford Lodge, 763 at Stansted and 1,754 at Baverstock. Dock detachments were located at Bristol, Liverpool and Hull and BADA personnel were on the airfields at Biggin Hill, Prestwick, Grove and Valley. Additional detachments were in France.

The total valuation of the facilities at Burtonwood in 1945 was estimated at $50 million. The station consisted of 1,823 buildings, 2.5424 miles of runway, 3.52 miles of perimeter track, 22.763 miles of road, 4.025 miles of railway track and a total acreage of 1,253. There were 4,006,842 sq feet of covered storage facilities and 7,097,181 sq feet of open facilities. Including Canada Hall, there was accommodation for 923 officers and 16,165 enlisted men. The original capacity had been 648! The total concrete surfacing created was 8,307,481 sq feet, nearly three square miles!

In 1945 General Eisenhower's personal B-17 came back for overhaul, engine changes, radio refits and modifications. All other work continued without a break. Suddenly it was all over. On 8th May 1945 Germany surrendered and VE-Day saw massive celebrations. The

American Forces newspaper *Stars and Stripes* carried a two-inch high headline 'GERMANY QUITS!' Work stopped for the day and a Sunday routine was adopted. A victory dance was held in Hangar 220, on Mary Ann Site, with two bands, Eddie Kistler's 'Swingtips' and Roger's 'Airmen' playing. The Post Exchange ran out of beer by the end of March and remained in short supply for another month, such was the demand. The weather was good, there was an average of 300 aircraft on the airfield each day and there were 18,071 personnel at Burtonwood on 31st May 1945. But the end was nigh! Suddenly trucks loaded with broken wings and fuselages appeared on the base roads as older aircraft were scrapped. Men and mechanics, who had worked flat out to get them into air, looked at them sadly. The base motto was 'Keep 'em Flying' but now the reason was gone, the war in Europe was won and thoughts turned to going home.

The war in the Pacific, however, was not yet won. A reception centre was prepared on Site 3 to handle an additional group of aircrews after notice was received that Burtonwood would receive 12 aircrews daily for a period of 30 to 45 days, mostly flying B-17 and B-24 bombers home across the Atlantic or preparing to fly them eastwards. Aircraft were still being produced but engine production was run down to close

P-47s at dispersal.

120

entirely by the end of June. Stocks of engines were adequate to supply the occupational air force and many mechanics from Burtonwood went to Compeign in France to man a new Base Air Depot there.

A programme to inspect and overhaul B-17s for the Pacific started immediately with 325 aircraft being worked on in May, 410 flight-tested and 388 made ready for delivery. With almost 10,000 men working on engine production a huge reduction in numbers started with only 15,416 being on site by the end of June. It would be a long time before Burtonwood's work would be finalized. On 6th June, the first anniversary of D-Day, all station personnel were given a day's holiday. Two propaganda films were shown *On to Tokyo* and *One Down, Two to Go*. Stations under command of Burtonwood were Warton, Baverstock, Poynton, Haydock Park, Stansted, Taunton, Sudbury, Liverpool Docks, Cardiff, Langford Lodge and various locations in London. Closure and reorganisation saw Poynton close in August, Warton by 1st September and Langford Lodge on 2nd August. Maintenance activities decreased, engine work stopped totally and the mood was 'return the new aircraft but scrap the rest'. In June 114 aircraft were salvaged (scrapped). Half of these were B-26s and a third were B-17s. It was a sad sight with aircraft on their backs, undercarriages in the air, and engines being cut off and wrecked. Huge numbers of aircraft were ferried in to Burtonwood from the front line squadrons to meet their end. The daily average was 300 on the field, rapidly rising to 500, including RAF P-47s and P-51s returned from Lease-Lend by the RAF. In return, 33 aircraft went back to the US and 200 A-20s were in storage ready to go.

In June 2,000 personnel left the base and in each edition of the *Warrington Guardian* there ran stories with statements: 'Sgt Wallace O McDonald USAAF married Miss Pauline M Jones, daughter of Mr and Mrs Herbert Jones, 72 Laburnum Road, Lowton at Lowton.' A sign of hundreds of GI marriages which took place and rapidly accelerated, once the guys were due to move out. Often the new wives had to wait until the following year before they could follow their husbands to the States. Many never returned to the UK or their families. During the Second World War 70,000 English girls married US men across the UK but it is believed that 10% came from the north-west. Another headline read: 'About 3,000 GIs and girls crowded into the Recreational Club on Tuesday for a variety show, "Pan American Fiesta" produced by Special Services, BAD No 1, from soldier talent. Soldiers meant both WACs and GIs and they really put on some professional entertainment.' A letter was sent to the *Guardian* editor entitled 'Yanks Au Revoir', and

A view of the second WWII tower, from the third tower built in 1953 at Burtonwood. 'A' Site is across the runway. (Reflections)

spoke of the 'American airman who had stood in front of "Oliver" (the statue of Oliver Cromwell in the town centre) and whistled at our girls, crowded us out on our buses, and laughed at our ways, only because an American, when he jokes about you it's a sure sign that he likes you.' Departing GIs also wrote to the editor saying to the people of Warrington such things as 'It's been a genuine pleasure to mix with you and to learn how to make an enjoyable evening out of such simple pleasures as friendly conversation and a game of darts.'

Total aircraft on the airfield remained at 500 despite the Back-to-the-States projects and wholesale scrapping. Whilst the longer-serving personnel moved out to go home and many were shipped into Europe to maintain the occupying air force, more men arrived from units closing in the UK, especially Warton and Langford Lodge, ready to be relocated. At 00.30 on 15th August VJ-Day was announced with the surrender of Japan. In the middle of the night members of the 513rd AAF Band appeared on the roads of Burtonwood with musical instruments and an impromptu parade started and toured the base, getting bigger as it went. The following two days were declared a holiday and now there was no more war effort, the aim was to get rid of the material as fast as possible. Approximately 200 American bombers had force or crash landed in Sweden or Switzerland and these were now to be repatriated. Three planeloads of mechanics flew from Burtonwood to Dubendorf Airport, Zurich in C-82s (converted B-24 Liberator bombers to carry passengers) to get them serviceable and fly them home. These men were specially chosen for this perk and given the chance to enjoy Switzerland for a few weeks. Sadly, one aircraft flew a missed approach and on the circuit crashed, killing all on board. The others assessed each bomber and salvaged several to cannibalise them for parts for the rest. With basic tools but a lot of know-how, they managed to return over 150 to Burtonwood with the first four arriving in the first week in September. They were placed on the Back-to-the-States project but eventually were unceremoniously scrapped at Burtonwood.

It was now a race to dispose of all equipment and get ready to close the base. By the end of 1945 personnel numbers stood at 6,129 but by the end of April it had dropped to fewer than 2,000. The sub units and stations were closed and items were either scrapped on site or returned to Burtonwood. Scrap material was everywhere but it could not be given or sold to the British as it was deemed that it could affect our post-war industry if the country was flooded with surplus US material

P-38 Lightnings being scrapped, 1945.

and stock. Instead it was burned, scrapped, buried or taken out to sea and sunk! On 25th May 1946 Burtonwood remained the last US base in the UK when HQ BADA and AAF 590 Burtonwood were deactivated. 'Mission Accomplished!'

Burtonwood was by far the largest USAAF base in the UK and Europe during the Second World War. Taking over the giant facilities of BRD Site, it could produce engines at four times the rate of Warton. It also had the advantage of a rail link running right into the base itself. Staggering numbers have already been given relating to size and output but the summary is amazing. In 32 months from 1st July 1943 to VE-Day on 8th May 1945 BAD1 produced 11,575 aircraft including 4,243 B-17s, 4381 P-47s and 1,004 P-38s, plus 694 B-24s and 444 B-26s. Engine Division overhauled 30,386 radial aero engines. Maintenance Division overhauled 2,476,462 spark plugs, 31,812 carburettors, 61,409 magnetos and 331,012 cylinders. Armament section overhauled or modified 38,526 machine guns, 836 20mm cannon and 330 turrets. Figures include 1,887 automatic pilot equipment, 4,521 stabilisers, 2,270 bomb sights, 71,422 parachutes, 13,796 life rafts, 28,394 oxygen masks and 11,798 propeller assemblies. 13,346 items of radio or radar equipment were attended to in the aircraft with 126,684 in the shop and a total of 968,158 modification kits for individual aircraft. It was an astonishing total.

RAF Burtonwood was returned to RAF control and 276 MU returned shortly afterwards followed by the reactivated 37 MU. The RAF Master Provision Office remained and this unit supplied parts for US aircraft in RAF service. American aircraft departed and RAF aircraft filled a small part of the huge gap left. No 5 Personnel Dispatch Unit also arrived holding RAF personnel ready for overseas deployment but even with all these units it was still strangely quiet. Not for long!

In 1948 the Cold War started. The Berlin Blockade commenced and US Air Force eyes once again turned to Burtonwood. The base was handed back to the Americans in September 1948 and it immediately started to service the C-47 and C-54 aircraft taking part in the Airlift. Over the next few years it was massively expanded with the runway being almost doubled in length. A new passenger terminal and control tower, massively improved living and mess accommodation and married quarters for wives and families were built. In 1954 Header House opened, the largest warehouse in Europe, with 47 acres or 3,000,000 sq feet of covered space. Throughout the 1950s there averaged 5,000 USAF personnel on base plus families. All types of new aircraft were maintained here including the latest jet fighters such

124

as F-84 Thunderstreaks and F-86 Sabres. The base grew and took over several other bases such as Sealand, Flint and Cranage, Cheshire for many years. With coal mining under the main runway and defence cuts, the USAF ran the base down and moved out in 1965 leaving it almost empty except for occasional RAF V-Bombers using the long runway as a safe satellite in case of nuclear war. The RAF had no requirement and it was thought that was the end of Burtonwood, but again the Americans realised its importance. President de Gaulle withdrew France from NATO in 1967 and the Americans had huge supply bases and airfields there. The US Army took over Burtonwood and moved in with massive supplies for use in the event of the Cold War becoming Hot.

The 47th Area Support Group, US Army, remained at Burtonwood until 1993 when it was deactivated due to the end of the Cold War. Much of the material was used in the Balkan wars around Bosnia and later it was to supply vast quantities of materials, mobile hospitals, NBC suits, MREs, medical equipment etc for the successful Desert Storm operation on Iraq. It officially closed in June 1994 with most sites torn down by 2000 and very little remaining in 2004. Most of the sites have been or will be redeveloped but already road names are reflecting the former American presence with California Drive and Moran Drive after one of the last US Army commanders. Part of the new Urban Village, Chapelford, is named Dakota Park after the C-47 Dakota aircraft and the RAF Burtonwood Association is keeping the memory alive with a Heritage Centre open at weekends.

Burtonwood was a mighty base, and its contribution to the US war effort is immeasurable. Its impact on the local communities, thousands of marriages and financial input to the local area in peace and war will never be forgotten. This base lived up to its motto to 'Keep 'em Flying' and can take its place in history being satisfied that it truly can claim 'Mission Accomplished!'

6
CARK

½ mile south of Flookburgh, off B5227
SD 374745

Cark was the most northerly airfield in Lancashire (just north of Barrow) sitting on the northern shore of Morecambe Bay and immediately south of the Lake District. The site was originally commandeered by Vickers Company in April 1916 as a result of the airship sheds at Barrow being shot at by an enemy submarine. The Admiralty wanted another site because Barrow was considered too vulnerable and although this site (named Flookburgh after the adjoining village) was on the edge of Morecambe Bay the sea was far too shallow for submarines to operate. Work commenced at an estimated cost of £110,000, which soon spiralled out of control. A railway line had to be built from the Carnforth to Barrow LMS line, and houses, roads, water and electricity had to be provided, as well as the huge airship shed. By November 1917 costs had escalated to £792,000 and construction was stopped. The airship shed was to be 900 ft long, 300 ft wide and 130 ft long but was never completed. The site changed hands between several government bodies and eventually the partly-built shed was dismantled and removed with virtually nothing remaining by the time the Second World War broke out.

The site lay derelict but was looked at again in 1941 as a fighter station within the Speke sector for No 9 Group, Fighter Command based at Barton Hall, Preston. Work commenced on the airfield which was called Cark to avoid confusion with the previous military occupiers. Like Barrow and Woodvale, Cark was designed and constructed as a temporary wartime fighter airfield in the Speke sector (later Woodvale) of No 9 Group Fighter Command (HQ at Barton Hall, Preston). The technical buildings, training area, messes, specialised

Oblique aerial view looking west 1944, note blister hangars with Ansons parked outside and main site buildings in centre. (Via D J Smith)

navigation and wireless lecture rooms, control tower etc were made of brick, while most of the airmen's accommodation and storage was a mixture of Nissen, Neve and Handcraft type hutting, all of cheap temporary construction. The airfield had three hard runways No 1 07/25, No 2 17/35 and No 3 13/31 being 3,900, 3,300 and 3,300 ft long respectively. The main site was very small and located immediately adjacent to the north-west corner of the airfield comprising squadron offices, main stores, workshop, parachute and dinghy stores and workshops, link trainer room, battle headquarters etc. There was a total of 11 sites. Site No 1 was the airfield, No 2 was the communal site with officers' and sergeants' messes plus airmen's dining hall and institute. No 3 was very close but with a mixture of sergeants' and airmen's quarters, Nos 4 and 5 were predominantly airmen's living sites, No 6 was the WAAF site, No 7 sick quarters, No 8 wireless telegraphy, Nos 9 and 10 were High Frequency Direction Finding (HFDF) and No 11 was the sewage disposal site. Accommodation was provided for 69 officers, 271 SNCOs and 518 airmen plus WAAF quarters for 6 officers, 6 SNCOs and 188 airwomen, a total of 1,058

All were located in the north-west corner of the airfield just south of the villages of Flookburgh and Cark. The railway station was at Cark with good sidings for materials and equipment for the base, provided during the First World War. A disused tramway from the earlier occupation still lay along the southern boundary of the airfield. Aircraft were dispersed in two areas, north-west and along the east side of the airfield with the hangars to the north-west corner. There was a strange mixture of hangars, one Bellman for maintenance, six enlarged over blister and four enlarged double over blister hangars to protect the aircraft from the elements. Essentially these blister hangars looked similar having curved roofs and doors at one end only with the double hangars being literally two normal ones built together to double the length. They had a span of approximately 69 ft and a height of 20 ft. There were three more enlarged over blister hangars on the east side of the airfield together with six two-aircraft dispersals and associated hutting for two flights of aircraft. The dispersals were surrounded by sand bags to protect the aircraft in case of enemy air attack. Like Barrow the airfield had the sea immediately adjacent and two runways had over-runs that led directly into the sea.

The first RAF units to arrive were 'F' and 'R' Flights of No 1 Anti-Aircraft Co-operation Unit. Both Flights had been formed at Farnborough with 'F' moving to Squires Gate in April 1939 followed by 'R' Flight in September 1941. The Flights towed targets for Light

Anti-Aircraft Practice Camps, 'F' for No 9 at Flookburgh, immediately adjacent to Cark, and 'R' for No 14 at Nethertown on the coast just south of Workington. As soon as Cark was ready to accept aircraft they flew in on 7th January 1942 to find a brand new, but not yet finished airfield to work from. They were dispersed on the east side of the base in the dispersals running just off the perimeter track so as to leave space for the main unit yet to arrive. These flights operated Henleys, Defiants, Lysanders, Hurricanes, Magisters and Tiger Moths as tugs operating whenever the weather allowed and liaising closely with the ground-based army units. 'R' Flight disbanded on 1st October 1942, officially due to lack of aircraft but its role was taken over by 'F' Flight which , in turn, disbanded on 1st November 1942 to be redesignated No 1614 Flight doing exactly the same job. This flight operated Henleys, Tiger Moths and Martinets and had a detachment at Morpeth from April to June in 1943. Target towing continued but the unit was again redesignated on 1st December 1943 by merging with 'D' Flight of No 289 Squadron and becoming No 650 Squadron flying predominantly Martinets and Hurricanes in the same role. The CO was Squadron Leader Verity DFC and the squadron continued its role as army co-operation, towing drogues. 'B' Flight was detached to

Pilots of No 6 Course Staff Pilots Training Unit 1943. (RAF Millom Museum)

Station WAAF contingent with only male being the Station Commander in the centre, 1944. (RAF Millom Museum)

Woodvale on 18th June 1944 under command of Flt Lt Trench. This unit remained until 18th November 1944 when it moved to Bodorgan, Anglesey.

Although built as a Fighter station and promised to No 9 Group, the station was not needed due to Hitler opening up the eastern front and the Luftwaffe being extremely busy elsewhere. Therefore Cark was transferred to No 25 Group, Flying Training Command on 16 March 1942 just as the Staff Pilots Training Unit (SPTU) formed on the following day. This unit was established with Anson I aircraft and its role was to train pilots in day and night flying for staff pilot duties at the Air Observer Schools for the (Observer) Advanced Flying Units where the role was both pilot and instructor. The establishment was set at 20 Ansons with a further 10 in reserve and by September 1942 had 27 Ansons and four Masters. Many of the pilots were tour-expired operational pilots and the first course started on 30th April with several more passing through before it was disbanded on 14th November 1942. However the unit was reborn on 12th March 1943 in exactly the same role with 30 Ansons and one Magister.

Another co-operation unit arrived on 15 March 1942 when No 6 Anti-Aircraft Co-operation Unit flew in from Ringway, Cheshire with a mixture of tug aircraft including Dragon, Leopard Moth, Scion, Battle, Blenheim, Lysander, Master and Oxford. This unit operated with army and navy artillery units and had detachments at Croft, Middleton St George, Newtownards, Rednal, Ringway, Sealand, Towyn and Wrexham. After a year here the HQ moved to Castle Bromwich on 8th March 1943.

Being close to the Lake District it was not surprising that there were several crashes in the area, but not from Cark-based units. Millom had an official Mountain Rescue Unit but resources at Cark were used on 2nd November 1942 to search for an Airacobra from the USAAC training station at Atcham, Shropshire, which crashed near Settle killing the pilot. The unit was often tasked to search for aircraft lost over the Irish Sea, usually without result. A near loss was avoided on 14th February 1944 when a USAAF B-17 42-38177 was inbound to the UK from Labrador and short of fuel, just making it into Cark before running out.

The SPTU had an excellent accident rate, probably because it had experienced students. The only local fatal accident was a high ground casualty on 20th March 1944 when Anson EG686 crashed on Swirl How near Coniston. Another accident was Anson LT433 which crashed in Snowdonia on 20th February 1944.

Sqn Ldr Kingsley and another by the station Miles Magister on 21 December 1944.
(RAF Millom Museum)

Millom was placed under care and maintenance in January 1945 and its Mountain Rescue Unit moved to Cark. Its first call out was on 11th January looking for an Avenger from RNAS Inskip which was eventually found wrecked at Wastwater. On 10th February a Mosquito of No 51 OTU at Cranfield, Bedfordshire, crashed on Hellvellyn but there were no survivors. The unit was very inventive. They practised using a boat on Lake Windermere and dogs to help find crashed aircrews but neither exercise was put into use. An 'At Home' day was held on Battle of Britain day, 15th September 1945, with the resident aircraft on display plus visiting Tempest, Spitfire, Lancaster, Halifax and Mosquito. Not too much room to spare for the bigger four-engined aircraft to land on this 'fighter' airfield. Only 3,000 people came to see the station indicating the sparse population in the area and lack of private cars and poor public transport.

The SPTU disbanded on 31st December 1945 and, except for the gliders of No 188 Gliding School, the base was empty for the first time since January 1942. With the RAF rapidly downsizing, this small 'temporary' airfield was closed and placed under care and maintenance but was never to see military colours again. The Gliding School had formed here by February 1944 to train air cadets using Cadet Mk I gliders. In May 1947 it moved to Barrow where it remained until 1955. Most of the dispersed living sites have long gone but many of the technical site buildings including the control tower (used as a dwelling) remain to this day. Civilian flying and some gliding have taken place for many years using part of one of the remaining runways.

7
HESKETH PARK BEACH, SOUTHPORT

1 mile north of Southport Pier
SJ 344194

Flying off Southport beach goes back to 1910 and can be dated back to 1st August that year when famous pioneer airman Claude Grahame-White arrived unexpectedly and landed his Farman biplane on the beach near to the pier. Naturally it was not long before a large crowd gathered to see the new fangled machine. Blackpool, just across the Ribble estuary, had seen the first aviation in Lancashire but the beach between Liverpool and Southport was ideal for these early airmen because there were miles of firm sand to use as a runway and no building or people to hurt in the event of accidents, which were frequent! Names such as Henry Melly, Charles Hubert, Clement Gresswell and John Gaunt were always in the newspaper and a far-sighted Southport Corporation built a hangar at Hesketh Park, just off the shore to be safe from the tide but convenient for the sand. However the original airfield was on what is now the Municipal Golf Course before the beach was considered.

John Gaunt was the first occupier and many others followed him whilst others set up hangars at Freshfield and Waterloo. A display in 1911 further established Southport as one of the most important aviation centres in the entire country with thousands flocking to see the aircraft airborne. H Blackburn was also allowed to use the hangar and he was later to form the large aircraft company carrying his name, which lasted until the 1960s.

The First World War was to change things forever but secured an airfield at Hesketh Park. Soldiers were being billeted in Southport and the Council allowed the hangar to be used for band practice, because it was far enough away from houses not to annoy the local residents. It was as late as 1917 that the War Office was in contact with Southport Council about taking over the aerodrome for military purposes. In due course this happened and the Royal Naval Air Service demolished the original hangar to build two standard bow-strung truss-roofed hangars side by side. These are commonly known as Belfast hangars after their roof construction. The slipway onto the beach was already constructed and the airfield was designated an Aircraft Acceptance Park (AAP) to accept new aircraft from the Vulcan Factory and nearby Crossens which was to build DH-9's with Liberty engines. Components were manufactured in many places in Southport including the old ice rink in Lord Street and other small toolmakers and fabricators. No 11 AAP was formed on 15th September 1917 changing its name to No 11 (Southport) AAP on 12th October 1917.

It is assumed that the aircraft were built complete at the factory then dismantled to allow them to be taken by road to the hangars for final assembly, test-flying and delivery to the active squadrons. The first aircraft to be built were BE 2d early biplane fighters. A test pilot came up from Farnborough to test the first aircraft and employees from Vulcan Engineering were given time off and allowed to bring their families to watch the flights. In the event, with men desperately required in the Army, many Southport women were to join Vulcan to do war work. The BE2d was soon outdated and production changed to the de Havilland DH4, DH9 and DH9A type aircraft. The DH9A was one of the most famous aircraft in the RAF rivalling the Bristol Fighter and Avro 504 for its longevity. It was designed as a two-seat day bomber with a 400 hp Liberty engine (some having 360 hp Rolls-Royce engines). Its maximum speed was 114 mph, it had an endurance of $5^3/_4$ hours, a ceiling of 16,500 ft and was armed with one Vickers forward-firing machine gun and one Lewis gun firing aft.

The Liberty engines were American-designed and mostly built there and shipped over. Some aircraft were dispatched to Russia in packing cases but most flew off the beach. At the end of the First World War Vulcan received an order for 600 ABC Dragonfly radial engines but the Armistice stopped all military contracts and none were built. No 11 (Southport) AAP closed down on 11th January 1918.

Vulcan Engineering turned to civilian manufacture including Crossley Cars, and the hangars at Hesketh Park were taken over by the Giro Aviation Company who, with its founder, Norman Giroux, was to be synonymous with flying at Southport until the 1960s.

Hesketh Park hangars mid 1930s. (E J Riding via John Mulliner)

Birkdale Sands became licensed as an airfield and was very close to the now demolished Palace Hotel at Birkdale, which could accommodate guests with their own aircraft and pleasure flying. Scheduled air services used Hesketh Park inter-war, linking Southport with Blackpool, Manchester and beyond but these were not maintained. The 1931 *Air Pilot* shows Hesketh Park as a licensed aerodrome with a circular landing area allowing 880 yards take off and landing run into wind in any direction. It warns that virtually the whole landing area is covered in water at high tide! There were no markings, signals or wind indicator, no floodlights or night landing facilities and no radio. It continues that handling facilities may be available from Giro Aviation Co who may also facilitate minor repairs and provide fuel, oil and fresh water. The two First World War hangars were 80 ft wide, 170 feet long and the door was 21 feet high and 80 feet wide. These facilities, or lack of them, were to remain until the 1960s especially the flying hours, because the landing area was normally clear of water for seven hours, from about three hours after high-water.

The Second World War brought about a much greater impact on the Lancashire coastline. Martin Hearn Ltd at Hooton Park, Cheshire was a civilian aircraft repair company contracted by the Air Ministry to repair and modify aircraft for the RAF and Fleet Air Arm. On 27th September 1940 No 7 Aircraft Assembly Unit was formed here and the Ministry of Aircraft production built a large hangar, with a door on the long side, at Hesketh Park to provide a dispersed site for this unit,

Avro 588 G-ABMB in hangar in 1930s. (E J Riding via John Mulliner)

operated by Martin Hearn Ltd. A large tarmac apron was built extending to three sides of the hangars to provide hard-surfaced external parking together with an elevated tarmac taxiway alongside the Municipal Golf Course extending from the apron for about 350 yards before reaching a ramp which led down to the sea. Deep maintenance to Mosquitoes and Ansons was undertaken from here in addition to various marks of Spitfires. All three hangars were pressed into service but there does not appear to be any record of numbers of aircraft passing through this facility. It is understood, however, that over 200 people worked there. It is assumed they were all civilians as no accommodation for personnel was ever built here. In fact it is difficult to see how so many people could have been fed here at lunchtime. There were no flying control facilities of any form with no control tower or similar being constructed until well after the Second World War and then for civilian flying. Martin Hearn Ltd assembled many US-built aircraft, which were towed from Liverpool and Birkenhead docks, similar to the work at Speke. It appears that he kept this work at Hooton Park and only utilised Southport for UK-manufactured RAF aircraft.

Number 1 Packed Aircraft Transit Pool established itself at Hesketh Park with a storage area by the Pleasureland fairground within No 40 Group, Maintenance Command. This unit had two detached sites at Carr Lane, Birkdale and Pleasureland but no permanent hangar space except at Hesketh Park. It held cased aircraft awaiting transit, usually

Hesketh Park from the air in 1960, with two remaining hangars and aircraft apron. (Tony Whelan)

out of Liverpool Docks and similar units were established near Barry and Glasgow docks. Crated aircraft were seen on the central reservation of the A565 outside RAF Woodvale, and on the reservation of the Southport to Preston dual carriageway. RAF Sealand was a major aircraft-packing MU and may have been the source of these aircraft. In 1945 it is noted that gliders were stored in cases at Pleasureland but were transferred to the unit at Fleetwood Road to clear the Pleasureland site which was closing. Possibly Pleasureland was used as a camouflage as few people would expect the fairground to be hiding military aircraft! Many crated aircraft arrived from the docks and up to 400 were sometimes seen at Carr Lane.

During late 1945 this unit was receiving and dispatching Spitfire Mks XIV and XVIII, Tempests, Ansons and Albacores but work was diminishing with end of the war. Crated Martinets and Waco gliders were held and in April 1946 57 cases of Waco gliders were brought to the hangars from Fleetwood Road and work was restricted to returning equipment and aircraft to No 47 MU at Sealand. Parts returned included 20 sets of Spitfire internal fittings, 57 Hurricane fittings and 25 Austers. The staff level was down to 14 but 20 sets of Barracuda spares were disposed of to No 5 MT Company at Woodvale and later 765 glider components were sold to a private firm by the Ministry of Supply. This firm could not move them all by the time the unit disbanded on 4th October 1946 and the gliders were left there after the de-requisitioning of the site back to civilian owners. The last crated aircraft to leave were three Martinets back to 47 MU at Sealand. The last aircraft to fly from Hesketh Park is said to be a Mosquito XXX in May 1946. A local young journalist, Malcolm Moore, was given the chance to fly with Indian test pilot Tony Chotia on that last flight. All remaining employees gathered to watch the event, waving as the Mosquito took off towards the pier. After a circuit of the town the Mosquito returned on a low run past the assembled crowd before turning away for its flight to Hooton Park. It is thought that over 1,000 aircraft had been assembled at Hesketh Park

Martin Hearn vacated Hesketh Park shortly after the cessation of hostilities. In mid-1946 the site was vacant. One of the First World War hangars was sold shortly after the war but the other two remained with Norman Giroux. Giroux was a flying instructor during the Second World War and it is understood that he became Station Commander or at least held a senior position at RAF Cark late in the war. He returned to Hesketh Park shortly after the Second World War to recommence pleasure flying off the beach, mostly at Birkdale Sands. The aircraft

Tiger Moth G-ANOD on the beach c 1950. (Quentin H Jones, via John Mulliner)

would be housed in hangars, maintained and prepared for flight at Hesketh Park and then flown to Birkdale early in the morning for the day's flying programme. He flew DH Fox Moths and an Avian, which had been stored in the roof of the hangar during the war and were now put back into flying condition. Fox Moths were the most common, with the author having his first ever flight in one around 1955.

It is understood that the Belfast hangar was sold to a holiday camp in Morcambe but the men sent to dismantle and move it were never informed of its size and age. After stripping off the roof they tried to pull the timber roof trusses down but they crashed to the floor and broke into thousands of pieces. The newer Second World War hangar was used by Southport Corporation as a bus depot.

In 1954 the Southport Aero Club began flying from Hesketh Park before moving to RAF Woodvale. The Club shared Giroux's hangar operating a Tiger Moth and Wicko high-winged two-seat cabin configured side by side. The Club received permission to build a clubhouse, which was built on the embankment overlooking the beach, and it incorporated a control tower for the first time ever! Control was all by the old Aldis lamp signals, red for 'stop' or 'do not land' and green for 'clear to land' or 'take off'.

Hesketh Park closed in 1965. Norman Giroux retired with over 30,000 flying hours and the two remaining hangars were demolished in 1966. Today a row of bungalows occupies the site of the hangars but the airfield remains and the sand and a length of apron and taxiway is clearly visible. Part of the site retains the concrete posts of the original perimeter security fence.

Pleasure flying continued for many years on Birkdale Sands (not a Second World War airfield so not included in detail in this book) first by John Lewery in another Fox Moth which he hangared at RAF Woodvale. Later he operated Piper Caribbean and was succeeded by Bill Robinson with a Piper Cherokee. By 1990 the flights had all but ceased but there is a move to relocate the airstrip further south and have it licensed again for pleasure flying.

8
INSKIP

7½ miles east of Blackpool
SD 450370

The Fleet Air Arm airfield at Inskip, known as a 'stone-frigate' in naval terms, remains a defence establishment today as a Radio Station responsible for military radio messages around the world. On first impressions it is hard to see what was there before. The flat farmland south of the village of Inskip is dominated by very high radio masts but with very few buildings visible. The site was originally identified in 1942 when the War Office started to acquire the 600 acres of farmland from its owner, Lord Derby. The acquisition was virtually simultaneous with that of HMS *Ringtail* at Burscough and both are of similar design to last the duration of the war and no more. The acquisition of land took place on 4th June 1942 allowing building work to commence immediately. In addition to the airfield site, part of Parrox Hall, Preesall was taken over for WRNS accommodation; Thistleton Lodge as mentioned below, for sick quarters; Higham Grange also as the sick bay and the Prefect Hotel at 204 Queens Drive, Blackpool for further WRNS accommodation.

Although some distance from Navy establishments the FAA required training bases around the country and especially somewhere close to the quiet coastline around Morecambe Bay. The Fylde was considered a good location with easy access to a coastal range at Cockerham Sand, Pilling Sand and Preesall Sand, all to the immediate north of Fleetwood and Knot End which form the southern edge of Morecambe Bay.

The airfield was built with the usual FAA four narrow runways, each

143

100 ft wide and of differing lengths. Two of the runways, 00/18 and 05/23, were 3,000 ft, 09/27 was 3,600 ft and 14/32 was 3,900 ft

The runways were all joined by a taxiway 40 feet wide and the six sites were dispersed around the airfield and designated 'A' to 'F' in an anti-clockwise direction from the south-west corner of the airfield. The main technical site was in the south-east corner adjacent to the Wharles to Inskip road with six hangar sites, an explosives area, a living and administrative area plus the control tower and adjoining technical and safety equipment buildings. The design was for a maximum of 145 aircraft to be accommodated at any one time. The sites had 32 Mainhill type hangars, measuring 60 ft wide by 70 ft long each with one door only, for squadron and storage use. They also had two larger, Callender Hamilton maintenance hangars each measuring 185 ft long, 110 ft wide and 25 ft high. There were two off-site living sites at Inskip village and Wharles, both within walking distance. Initial accommodation was provided for 171 officers and 954 of other ranks, and 64

Vertical of Inskip taken on 14th April 1944. (Fleet Air Arm Museum)

WRNS officers and 425 WRNS of other ranks.

A battle headquarters was established at Higham Slip Inn Farm, Inskip, HF/DF at Shorrocks Farm, Catforth. The GCI installation was at Inskip Lodge just west of the village. Thistleton Lodge was requisitioned as a military hospital and nursing home for units in the area and much used by Inskip. The control tower was the traditional FAA three storey type, of brick construction and still in use today as Sea Scout accommodation and offices, albeit surrounded by newer buildings.

Originally named Elswick after the adjacent village, RNAS Inskip was commissioned as HMS *Nightjar* on 15th May 1943 and its main role was the operational training of anti-submarine and two-seat strike crews. The first squadron to arrive was 747 Squadron from Fearn, Scotland on 9th June 1943 with a mixture of Fairey Albacore, Fairey Swordfish, Fairey Barracuda and Avro Anson aircraft. It was joined two days later by 766 Squadron arriving from Macrihanish, Scotland with the same types plus Fairey Fulmar, Boulton Paul Defiant, Fairey Firefly, Gloster Sea Gladiators and Hawker Sea Hurricanes. Together these training squadrons were also known as No 1 Navy Operational Training Unit. Originally, 747 Squadron had formed as a Torpedo Bomber Reconnaissance Pool squadron with three Barracudas and a few Ansons but changed to an OTU with the Ansons being used for radar training. At Inskip, Albacores were added for an intensive crew training course. The CO was Lt Cdr J A Jevern who was succeeded by Lt Cdr F A Swanton in September 1943. Lt Cdr W F C Garthwaite DSC, RN took over 766 Squadron just after arrival at Inskip. The squadron gave up its Albacores in October 1943 and received Anson Is in January 1944 and Defiants in March 1944.

The Fairey Swordfish was the most common aircraft at Inskip. Although a very large and slow bi-plane its most remarkable attribute was its longevity. Strictly obsolete at the beginning of the Second World War, it remained as an effective aircraft until after VE-Day and outlived its intended replacement, the Albacore. It was designated as a carrier-based torpedo-spotter-reconnaissance aircraft or twin float seaplane for catapult operations aboard warships. It carried a crew of three for reconnaissance or two for torpedo operations. It was constructed of metal but was covered by fabric and was powered by one 690 hp Bristol Pegasus IIIM engine, or the more powerful Pegasus XXX rated at 750 hp. It was 36 ft 4 in long and 12 ft 10 in high and the wings spanned 45 ft 6 in. The amazing thing about it was its maximum speed of only 139 mph and a cruising speed of 104-129 mph. It took ten minutes to climb to 5,000 ft and carried one Vickers gun forward and one Lewis or Vickers gun aft plus provision for one 18in torpedo or one 1,500lb mine. The Swordfish II could carry eight 60lb rocket-projectiles below the wings instead of torpedoes or bombs.

During their stay at Inskip, 766 Squadron had at least six accidents with Swordfish. As a result of a forced landing when the aircraft ran out of fuel HS168 was written off. Fortunately, Sub Lt C H Barker was not hurt. On another occasion HS547 force landed after the engine cut out on an anti-submarine bombing exercise and HS556 hit a hillside injuring Sub Lt R B Cassels. Finally, HS346 force landed on 24th August 1944 after engine failure with no fatality. There were others, more of which later.

On 1 August 1943 735 Squadron was formed, under Lt Cdr E S Carver DSC RN, with Swordfish and Anson aircraft. After working up as an anti-submarine training unit, using the experience gained by the other resident units, the squadron moved to HMS *Ringtail* (RNAS Burscough) in March 1944 to continue the same role there. It operated as two flights, 'A' Flight for radar training and 'B' Flight for radar trials. The incoming flow of units started to grow even though the base was fully committed to training. The first operational unit, 819 Squadron, disembarked from HMS *Activity* in September 1943 bringing its Swordfish and Wildcats to Inskip for four weeks to have air-to-surface Mk X radar fitted to its Swordfish prior to flying to Belfast ready to re-embark on HMS *Activity*. HMS *Activity* had been active in North Sea patrols and then went on to support the Russian convoys in 1944. No sooner had 819 Squadron departed than 825 Squadron arrived from Donibristle, Scotland with Swordfish and Sea Hurricanes commanded by Lt Cdr A H D Gough RN. The squadron had joined the carrier HMS *Furious* for anti-submarine operations during convoy escorts from Scapa to Iceland. After four weeks' intensive anti-submarine training at Inskip, the squadron left for HMS *Vindex* on 18th December 1943 for anti-submarine protection for Atlantic convoys. Terrible weather did not stop continuous flying and the squadron shared the sinking of U-653 with surface forces on 15th March 1944 and U-765 on 6th May.

Inskip was never attacked or bombed by the Luftwaffe and although the accommodation was rather basic the ratings based there made the most of their service career. For many it was the first time they had been away from home and with Blackpool close by and Preston in the opposite direction there were many places to pass free time. The nearest railway station was Kirkham (linking Preston and Blackpool) and although a long walk from Inskip, many did walk it and get the train into Blackpool for a drink or dance at the Tower Ballroom. The local pubs included the Derby Arms located very close to the airfield between the main entrance and the Inskip living site and the Running Pump, both of which saw a huge increase in business during the war years. The Eagle and Child at Wharles was also very popular.

For those arriving at Inskip they would be picked up by service transport from Kirkham Station to the new camp. On arrival they would report to the guardroom (Quarterdeck in naval parlance) with their joining instructions. Here they would be told which section they were to report to, where they would be billeted and where to eat, together with all local rules. Like all airfields, Inskip was remote from towns and also well dispersed involving walking everywhere or, as was often the case, a bicycle trip which was so much quicker. To get from the barrack hut to work could take a long time and then meals would also be a long walk away. The Salvation Army and NAAFI would use vans to bring tea and snacks to all sections to allow mid-shift snacks and drink and save time. In the winter it was often very cold, heating was often by means of a coke stove which took forever to get alight and then would go out overnight unless stocked up. Coke

Front and back cover of the Nightjar *station magazine Xmas 1943.*

was also difficult to get, necessitating late-night sorties and raiding parties to keep warm.

'Z' Flight of 787 Squadron had formed at Lee-on-Solent, Hampshire in January 1943, moving to St Merryn, Cornwall on 24th February. Here it equipped with Swordfish, Fulmars and Sea Hurricanes as a development unit for the use of rocket projectiles by naval aircraft. It was also responsible for training front line squadrons in rocket projectile firing and it was in this role that it moved north to Inskip in November 1943, no doubt using the Preesall range. It moved back to Treligga, a satellite airfield of St Merryn, on 14th January 1944.

The Navy List for 1944 shows Captain J B Heath as CO from 15th May 1943 (commissioning date) and from 8th September 1945 he was replaced by Captain J F Milne-Home. In 1944 the units were shown as 735 Squadron with Lt J P Inderwick as CO; 747 Squadron, with Lt A D Michie; 760 Squadron from 1 May 1944 with Lt J D Kelsall as CO; 763 Squadron with Lt Cdr R J G Brown as CO; 766 Squadron with Lt Cdr E B Morgan as CO; the Fleet Facilities Unit, training department and the WRNS under command of First Officer A I Watt. The list for October 1945 shows 735, 762 and 763 Squadrons plus the facilities and training unit and WRNS commanded by First Officer O Nepean.

The Preesall range was extensively used by the training squadrons at Inskip and had two substantial targets. One was a mock aircraft constructed of steel and mounted on a gantry whilst the other resembled a submarine conning tower. On 5th September 1943 766 Squadron lost Swordfish DK689 when it suffered engine failure over the range and crashed in the resulting forced landing on the sea. Sub Lt T E R Judd and his crew survived. The squadron also lost a Firefly (DK448) on 26th May 1945 when it crashed into the sea seven miles north of Blackpool Tower killing Sub Lts Jamieson and Grainger.

Another serious accident occurred on 22nd October 1943 when Albacore X9152, also of 766 Squadron, crashed just after take off from Inskip just to the east of the village. The pilot, Sub Lt W Thirlaway RNVR, and his crew were killed. Thirlaway was cremated and is commemorated on Panel 5 at Carleton crematorium. Swordfish NF337 crashed to the north of the airfield on 17th November 1944 killing Sub Lt D A G Tomlinson and Petty Officer Nelson. Sub Lt Tomlinson is buried at St Peter's Church, Inskip. At least two others crashed in the same area but without fatalities. Two more Swordfish of the squadron crashed into the sea near the Preesall range; HS615 whilst on a night exercise on 11th February 1944 killing the crew of three, Sub Lt Meat,

Sub Lt Camps and Leading Airman N A Dennis. A similar accident occurred on 30th May 1944 when Swordfish HS615 crashed killing Sub Lt Ferrier and Petty Officer Diggins.

Sharing the dispersals at Inskip simultaneously with 787 'Z' Flight, was 811 Squadron, which flew its Swordfish and Wildcats in from Donibristle, Fife in December 1943. Whilst embarked on HMS *Biter* earlier in the year its Wildcats had attacked and damaged U-203 on 25th April and then U-89 on 12th May, both of which were later sunk by surface shipping. Mostly operating in the North Atlantic the squadron visited Inskip for more training on anti-submarine tactics for one month, prior to re-embarking on HMS *Biter* on 12th January 1944. The flow continued with 813 Squadron arriving from Dunino eight days later also equipped with nine new anti-submarine Swordfish. Again utilising the expertise at No 1 NOTU the squadron spent a month here before moving on to Burscough on 15th February and then moving to Machrihanish prior to embarking on HMS *Campania* for North Atlantic and Russian convoy protection work.

On the night of 20th December 1943 747 Squadron lost Barracuda P9828. The plane was flying over Coniston Water, in the Lake District, in the direction of Skelwith Bridge. As the pilot left the lake, he turned to the right and whilst climbing on full power, struck rising ground at High Arnside Farm. The aircraft was carrying a load of high explosives which exploded on impact causing total disintegration of the aircraft and crew. The remains of Sub Lt W H R Young, aged 19, one of the crew, are buried at Inskip Church, the other two fatalities being Sub Lt Hopewell and an unnamed trainee air gunner. The squadron also lost Barracuda DN641 when it crashed into the sea on 7th September 1943 and BV758 a few weeks later on 23rd October. On each occasion the pilot was Sub Lt J H M Lawrence who survived both incidents!

Air Mechanic A W Hodgins spent most of 1944 on HMS *Nightjar* and recalls: 'I was drafted to Inskip with another air mechanic and a Petty Officer. We arrived at Kirkham by train at about 9pm. As it was too late to allocate us a mess the other lad and I slept in the cells. The next day I reported to the Engineering Officer and was told to report to PO Pyecroft in the MU hangar. This was situated by the side of the road near to a small wood and a bridge.

'On the flights the aircraft got a daily Inspection (DI) but when they had logged 40 flying hours they were sent to the MU for a more thorough inspection. I was to spend the next 10 months there. All the trades (airframes, engines, electricians, and radar mechs) and later radar, worked in the hangar on the aircraft. Only Fairey Swordfish were serviced in the MU. During my time there I saw only Swordfish and Avengers.

'On the whole it was a very happy easy going environment. For some reason electricians were not popular with the other trades. I found this situation wherever I went. As electricians we kept a wary eye on radio mechanics who had a habit of running our batteries down. Mechanics, including WRNS, except radio and radar lived at Wharles. The only amenity was the NAAFI, everything else was at Inskip. To go to concerts, dances and other events the lads went by lorry and the girls went by bus. Four WRNS Air Mechanics were employed in the MU namely Liz Field, Molly Fidgeon, Margaret Eagan and Gerri Lobley. Gerri married AF/L Fred Moisan at Inskip in 1945.

'We all worked in pairs and sometimes the girls might work together but most times they worked with one of the lads. We all got on well together enjoying jokes and leg pulling and the odd prank. There was mutual respect for each other especially for our ability to do the job for which we had been trained. Our social life, which took prominence after work, revolved around dances. Every Saturday or Sunday afternoon, when off duty, we would take a trip to Blackpool. Those

Aerial view of maintenance area, hangars and hard-standings 22nd November 1945.

Radar controllers at Inskip 1944.

of us with girlfriends would go by bus, the other lads went by lorry. Living conditions could only be described as rough. Nissen huts with a stove in the middle and only coke to burn. The stoves were terrible to light. On one occasion I remember quite clearly someone tried to start their stove by using a Very light cartridge; they blew the chimney off!

'It was at Inskip that I flew for the very first time. I had done a service on a Swordfish and the pilot had taken it up on an air test. He brought it back, which was unusual and said that the air speed indicator was not working and it should be put right. I explained that it had been checked on the ground test but he insisted that it couldn't have been. Two electricians performed the check on the aircraft and the other at the pilot head. We knew it was OK but the PO said, "Do it again" and he stayed with us until it was done. Showing the same result as before, the pilot took it again but the same thing happened. We were told to do it again and if it was not corrected this time I would be put on a charge. Again we checked it and sent for the pilot, he told me to get a parachute as I was going with him. There was an ASI in both cockpits and as we were running round the perimeter track I saw that my instrument was giving a reading. I looked over his shoulder

151

and saw that his was also registering air speed. I sat down saying nothing as I was not going to have this experience lost. After we had taken off I again checked both instruments. Both were working correctly. I leaned over and pointed to his ASI, he brushed my hand away. Eventually we landed with me muttering things about pilots, as a result of which I had to walk back to the MU from the flights. What he had been looking at I have no idea!

'Another time when Margaret [Eagan] and I had finished an inspection we asked the PO if we could go on the test flight. He said it was OK with him. The pilot was agreeable and took us out over the Irish Sea as far as the Isle of Man and over a homeward bound convoy.

'Fred Moisan and I were going to the Major Repair Hangar when we looked up and saw a Swordfish on fire. The fire appeared to be in the vicinity of the alternator on the port side of the engine. We then saw it nose dive into the ground on the far side of the airfield. Alternators had been fitted to provide AC current for the radar. Why the crew made no effort to get out I have never been able to understand. They were high enough, I wonder if these two airmen are the ghosts seen walking down the remains of the main runway?'

AM/L Hodgins went on to explain how their CPO suggested all units should have a badge and he made one on plywood with the mock Latin motto 'UBENDUM WEMENDUM'. Also how there was a floodlight positioned at the end of the runway which they switched on when they were told. There was a beacon that flashed the letters of the day when flying was on. There were also three Sandra lights (search lights) placed around the airfield, manned by electricians and an engine mechanic one hour before sunset and one hour after sunrise. These were switched on to guide lost aircraft. The three beams intersected over the middle of the airfield.

On 6th February 1944 813 Squadron was joined by 838 Squadron, commanded by Lt Cdr J M Brown DSC, RN and flying its Swordfish in from Dunino. This squadron had reformed at Belfast on 1st November 1943 as a torpedo bomber reconnaissance squadron with four Swordfish IIs. A month later it was working up on HMS *Nairana* on the Clyde before flying to Inskip where it increased its establishment to nine Swordfish on 14th February. The squadron moved out to Machrihanish on 18th March where it received four more aircraft. After fully working up it moved to Harrowbeer for anti-submarine patrols in the English Channel working jointly with RAF Coastal Command.

Another training squadron, 737, reformed at Inskip on 15th March

Barracuda over Gibraltar. (FAA Museum)

1944 as an Air-to-Surface Vessel Radar Training unit equipped with Swordfish and Ansons. Working with No 1 NOTU, this squadron trained aircrew in the use of ASV Mks X and XI radar for anti-shipping operations. It moved to Arbroath in August 1944. Yet another training squadron reformed here on 14th April 1944 when 763 was re-established from part of 766 as an anti-submarine Operational Training Squadron. It was equipped with Grumman Avengers, having originally been intended to be the Avenger flight of 766 Squadron until plans were changed. A photographic flight was added in March 1945 equipped with Swordfish but the unit disbanded on 31st July 1945 with its remnants being absorbed into 785 Squadron at Crail.

Avenger II JZ390 of 763 Squadron was lost on 16th January 1945 whilst on a night 'Navex' over the Irish Sea. The aircraft crashed into an almost vertical rock face near Wastwater in the north of the Lake District. The crew comprised the pilot, Lt Bernard J Kennedy RCNVR, G Fell and Leading Airman P R Mallorie who were all killed. Mallorie is buried at St Peter's Church, Inskip. Kennedy is buried at Lytham St Anne's (Park) Cemetery and Fell was buried at his hometown of Accrington, Lancashire.

Like all Fleet Air Arm bases Inskip had its share of accidents and

The Station Flight on a Martinet in June 1944.

fatalities as has already been shown. It was an unfortunate result of war and intensive training. A mid-air collision between Avengers FN784 and JZ310 of 763 Squadron occurred on 10th July 1945 but there were no fatalities. On 14th June 1944 JZ130 was written off when the engine cut out on take off. Sub Lts Hughes and McQuarter were killed on 12th May 1945 when their JZ471 crashed at Port Soderick, Isle of Man. A night dummy deck landing on 21 August 1944 resulted in JZ475 hitting HT cables. The pilot, Sub Lt J C Arbuthnott, survived to become Lord Arbuthnott DFC. There were no fatalities, either, when JZ502 hit trees and crashed on 24th August 1944. Sub Lts Hemming and Callander were not so lucky, however, when their JZ304 flew into a merchant ship, *Glen Maroon* (which sank). On 21st August 1944 JZ519 damaged its undercarriage on a night aerodrome dummy deck landing exercise.

The pattern continued with 760 Squadron reforming on 1st May 1944 also as an Anti-Submarine Operational Training squadron equipped with Sea Hurricane IICs. The pupils practised rocket attacks and anti-flak cannon fire on the Preesall range. After six months the unit again disbanded and was absorbed into 766 Squadron as part of No 1 NOTU.

Harry W Woodford was posted to Inskip in June 1944 and paints a very clear picture of what life was like on the base at that time.

'In June 1944, just after D-Day I was posted to 763 Squadron at RNAS Inskip. This caused some consternation as nobody could tell me anything about the squadron or the station, so it was with great interest that I finally arrived at Kirkham station. We were met by a standard three tonner driven by a Royal Marine. No information could be gathered from the driver, so we set off towards the camp. It was a beautiful summer evening (we were on Double British Summer Time) and after passing the main airfield entrance we saw some aircraft, Grumman Avengers, parked on a dispersal. I idly wondered who operated them.

'We arrived at the main gate of the domestic site at Inskip, and were dropped off at the guard room. I was shown to my Nissen hut, dumped my kit, and was introduced to the C & PO's Mess, another Nissen hut. It was there that I finally got the "gen" on Inskip. The Avengers I had spotted on the way were operated by 763. In addition 760 had Sea Hurricanes and 766 flew more than thirty Swordfish.

'Inskip station letter was "K" and all aircraft based there had a three letter code "K", then the squadron number (in the case of 763 it was "5") followed by the squadron individual letter, so a typical Avenger would have the code K5H painted on each side. We had 24 Avengers

Avenger of 703 Squadron based at Ford. (FAA Museum)

and two Ansons used for training observers on our American radar. Our task was to produce Avenger aircrew fully trained, and to achieve this each course contained an equal number of pilots, observers and air gunners who were formed into crews. The same crew went through training together, and finally left Inskip as a team of three.

'The manning of Inskip was typical of an FAA wartime airfield. There was a proportion of regulars, of which I was one, who by 1944 were mainly Chiefs or POs, a lot of HO POs, but nearly all the junior rates were HO. In addition we had quite a number of pensioners who had been recalled for the duration of hostilities, nearly all POs and all of them general service. The torpedo specialists, for instance, manned the torpedo section and, as our Avengers did quite a lot of torpedo work, we got to know them very well. Some of the other pensioners had appropriate jobs, a signals PO ran the PCB but the majority had regulating jobs etc. Although they were rather amazed with the FAA and probably thought we were all mad, I do believe that most of them thoroughly enjoyed the experience, although we did hear one of them confide to his chum that "this would be a wonderful place if we could get rid of the aeroplanes"!

'One thing was certain, Inskip was a very happy air station, the

Swordfish 816 Squadron invasion markings. (FAA Museum)

General service, Fleet Air Arm, regulars, pensioners and HOs all got on very well together. The boss of this miscellany of personnel was Captain J B Heath. Captain Heath was an ideal man to head the team; he gave the impression of knowing everyone by name, and he was always prepared to roll up his sleeves and get stuck in. I remember one Saturday afternoon I had to taxi one of our Avengers from one side of the airfield to the other, when about half way round I came across a refuse cart parked on the perimeter track. I did not realize that behind me was the Captain's car until I saw the Captain telling the crew of the cart to move, and, once moved, the Captain waved me on. That was Captain Heath.

'Blackpool was a great place for recreation and I remember leaving the Red Shield canteen at 23.00 after a very good run ashore. There were plenty of pubs, cafes, cinemas, shows, dances and of course the Pleasure Beach, so almost every taste could be catered for. Nearly all the theatres put on shows prior to being shown in London, and periodically a bus went from Inskip to one of these where we were admitted at a greatly reduced rate. I remember seeing Celia Lipton in the *Quaker Girls*, John Mills in *Duet for Two Hands* plus variety at the palace.

'On one occasion my whole squadron was bussed to Blackpool to see a film called *Wing and a Prayer*. This was about a US Avenger squadron, and one sequence shows a TBF ditching and then getting the dinghy out. This dinghy drill was considered so perfect that it was decided that the whole squadron should see it!

'We also had visits to the camp from top artists, again I remember seeing George Formby live in the Inskip cinema. The cinema had another function. One night every week it became a dance hall. Although it was called the station dance, it was organized every week by a different department or squadron, and the ideas and stunts that came out of this arrangement had to be seen to be believed; every section vied with each other to produce the best dance ever, so the standard improved all the time.

'Early in 1945 the FAA decided to put all aircraft maintenance onto a centralized basis, and I was sent to head the team in the new "Avenger Maintenance Hangar", which was set up on the opposite side of the airfield to our old dispersal. This meant another upheaval, as it was decided that all who worked in our new hangar would be moved to Wharles for accommodation. We wondered why HMS *Nightjar* should have two camps, Inskip and Wharles, on opposite sides of the airfield, but it did!

'Wharles was a very similar camp to Inskip, but did not have a cinema. Again it was a pleasant spot, and very handy for access to the new hangar. It was a lot nearer Kirkham, and had its own collection of local pubs, whose names are long forgotten.

'Later in 1945 came VE-Day. Most of us went to the church service held in the Nissen hut chapel at Wharles, then to the Mess to celebrate, and then to Blackpool to join in the celebration there. Then back to work with the news that the squadron was to be disbanded and all the aeroplanes plus a dozen or so key personnel moved to form 785 Squadron at Crail.'

Another operational squadron arrived in February 1945 when 828 Squadron moved in from Fearn where it had re-equipped with 21 Avenger Is and IIs. In 1944 this squadron had been involved in strikes against the German capital ship *Tirpitz* in Operation Goodwood then in shipping strikes off the Norwegian coast with Barracudas. Returning to Fearn after radar training at Inskip the squadron joined HMS *Implacable* travelling to the Pacific where it was involved in attacks on the Turk and Caroline Islands before making a series of attacks on the Japanese mainland just prior to the Japanese surrender.

Number 1791 Squadron had formed at Lee-on-Solent, Hampshire in

March 1945 as a night fighter squadron equipped with twelve Firefly INFs. The unit moved to Inskip as part of its work up, prior to embarking on HMS *Puncher* on 11th June for deck landing practice, but the squadron was no longer needed after VJ-Day. It disembarked to Drem on 18th June and then flew to Burscough on 18th August where it disbanded on 23rd September. A similar unit, 1792 Squadron had also formed at Lee-on-Solent on 15th May 1945 and also with Firefly INFs. Again it was a day fighter squadron working up at Inskip from June to August prior to flying north to Drem and joining HMS *Ocean* in the Mediterranean until April 1946 when it returned to the UK and was disbanded.

On 14th March 1944 762 Squadron reformed at Lee-on-Solent as the Twin Engine Conversion Unit, moving to Dale at the end of the month. The squadron was equipped with Beauforts and Oxfords. A detachment was sent to Inskip in June and the whole squadron moved to Halesworth in December. Records are scant but it is assumed that twin engine training was carried out at Inskip in Oxford aircraft. The last unit to arrive at Inskip was 816 Squadron on 11th August 1945. It came from Woodvale, where it had replaced its Barracudas with twelve Firefly FR.1s. Woodvale (HMS *Ringtail II*) was running down due to the end of the war in the Pacific. The unit stayed at Inskip for training on their new type before moving north to Machrihanish on 11th October for deck landing practice on HMS *Nairana* in the Clyde and then

Squadron in front of a Firefly on E Site 1944.

moving south to join HMS *Ocean* for a Mediterranean cruise in peaceful post-war waters. There was one fatality for 816 when Firefly MB688 spun in on a turn near Tarleton, five miles north of Southport, killing the pilot, Sub Lt Davies and another. With the departure of 816 Squadron, Inskip remained with only No 1 NOTU in residence which continued anti-submarine training until 26th January 1946 when it closed down and Inskip was left with no aircraft. In only 30 months operational service Inskip had been home to 17 different units, seen over 13 different types of aircraft, had a population over 1,600 and made a huge impact on the local area and economy.

HMS *Nightjar* held its only open day on Saturday 20th October 1945 to celebrate the end of the war. Aircraft present were Avengers, Master, Firebrand, Seafire, Corsair, Wildcat, Hellcat, Reliant and Barracuda. Four Fireflies formed the flying displays and also demonstrated deck landings on the dummy deck, set out on at least one runway. The Americans at BAD#2 Warton sent a UC-43 Traveller as a token gesture although they were in the process of closing down.

Inskip was paid off and de-commissioned on 2nd July 1946 but retained as a Transport Pool and storage sub site for HMS *Blackcap* at Stretton, Warrington with the hangars utilised for general storage. The runways were never used again by aircraft but were put into service by nearby RAF Weeton (No 8 S of T T) which housed the RAF Driving School. Many RAF drivers received their driver training on Inskip's runways. Most dispersed buildings on the two living sites were allowed to become dilapidated but lasted a long time before demolition. With the growth of nuclear energy the hangars were taken over by British Nuclear Fuels Ltd as a secure storage site and remained as such until 1994. Never being passed back to its original owner, Lord Derby, the site was developed as a major RN radio station, opening on 12th January 1959 with about 90 masts and aerials scattered across the airfield and used for ship to shore radio communications. Four of the masts are 600 ft high. The site was re-established and known as RN Wireless Station, Inskip but was commissioned as HMS *Inskip* in 1966. Limited living accommodation was constructed adjacent to, and literally connected to, the old control tower capable of accommodating senior NCOs and ratings, who operated the signals unit. Housing for married officers and SNCOs was provided in Inskip village. A purpose-built operations building with transmitters and receivers was constructed at the junction of runways 05/12, 09/27 and 14/32. This building remains in use, with a full set of stand-by generators in case of power failure and visitors are discouraged!

The substantial three storey Second World War tower with the newer 1950s addition to the left. (Philip Waite)

The hangars were demolished in two phases, the first in the 1980s and the second in 1994–5. The runways were broken up in 1974 by McAlpine Ltd for use as hardcore for the M55 Preston to Blackpool motorway. The contractors left the width of a road for on site communication and they are still used today.

HMS *Inskip* was paid off on 8th March 1995 when its last CO, Lt Cdr R C Beveridge RN, presented the base's last White Ensign to St Peter's Church, Inskip where it hangs to this day, close to the four graves noted above. The radio unit remains, now known as Defence Communications Service Agency Radio Services Inskip with the control tower and adjacent accommodation utilised by the Sea Cadet Corps and known as Training Ship (TS) *Nightjar*, Sea Cadet Training Centre, Inskip.

The role of Inskip today is world-wide communications for all three services; naval broadcasts to ships; special broadcasts to individual ships and frequency airing for dormant frequencies.

162

9
KNOWSLEY PARK

1 mile north of Prescot, off A58
SJ 465945

Threat of enemy air attack on our airfields was a constant concern once we were at war with Germany. Specific rules about dispersing aircraft were made by HQ 41 group, Maintenance Command at RAF Andover, Hampshire which called for massive dispersals to achieve the requirement. MAP developed Robin hangars for safe dispersal but the maximum was two aircraft per hangar. No more than three Spitfires or Hurricanes were to be in any one hangar or parking area. The number of aircraft acceptable in E or L type hangars was 30 with only eight in a C, D, J or M type with a maximum of six large types in a C type hangar. There had to be 800 yards between each aircraft park and 100 yards between individual aircraft in the open or 50 yards if partly concealed and not more than twelve large aircraft in a park. Aircraft in hangars or parks were not to have petrol in their tanks other than in the readiness park.

This was a tall order, which required huge parking areas and was used as a guideline to choose and requisition Satellite Landing Grounds (SLGs) and Maintenance Units (MUs). With MUs getting more and more congested and providing very susceptible targets to the Luftwaffe it was decided to open SLGs for specific MUs to allow them to disperse their aircraft safely. Sites across the country were looked at and several were placed in the grounds of country houses and estates where there was open space large enough for a grass runway but trees under which the aircraft could hide. Initially approximately 50 sites were prepared by Rendall, Palmer and Tritton, each being allocated a number from 1 to 49. Later an additional fifteen were selected but of those only eleven appear to have been used. In one or two cases these sites were eventually developed into full airfields.

Normally these sites do not appear on military charts and they must not be confused with RAF satellite airfields, which were properly equipped airfields. Building work was deliberately kept to a minimum to avoid aerial reconnaissance spotting them and to keep the cost down. Runways were levelled and rolled to consolidate them and often laid with Sommerfeld tracking to allow heavier aircraft to use them in wet weather. Some had Robin hangars erected and as these were not much bigger than houses, they were camouflaged by adding dummy doors and windows and chimneystacks. Normally SLGs were allocated to a specific MU and in the case of Knowsley Park, numbered 49 SLG, it was allocated to No 37 MU at Burtonwood. Knowsley Park was part of the estate of Lord Derby who was also to lose much of his land at Inskip for HMS *Nightjar*. His estate had a flat area of grass surrounded by trees and running roughly north-west to south-east, located to the north of Knowsley Hall, his ancestral home. This area and large areas of surrounding parkland were acquired by the Air Ministry to allow plenty of space for hiding aircraft under trees and spreading out the few buildings that were to be constructed. On 14th October 1941 a detachment of one officer and 40 NCOs and airmen together with the necessary equipment, stores and MT proceeded to Knowsley to prepare for the opening of the SLG. Personnel comprising this detachment were billeted in Prescot, about a three-mile drive from the SLG. Owing to the SLG not being in a fit state to receive aircraft, instructions were received that all personnel and equipment were to be withdrawn and returned to the parent unit by 7th November. In the meantime 37 MU was obliged to use 21 SLG at Ollerton, Salop which was eventually to become Hinstock airfield. Ollerton was a long way from Burtonwood and not convenient so the pressure was on the engineers to get Knowsley Park open as soon as possible.

On 13th November 1941 HQ 41 Group called for a report and the response was that the turf was very soft and waterlogged and it was impossible to give any date when it was considered it would be fit for aircraft to use. Optimistic estimates were Spring 1942. The site was looked at again on 8th December by Sqn Ldr Gray and the site engineer who determined that it could probably be used but it would benefit if left until the spring. The first aircraft to land was a Miles Magister that made a forced landing here at one extreme end of the runway and sunk to a depth of approximately three inches. This was a very light aircraft so it proved the engineers were right.

On 24th March another inspection stated the runway was completed and knitting well and should be ready for use by the end of April. It

Typical of the types stored at Knowsley Park, this Westland Lysander was a type seen on main airfields in Lancashire during the Second World War. (Via Peter Yuile)

also stated that hardstandings for 50 aircraft had been completed, buildings were finished and work on the access tracks was in progress and should be complete in three weeks.

The SLG officially opened on 13th May 1942 and personnel comprising the detachment of one admin and one engineer officer and 44 NCOs and airmen went back on that day, again to be billeted in Prescot. The first aircraft was a Wellington landing on 15th May and dispersed to the west side as not all hardstandings had been completed. Several more aircraft arrived over the next few days. On 22nd May an ATA officer landed a Fairchild aircraft, inspected the runway and after a conference with Fg Off Edwards (detachment Commander) and on the statement of the contractors he condemned the landing strip as unserviceable. It was decided to divert three Wellingtons due for delivery here to Burtonwood. Nonetheless, the next day Wellington X3896 arrived from Burtonwood but the tail wheel was slightly damaged on landing and it could not be moved off the landing strip. The propellers were removed and returned to Burtonwood as they were in short supply and were to be used to ferry another Wellington over to the SLG! The same props powered Wellington X3868 in that evening and several more landed the next day, also to have their props removed. By the end of the month the site held 19 aircraft but none had been delivered out.

Sqn Ldr Brackenbury and Flt Lt Duke from HQ No 25 Group, Flying Training Command were flying a Gloster Gauntlet and Gladiator respectively nearby on 14th June when the weather deteriorated and they made a precautionary landing on the SLG. Once sure of where they were they took off again for Speke. Asked how they located the aerodrome they stated that the runway was very noticeable from the air and could not be mistaken for anything else! So much for the camouflage!

Knowsley was not too successful for 37 MU and with Burtonwood being handed over to the Americans and 37 MU disbanding the SLG was transferred to 48 MU at Hawarden, North Wales on 7th July 1942 together with personnel, equipment and aircraft. In August its use by 48 MU was reconfirmed. This unit dispersed Lysanders and Halifaxes at Knowsley Park. It also utilized the SLG at Tatton Park near Manchester, set in another stately home's gardens but larger and more open than Knowsley Park. Tatton Park became a dropping zone for the parachute school at Ringway, Cheshire so Bodorgan in Anglesey was taken over to relieve the pressure on the parent unit. In July 1943, 293 aircraft were held by 48 MU at Hawarden, Knowsley and Bodorgan.

On 5th April 1944 HQ 41 Group called for the de-requisitioning of ten SLGs including Knowsley Park and for the aircraft held there to be ferried back to the parent unit but it appears that Knowsley Park continued until late 1944. Hooton Park, Cheshire had been taken over by 48 MU for storage as it had clear open space and hard runways, and camouflage was no longer necessary. Knowsley Park was closed down. The Robin hangars and temporary buildings were removed and the land given back to Lord Derby

The site was well chosen and Lord Derby used the runway for his one private aircraft in the 1950s. The site is now in the centre of Knowsley Safari Park and virtually nothing remains to show what was once here except the bases of a few buildings and blast shelters.

10
SAMLESBURY

6 miles east of Preston, on A59
SD 637331

Located close to junction 31 of the M6 motorway, Samlesbury today covers 142 hectares (350 acres) in the Ribble Valley with the 14th-century Samlesbury Hall outside the south-west corner of the site. Over 4,000 people work at Samlesbury in 128,000 sq metres (1.38 million sq feet) of covered space.

Samlesbury was built as a factory airfield, just before the Second World War. The factory is now a much enlarged, high technology aircraft factory without an active airfield. There is no longer a control tower but Air Cadet gliding still takes place there.

The factory now makes components and assemblies for Airbus wings, Eurofighter Tyhpoon front fuselages and empennage surfaces, as well as T-45 Goshawk and joint Strike Fighter, with the Americans, plus other work.

A major claim to fame was that, during the war, work was of such a high standard that ferry pilots would report that aircraft built at Preston and Samlesbury flew better and more consistently than the same aircraft from other shadow factories. It helped when the company needed support from the Ministry in establishing its new design team at a time when established firms were being cut back. This led to the Canberra, Britain's first jet bomber and its successors.

Thousands of motorists pass by every day but I doubt that many will realise what a huge contribution the base made, and still makes, to our military aviation industry.

The beginning of Samlesbury airfield can be traced back to 1922, when it was proposed that an aerodrome be built to serve Blackburn and Preston. In November of that year, the Secretary of the Preston and

District Regional Town Planning Committee wrote to the Air Ministry seeking advice on the siting of the aerodrome. The committee was a joint organization of the Preston and Blackburn municipalities and the local Rural District Councils, and was encouraged to appoint a consultant from the Air Ministry's approved list to advise it on the selection of a site and other related matters. In due course the aviation adviser to the Automobile Association was appointed to act for the committee. At the time the AA was very much involved in the private side of civil aviation and published a list of landing strips approved by its aviation department.

The AA's final report to the committee recommended the siting of the aerodrome to the north-east of Samlesbury Hall. The site was judged to be the only one within easy reach of both Preston and Blackburn, which allowed the development of a full-sized aerodrome to the standards then recommended by the Air Ministry.

After due consideration, the report was submitted to the Air Ministry on 17th September 1934. On 9th May 1935 the announcement of a compulsory purchase order appeared in the local Press, applying to a 915 acre (370 hectare) site for purely aviation purposes.

The proposal was for a standard civilian aerodrome, all runways to be grass, with a main runway 1,300 yards long and 400 yards wide plus two other runways 1,000 yards long.

The layout of the airfield was by now established and awaited trials with a portable radio beacon to confirm that the selected runway centreline was suitable for installation of radio larding aids. The proposed location was on the southern part of the current airfield, lying between Preston New Road (the present southern boundary) and Myerscough Smithy Road, which was a road roughly parallel to Preston New Road but lying further north. Whalley New Road which now skirts the northern boundary of the aerodrome was already planned in 1935 as a bypass which would replace Myerscough Smithy Road as a route from Preston to Whalley and it was intended at the next stage of the development to extend the airfield to the line of Whalley New Road. The municipal aerodrome's administrative buildings were to be adjacent to Preston New Road at the south-east corner of the airfield.

In 1937 the Air Ministry was looking not only for new airfields for use by the RAF, but for suitable civilian airfields which might be used by RAFVR flying training schools to be operated by civilian companies. In November 1937, with encouragement from the Joint Committee, an Air Ministry team visited Samlesbury to consider its suitability for a new RAFVR Centre and associated Elementary and Reserve Flying Training school to recruit and train aircrew reservists from the Preston area. Plans were made to proceed with levelling and draining the southern part of the site at a cost of £12,000. This work had started when the Committee heard from the Air Ministry that they did not consider the site as suitable but it might be considered again if further expansion of the RAFVR took place.

In October 1938 the Joint Committee revisited the Air Ministry in London to try to have the site re-evaluated and approved for an airfield. There had also been press reports that English Electric were seeking an airfield for their proposed aircraft production but a site on the west side of Preston, at Freckleton, had been proposed in competition with Samlesbury. The Committee was told that the site for a RAFVR centre would need to be open by April 1939 and it would not be possible for the Samlesbury site to be completed by then; also the Freckleton side was flatter and easier to prepare. Not to be deterred the Committee received some hope that an RAF Maintenance Unit and/or a Vickers Armstrong shadow factory might, in fact, be built at Samlesbury, and might employ up to 4,000 people.

Again the excuse that the site could not be developed fast enough to keep up with expansion plans caused the cancellation of this proposal but by November 1938 more positive moves were afoot. Expansion Scheme L called for 12,000 new aircraft to be constructed for the rapidly expanding RAF and to achieve this, a massive amount of sub-contracting would be necessary. On the strength of this requirement English Electric re-entered aircraft manufacture and would urgently require an airfield from which to test-fly new aircraft. The Air Ministry now agreed that the airfield development could start. Blackburn maintained that the cost of the airfield had been or would be shared equally between Preston and Blackburn, but the main beneficiary in terms of employment would be Preston with up to 4,000 jobs being created at the newly enlarged English Electric Strand Road works, and only 150 or so at the airfield. The Air Ministry inspected the site again to assess its suitability for an Aircraft Storage Unit, but in December they confirmed their decision that the site was unsuitable for such a unit because the surrounding area was too restricted and undulated too much to allow the construction of properly dispersed storage sites.

In January 1939 the Air Ministry considered that the aerodrome should go ahead and an English Electric Co flight shed should be built on the north side. By mid 1938 agreement was reached between the Air

Aerial view of the whole airfield looking south-east with main runway clearly visible together with the three production areas. (BAE Systems North West Heritage Group)

Ministry and English Electric that they would build the twin-engined Hampden bomber at Preston with a production rate of seven aircraft per week anticipated on a two-shift working pattern. The initial contract, placed on 21st December 1938 for 75 Handley Page Hampden twin-engined bombers, envisaged production at half this rate but English Electric were warned this was the first of many contracts proposed. It was agreed that a canteen for 250 workers be built at Samlesbury but eventually the labour force reached a maximum of 1,100 personnel. Fine tuning in layout called for the first Flight Shed (No 1) to be built at right angles to the original layout. This was to bring the hangar doors into the lee of the building to ease ground handling of the aircraft. Only after the building was erected was it revealed that the change also caused the building to infringe the safety zone for one of the runways.

Forward planning now took into account that the site must be large enough to allow the eventual construction of three runways, since four-engined Halifaxes were to follow the Hampdens down the production line. At this time it was still assumed that the RAFVR school would still be built. The November 1937 survey had allowed for a site for the school adjacent to the intended civilian administration buildings, but the later plans showed a detailed layout with two entrances from the Whalley New Road approximately where flight shed 3A was later built and including two Bellman hangars and two larger 'semi-permanent' hangars, amongst many other buildings. In the event, the RAFVR scheme never proceeded. No 49 Elementary & Reserve Flying Training School was scheduled to form at Samlesbury in 1939 with Hind and Audax aircraft but the airfield was not ready and it never actually formed, being officially disbanded at the outbreak of war in September 1939.

Work commenced on Flight Shed No 1 on 10th April 1939 and the shed was taken over from the contractors on 1st November. Meanwhile, the Strand Road works in Preston had been greatly extended and the first Hampden, P2062, was delivered by road to Samlesbury on 31st December. At this point English Electric held three contracts for a total of 350 Hampdens and they had an 'Instruction to Proceed' on a batch of 100 Halifaxes, although no contract had been placed for the latter. By 10th January 1940, work was complete on the grass runways well ahead of the first flight of P2062, which took place on 22nd February. On 30th March, P2062 flew to Boscombe Down for comparison with Hampdens built on other production lines, a precaution taken with the first aircraft from a shadow factory. By the end of April, five aircraft per month were being produced.

Meanwhile, Preston and Blackburn Corporations remained the owners of the airfield and were closely involved in the supervision of the aerodrome layout and construction work.

Records show that Samlesbury was requisitioned by the Air Ministry on 8th October 1940, although a map of the airfield dated 26th November 1941 shows buildings in the south-west corner of the airfield labelled as 'Burnley Aircraft Products' (these were the Bellman hangars nearest Samlesbury Hall). The buildings were used by Samlesbury Engineering Ltd in the post-war period for aircraft component manufacture.

On 30th April 1940, English Electric received a firm contract for 200 Halifaxes and on 27th May work started on Flight Shed No 2, which was built next to the original building. On 30th June the fiftieth Hampden was delivered and on 6th July a further contract for 300 Hampdens was placed, followed on the 23rd July for a final contract for 250 more Hampdens. In April 1941, 130 aircraft were deleted from the final contract. Meanwhile, on 24th July 1940 a contract was placed for the repair or salvage of crashed Hampdens and on 30th July the final Hampden of the first contract, P2145, was advised as 'awaiting collection'.

On 14th August 1940, the construction of Flight Sheds 3A and 3B

Hampden fuselages under construction at the Strand Road factory in Preston.
(BAE Systems North West Heritage Group)

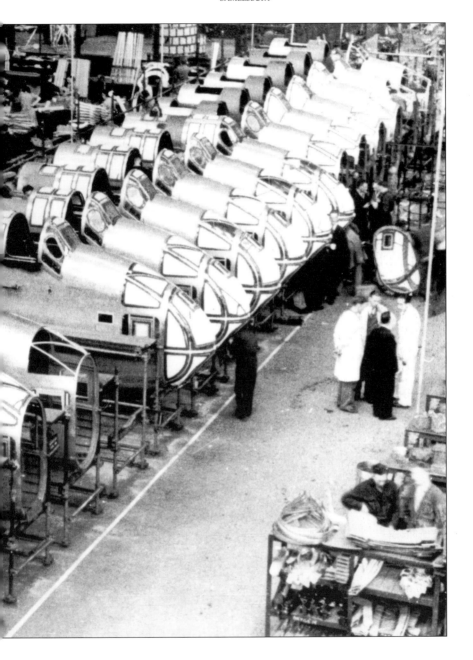

was authorised, with work starting in February 1941. These sheds were dispersed around the aerodrome perimeter from the original flight sheds. Shed 3A was adjacent to Whalley New Road but located in the north-west quadrant between runway No 1 and No 2, with 3B being right on the eastern boundary of the airfield by Mellor Brook. When it opened in September 1941, Flight Shed 3A was used for repair and modification work of Hampdens returned from service. Shed 3B had an annex attached, which was first used for the build up of the engines. Here the mounting structure and auxiliary were fitted ready for the engines to be installed in the aircraft.

Incidents were bound to happen and a large number of Hampdens returned for modification and repair, which meant that on some occasions various items were still on board the aircraft when they arrived from their operational squadrons. Flares were often found in the flare shoots and on one occasion a bullet was left in the breech of the pilot's gun. Whilst the aircraft was being checked for acceptance by the AID Inspector he accidentally pressed the firing button and fired it through the hangar doors and across the airfield, fortunately no damage was reported. Another mishap occurred when a detonator was left in the barrage balloon cutters which were situated in the leading edge of the Hampden's wing. It was only discovered when moving the aircraft up the production line and the chain blocks caught in the cutter and severed the chain, again no-one was hurt. One evening a modified Hampden was ready for delivery and the crew arrived to fly it away. However a snag delayed the departure so the pilot requested two cars be positioned at the end of the runway with headlights on. At this time there was no runway or airfield lighting of any form and the aircraft was desperately required for operations that night.

The Hampden production was completed without any accidents and during the Halifax production only three were recorded. One involved a Halifax which had a puncture on landing and the aircraft ground looped and a wing hit a concrete mixer at the side of the runway. The undercarriage collapsed and the wing dropped onto the runway. The second was when a Halifax was parked on the apron after a test-flight when the port undercarriage started to retract due to the under-carriage-up button being accidentally pressed. This aircraft required extensive post wing repairs. The final one involved an RAF crew who came to collect a Halifax but the flight engineer closed the throttles by mistake on take off causing the aircraft to run off the end of the runway where the wheels sank into soft ground. The aircraft stood on its nose, broke its back and was written off. The crew escaped injury as they were strapped in and there is no note of the disciplinary action taken against the flight engineer

As noted earlier, the airfield was requisitioned on 8th October 1940, because of the forthcoming investment by the Air Ministry and MAP in facilities to support Halifax production, including the extension of the grass runways, which commenced on 7th October.

The following is extracted from part of a history series by BAE Systems, North West Heritage Group:

'Many male workers above call-up age were directed to where in the country they were needed and large numbers of women of all ages were employed in factories for the first time. Many of these women had husbands in the armed services, some losing their men in the conflict. Those who operated machine tools usually had their machines set up by a skilled "setter" so that parts made would satisfy an inspector. Most workshops were very noisy, with "tin-bashers", riveters or clattering machines. For the men, shift work was normal as were long hours. Sometimes all staff would go on ten-hour days and/or seven-day weeks for a while and it was not unusual for a few men to work for several days without going home. Some workers also did Air Raid Warden or other duties. Most production workers were paid according to how many pieces they made, after times per piece had been established by a ratefixer watching a skilled man do the job (who tried to make it take longer without seeming to). Good money was earned and there was much fund-raising to buy aeroplanes and the like and for servicemen, widows and others.

'There were some air raid shelters but work would continue after the siren, until the wardens warned that the raid was imminent. Because many workers did not see much sunshine for months at a time, the Company arranged visits to a room with about a dozen powerful sun lamps, where you stood for one minute in each of four positions.

'Delivery of wing and fuselage assemblies were by "Queen Mary". This articulated lorry had a low-loading trailer that could carry a 50 ft long component. Test flights of these bombers were flown single handed (in service a Halifax would have two pilots, an engineer, a navigator, a radio operator and two gunners) and pilots sometimes tested and delivered two planes a day to an RAF station in Scotland, catching the train back to Preston at midday and evening. During the period of the war these pilots did not lose one of the 2,916 aircraft built.'

The second Hampden contract was completed on 5th December 1940 with the delivery of X3154 to No 12 MU at Kirkbride, whilst the third runway was completed on 8th March 1941 when AD873 was advised as awaiting collection, flying to No 44 MU Edzell, Scotland on the following day. By the end of December 1940, 260 aircraft had been delivered. In January 1941 No 2 Shed was opened and by the end of the month 300 Hampdens had been delivered at a rate of 6.78 per week. The work rate was still building up, the peak production of Hampdens being in April 1941 when 53 aircraft were delivered. The production rate of Hampdens then slackened with the cancellation of part of the contract at the end of April, as priority turned to the Halifax. The last Hampden was delivered to No 489 Squadron at RAF Thorney Island, Hampshire on 15th March. By the end of 1941, 714 Hampdens and 7 Halifaxes had been delivered. By mid March the last of 770 Hampdens had been delivered at the average rate of 1.06 aircraft per day; by the end of July 1942 Halifax production was a total of 36.

By this time, work was in progress on Flight Shed 4 (authorised on 5th February 1942), built to the south-east of the original Sheds 1 and 2 and divided from them by the tarmac parking area. This perhaps emphasises the limitations of the site because even at this stage of the war, dispersal was a major consideration in the siting of buildings to avoid damage from enemy air attacks. The only other site which could have been used, however, was that in the south-east corner of the airfield, originally intended for the Preston/Blackburn municipal airport buildings. Since this area is the highest ground on the whole aerodrome, there were restrictions on the height of buildings which could be erected without infringing the runway safety zones and this may have prevented its use for the erection of Flight Shed 4. The Luftwaffe flew reconnaissance flights across Britain and had already correctly spotted the Strand Road factory as an aircraft production facility and the construction of Samlesbury airfield. Although dispersal was a serious consideration the airfield was never attacked. A few incendiary bombs did fall in the vicinity, however, and on the village of Balderstone, which is half a mile north-east of the airfield.

On 7th December 1942, work commenced on laying concrete runways, the whole layout being completed by 8th May 1943. The runways were No 1 bearing 07-25 5,100 feet (1,554 m) long, No 2 bearing 17-35 being 2,880 feet long (878 m) and No 3 bearing 11-29 3,300 feet long (1,006 m). Due to its very short length and the fact that both over-runs are on public roads No 2 was soon closed! During the period of the war, Samlesbury was used by Burnley Aircraft Products, whose activities do not seem to have been detailed in any surviving

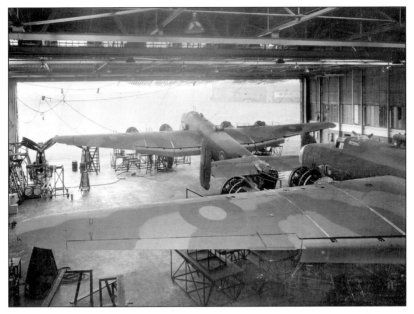

Halifax production line, 1944. (BAE Systems North West Heritage Group)

record, and by the Communications Flight of No 9 Group, Fighter Command.

Number 9 Group had its HQ at Barton Hall, just off the A61 to the north of Preston, and its Communication Flight was based at Samlesbury from its formation in October 1940 until the Group disbanded into No 12 Group on 15th September 1944. The flight was a small unit with a very mixed fleet of aircraft including Hurricane, Master, Leopard Moth, Cleveland, Oxford, Mentor, Dominie, Lysander II, Vega Gull, Magister, Tiger Moth, Martinet, Blenheim and Spitfires for communications duties. No permanent hangar was set up and the unit possibly operated from a Bessonneaux canvas hangar, which was erected near Flight Shed 3A. The flight operated out of Woodvale for a month in 1943 whilst the runways at Samlesbury were being resurfaced. The Lancashire Aircraft Corporation Ltd had works in Burnley and was awarded a contract from Air Ministry for Bristol Beaufort and Beaufighter repair and modification, some of which is reported to have been undertaken at Samlesbury from 1941.

On 13th November 1942, a further 360 Halifax IIIs were ordered from English Electric, the first part of contract No 2533, the second part comprising 200 aircraft being placed on 20th August 1943. Four days later, the final aircraft of the third contract, placed in February 1942, was completed. On 9th November contract No 3362 was signed for a further 400 Halifax III and VIs. During 1943 Halifax production was rising steadily towards the target of 60 aircraft a month with the maximum output achieved in February 1944 when 80 aircraft were built. This reflects a rate of 2.58 per day! It was an amazing achievement for war-torn Britain for a comparatively complicated four-engined bomber. At about this time, English Electric received instructions to prepare for the production of a fighter aircraft, the Folland FO.117A designed to specification F.18/43 which was considered to be a successor to the Tempest, then in service. This was a single-seat fighter with a Bristol Centaurus radial engine driving contra-rotating propellers and similar in layout to the Hawker Tempest and (Sea)Fury. After some months of preparation this project was abandoned in favour of the de Havilland Vampire jet fighter. The Vampire was the second jet fighter to enter RAF service after the Meteor and was too late so see active service in the Second World War.

Handley Page Halifaxes outside camouflaged erection shed, 1944. (BAE Systems North West Heritage Group)

Handley Page Halifax bombers lined up ready for test-flying in 1944. (BAE Systems North West Heritage Group)

It was initially known as the Spider Crab because of its unusual twin tail boom configuration which was designed to keep the length of the jet tailpipe as short as possible to prevent loss of power. First flight was at the de Havilland home factory at Hatfield, Hertfordshire in September 1943 powered by a 2,700 lb thrust de Havilland Goblin turbojet. Production of the Vampire F1 was subcontracted to English Electric, Preston, where the initial order of 120 was placed on 12th May 1944 and increased to 300 on 7th May 1945.

In 1944 English Electric considered fitting two Bristol Mercury engines, which were to be obtained from Blenheims, to Hamilcar gliders. Investigation showed that the airfield at Samlesbury was too small to permit safe operation of these lumbering aircraft so the proposal was dropped.

On 22nd May 1944, a further 175 Halifaxes were ordered, to be followed on 19th July by 400 more. In the event only the first 25 aircraft of these contracts were completed. However the order for 120 DH Vampire F.1s, was more productive. All were completed, and the first aircraft, TG274, flew from Samlesbury on 20th April 1945. The first 40 aircraft had the same engine as the prototype but from the 41st they were fitted with an improved version producing 3,100 lb thrust, known as the Goblin Gn.2. The first 50 Vampires were unpressurised but subsequent aircraft had a pressurised cockpit and the original three piece cockpit was replaced by a bubble hood. The aircraft was not large having a wing span of only 40 feet, a length of 30 ft 9 ins and a height of 8 ft 10 ins. Fully loaded it only weighed 12,390 lbs (5620 kg). Maximum speed was 540 mph, considerably better than the advanced fighters of the Second World War such as the Hawker Tempest (427 mph), and a range of 730 miles. The aircraft was fitted with four 20mm guns.

At the end of the war in Europe Halifax manufacture was rapidly reduced and production at Preston soon reduced to ten per month before ceasing totally in November 1945. Samlesbury had been responsible for the assembly and test flight of 2,145 Halifaxes. Production of the Hampden and Halifax by all manufacturers was a total of 7,762 of which English Electric was responsible for a share of 37.5 per cent.

English Electric was determined to remain in the aviation business after the war and saw this contract for an aircraft of the post-war generation as an essential stepping stone in achieving their aim. With this the Ministry of Aircraft Production (as it was at the time) were

Vampire I production, 1945, note the Halifax refurbishment and modification line on far right. (BAE Systems North West Heritage Group)

happy to concur, there being substantial evidence that, unlike some other 'shadow' manufacturers, English Electric really approached the production of aircraft seriously. The company took a pride in the job, turning out a superior product with fewer delays and problems than their motor trade contemporaries. By the end of the war, a further 180 Vampires had been ordered, and although those orders were later cut back, during 1946, 184 Vampires were delivered of which 52 were for export. As they were so much smaller than the Halifax there was spare capacity in the Flight Sheds at Samlesbury and English Electric secured a contract to modify Avro Lincoln bombers. Five major systems were modified or fitted including radio navigation when Loran, Rebecca and Gee were installed plus H2S radar. The fifth was an automatic gun-laying turret, the existing rear gun position modified to be auto-matically aimed by the system using rearward-facing radar. The Lincoln modification programme lasted three years during which time over 200 aircraft passed through Samlesbury. Vampire production totalled 180 in 1947 with the improved Mk 3 coming off the assembly lines followed by the Mk 5. Production in 1948 was just under 200 eventually to cease on 12th February 1952 by which time the Meteor F8 had replaced it as the front line RAF fighter.

The RAF and Fleet Air Arm received 1167 Vampires/Sea Vampires from the Samlesbury production line. The first RAF squadron to receive them was No 247 Squadron at RAF Odiham, Hampshire, which flew their new aircraft in the Victory Fly-Past over London on 8th June 1946. In September they were joined at Odiham by Nos 54 and 72 Squadrons to form the first Vampire Wing. Additional Vampires were built for overseas customers, since de Havilland were too busy to undertake production of their own design until about 1950, after which the work was shared for a while.

Immediately after the war No 182 Gliding School formed at Samlesbury with Cadet Mk I and III, Grunau Baby and Sedbergh TX1 gliders but disbanded in December 1949. Gliding returned when the giant American base at Burtonwood was no longer available and No 635 (Volunteer) Gliding School relocated from there in June 1984 and remains to this day flying Venture and Vigilant gliders.

Post-war, No 35 Maintenance Unit at RAF Heywood, Manchester, an Aircraft Equipment Depot, took over part of the base for storage from November 1947 until November 1951. It is not known what was stored there but it was probably parts and equipment relating to English Electric manufactured aircraft.

The Vampire production total is given as 1,369, although different

Vampire production at Samlesbury. (BAE Systems North West Heritage Group)

sources quote different figures. Of those the RAF and Fleet Air Arm received 1,167, Canada 85, South Africa 10, Sweden 70 and Switzerland 4, a total of 1,336. The RAF figures include examples to France, Norway, and elsewhere, which were built on RAF contracts but delivered to other Air Forces without being accepted by the RAF. The balance of 33 aircraft remains unexplained.

The empty manufacturing space was immediately put to use for the construction of the new Canberra Bomber, designed, built and test-flown by English Electric having made its maiden flight on 13th May 1949 from Warton. Canberra production continued at Strand Road, Warton and Samlesbury for nine years with virtually all aircraft making their first flights from Samlesbury and flying to Warton for test-flying. Samlesbury was too small with short runways for safe test-flying of jet aircraft but the manufacturing capability was excellent, hence it remained fully operational for construction. Warton is situated west of Preston immediately north of the Ribble estuary and had been vacated by the USAAF at the end of the Second World War. It was considerably larger than Samlesbury with scope for easy expansion and with clear approaches to the runways plus being close to the sea over which much test-flying was undertaken to minimize the noise.

Canberra work was joined by the development of the P1 twinjet fighter, later to become the Lightning. Manufactured at Strand Road, final assembly was undertaken at Samlesbury starting in 1956. The first flight, like the Canberra, was direct to Warton but most Lightnings first flew from here, although landing would have created all sorts of problems! In the 1960s the newly named British Aircraft Corporation (BAC) was fully committed to TSR.2, Lightning and Concorde work plus constant Canberra modification and upgrading work. Samlesbury was involved in all projects with the pre-production TSR.2 XS660 being assembled here. The Government scrapped TSR.2 in 1965 but Samlesbury continued with aircraft and component manufacture. Today it is responsible for upgrading the Tornado, Jaguar, Hawk and Harrier and manufacturing the next generation European air superiority fighter the Typhoon. These aircraft no longer fly from Samlesbury but the legacy lives on.

11
SPEKE

7 miles SE of Liverpool city centre
SJ 415835

Speke made an immense contribution to the Second World War with very close links to the Fleet Air Arm, providing fighter cover for Liverpool and the surrounding district, and manufacturing no fewer than 2,480 Blenheim twin-engined bombers and 1,070 Halifax four-engined bombers. The Merchant Navy was represented by the Merchant Ship Fighter Unit providing Hurricanes on catapults for convoy protection; calibration and co-operation units working with the army and navy gunnery; and prediction units and radar stations and the erection of thousands of American-built aircraft for the RAF, FAA and USAAF.

Five sites were seriously considered for Liverpool's airport, four on the Speke Estate and one in Walton Hall Park which was close to the proposed East Lancashire Road running directly east to Manchester. Aintree Race Course and Hooton Park were also considered but rejected. The favoured site at Speke was part of the 2,200 acre Speke Hall Estate acquired by Liverpool Corporation from Miss Adelaide Watt for development of housing, industrial and commercial sites and the airport. Work commenced around March 1930 with the first licence issued on 16th June 1930 on which day Imperial Airways commenced a service from Croydon to Liverpool via Birmingham and Manchester using Armstrong-Whitworth Argosy airliners.

The airport was opened for public use on 1st July 1933 with the longest grass runway only 800 yards. The only building was a timber office on the north-east side of the landing ground. Soon Chapel House Farm was taken over and adapted for use as terminal, offices and basic hangar. A new hangar was erected adjacent to the farm and a huge

A Hawker Hart of 611 Squadron at Speke in 1937. (Author)

flying display marked the opening ceremony.

The main flying activity was by the Liverpool and District Aero Club followed by Blackpool and West Coast Air Services flying to Blackpool and the Isle of Man and, later, Dublin. Railway Air services subsequently took over the Isle of Man service and extended routes to include Hull, Amsterdam, Glasgow, Belfast in addition to London, Birmingham and Manchester. Now firmly established as a civil airport the design and construction of permanent buildings commenced in 1936 with the construction of hangar No 1 and the control tower was formally opened on 11th June 1937 by Lord Derby. The huge hangar was steel framed and brick clad and remains an impressive structure to this day, as does the tower and terminal building now used as a luxury hotel. The classic art nouveau style terminal was started in 1938 and completed in 1939 just in time for civil flying to be terminated due to the imminent threat of war with Germany.

The RAF had come to Speke in May 1936 when Liverpool granted five acres of land on the west of the airfield to the RAF for use by 611 (West Lancashire) Squadron, Auxiliary Air Force. This unit had formed on paper at Hendon, Middlesex, but moved to its intended home (without aircraft) where a canvas hangar and timber buildings were erected. This squadron was one of 20 set up as a reserve in the Auxiliary Air Force having a cadre of regular officers and mechanics but manned by local volunteers who would train to fly, operate and maintain the aircraft and their associated equipment. The CO was Squadron Leader G L Pilkington of the famous St Helens glass manufacturing family who became the first station commander at Speke when war was declared. The unit worked at weekends and one night a week, plus a compulsory two-week annual summer camp to train up as a fully operational unit. Initially a bomber unit, they were equipped with Hawker Hart bi-planes and used Avro Tutors as trainers. Pilots were trained on the unit and graduated from the Tutor to the Harts on proving proficiency. The Harts gave way to more powerful Hinds but the squadron reformed as a fighter unit on 1st January 1939 and was one of the first auxiliary units to receive Spitfires, in May 1939. Two Fairey Battles were loaned to the squadron to give pilots dual instruction in the more powerful Merlin engine, retractable undercarriages and fully enclosed cockpits. On 13th August 1939 611 Squadron travelled to Duxford, Cambridgeshire, for summer camp, taking its Spitfires with it. On the outbreak of war it was immediately embodied into the regular RAF as a fighter squadron and had a very eventful and successful war career taking part in most major events such as Dunkirk, Dieppe and Normandy. The squadron ended the war as a Mustang-equipped unit carrying out long-range patrols and

An aerial view of the original terminal, club house and hangar at Speke, with 611 Squadron hangars to the right. (Via Phil Butler)

escorts to bombers. It never returned to Speke but reformed at Woodvale in 1946 (see chapter on Woodvale).

On 24th August 1939 RAF station Speke was formed to control military units operating there, utilising several members of 611 Squadron. On the east side of the airfield a very substantial 'shadow' factory had been built for the construction of aircraft. Considered to be far from German bombers and with a large local work force, a Bristol Aeroplane Co factory was planned with 97.23 acres on the opposite side of Speke Hall Avenue being acquired by the Air Ministry in January 1937. The factory was to be initially 1,440 ft long and 400 ft wide with roof heights increasing in steps from 20 ft to 30 ft and 40 ft. The factory was to produce aircraft from receipt of raw materials to the dispatch of complete aircraft at the other end. It was to be managed and run by Rootes Securities Ltd who had extensive experience in the motor car industry. Whilst the factory was under construction Rootes rented a factory in Edwards Lane, Speke to train staff and store new machines and equipment. The first part of the factory opened in September 1937 with sub assembly of aircraft parts emerging in February 1938. The first assembly of wings to the fuselage took place in June 1938 with the first Blenheim taking to the air in October 1938.

The first contract was for 600 Blenheims and after 250 Mk I's had been constructed the remaining 350 were the improved Mk IV version. Further contracts were placed in 1939 for a further 250 Blenheims plus spare parts and modification kits. This contract was extended several times with 400 ordered on 27th September (days after the outbreak of war). A further 800 were ordered on 22nd December and 600 in June 1940. Rootes were also considered for the production of the Short Stirling four-engined bomber. This would require a larger factory so the main building was widened to 600 ft and other factories were taken over to disperse the production in case of bombing. The factory survived the Liverpool Blitz but was the target for a Luftwaffe attack in October 1940, described later in the chapter, when a Ju88 was attacked and downed by 312 Squadron. The Edwards Lane factory was then pressed into service and the power station at Lister Drive, Tuebrook was taken over together with a second factory in Edwards Lane and more in Widnes New Road. The Stirling was not to be and instead Rootes started to tool up for production of the Handley Page Halifax bomber. The factory was again expanded by the construction of four Bellman hangars to the west of the main factory, this time to produce the prototype of the Bristol Bisley, despite furious protests from the

Blenheims under construction in the Rootes factory 1939. (Phil Butler collection)

Bristol Blenheim V prototype DJ702 outside the Rootes factory in August 1941 – the first to be built at Speke. (Museum of British Road Transport, Rootes Archive)

parent company who considered that they should make prototypes. These hangars were also used for tropicalising Blenheims and repairing battle-damaged aircraft.

The initial plan was for Rootes to produce 32 Halifaxes a month whilst also building 20 Blenheim Vs per month. It was a tall order. Additional sub assembly plants were opened at RAF Burtonwood, Lancs; Edwards Lane, Speke; Meir, near Stoke-on-Trent and RAF Shawbury, Shropshire. The prototype Blenheim V and 50 production aircraft were built at Speke between September and December 1941 with the first Halifax being rolled out in March 1942. Altogether 1,070 Halifaxes were constructed here at a final production rate of 60 a month. The last 620 were cancelled due to the end of the war but the factory produced an amazing number when one considers there was no aircraft production in the Liverpool area in 1937. The factory was passed over to the Dunlop Rubber Co after the war where tyres, belts and other rubber products were made. It finally closed and was demolished in the 1980s.

Rootes were not the only civilian contractor working at Speke. An order had been placed by the Air Ministry for 200 Lockheed Hudson aircraft from the USA in 1938 and Lockheed Aircraft set up an operation in hangar No 1 to reassemble the aircraft. Hudsons did not have the range to fly safely across the Atlantic so they were built in California, then disassembled, put onto ships to Liverpool where they were taken to Speke and reassembled by what became known as Lockheed British Reassembly Division. Work commenced in February 1939 but the demand on space was so great that a further hangar was required and a Bellman was built alongside the permanent No 1 hangar, to be followed by three others. This was still not adequate so permission was obtained to use hangar No 2 which had been built in 1939 by the Air Ministry for the formation of an Elementary and Reserve Flying Training School but this formation was cancelled on the outbreak of war.

With tooling, screw thread and standard nut and bolt sizes different in US- and UK-manufactured aircraft it was necessary to have specific bases to handle US-originated aircraft so they had the correct tools to work on them. The expertise here at Speke was soon realised and when the UK ordered Douglas Boston bombers, it was agreed Lockheed would handle them together with the huge numbers of different types and sizes which were to follow. Before the USA joined the Second World War this plant was renamed Lockheed's No 1 Aircraft Assembly Unit. Eventually Hudsons were allowed to fly from the US, 141 were assembled at Speke and the others flew via Gander to Aldergrove in Northern Ireland and then to Speke for pre-delivery checks before being flown to RAF units.

The first Hudson contract was delivered to the RAF by January 1940 but not before one crashed on air test on 28th July 1939 killing the three Americans on board at Thurstaston on the Wirral. Apparently part of the tail broke off in flight and although the crew attempted to bale out, they were too low. History was made on 12th November 1940 when the first of seven Hudsons flown from Canada arrived at Speke thus opening the great air-bridge across the Atlantic.

The aircraft's journey to Speke was not a simple one. Once safely in Liverpool they were lifted by crane from the ship and placed either onto their own undercarriage or onto a specially constructed trailer and towed to Speke down the public roads. The Mersey at the point of Speke was too shallow to accept ocean-going ships so a well-worked-out route was soon developed. They had to pass under the overhead railway, normally at the Pier Head and then travel eastwards up the Dock Road and eventually up to Allerton Road and down through Garston to Speke. Light standards and traffic signs were repositioned to give clearance for the larger aircraft and all travelled in convoys with police supervision. Trams, buses and general traffic gave way to aircraft. The assembly of aircraft for the RAF and FAA continued with

Grumman Martlet of the Fleet Air Arm outside the Lockheed facility 1944. (Brian Jones via Phil Butler)

P-51s lined up at Speke in 1945 with the terminal beyond. (IWM EA 74243)

A P-51 Mustang under erection in the Lockheed hangar. (Via Millom Museum)

Hudsons, Bostons, Martlets and many US-designed and built aircraft.

Once the US was in the Second World War, the unit worked for the USAAF doing the same role and was contracted to assemble and test-fly the Fairchild UC-61 Argus, Cessna UC-78 Bobcat, Lockheed P-38 Lightning, North American AT-6 Harvard, Noorduyn UC-64 Norse-man, North American P-51 Mustang, Piper L-4 Cub, Republic P-47 Thunderbolt and others. In October 1943 the unit reassembled 135 aircraft for the RAF comprising Mustang, Bermuda, Hudson, Harvard and Stinson Reliant trainers; 33 for the Fleet Air Arm comprising Wildcat, Corsair, Hellcat and Avenger types and 120 for the USAAF comprising P-38, P-47, P-51, UC-78, UC-61 and L-4 types; a total of 288 in one month. The unit was renamed Lockheed American Overseas Corporation on 30th September 1944.

An article in the *Aeroplane* magazine dated 12th December 1941 describes the way aircraft were packed and prepared for the Trans-Atlantic voyage:

'Packing the aeroplanes has received special consideration. Great care is taken to prevent corrosion of metal parts by seawater. The arrangement of cargoes has called for the packing to be thorough. Wings and tailplanes are removed and packed separately, fighters are stored in the holds and most of the medium bombers lashed to the forward and aft well-decks. When shipped in the holds only the motors are greased for protection against corrosion, but when carried as deck cargoes, as are the Bostons, for instance, the whole of the fuselage, undercarriage and motor are sprayed with a black composition called Para-al-tone and the joints and openings masked with protective tape. Without this protection damage of as much as £5,000 may be caused to half a dozen medium bombers during the course of the voyage.'

Mixed personnel worked on the aircraft and included men from Lockheeds, civil mechanics, NCOs and men of the RAF and members of the WAAF.

Most of the USAAF aircraft were divided between the two Base Air Depots in Lancashire, No 1 at Burtonwood and No 2 at Warton (see separate chapters). Burtonwood mostly handled P-47s and P-38s whilst the P-51s went to Warton. After re-assembly they were test-flown by civilians and then flown to the respective BADs for acceptance into the military. One crashed at Croston, between Southport and Preston, on 15th January 1943. Three P-38s took off for the ferry flight to Burtonwood but 2nd Lt Kenneth V Burnett flew north for some reason and in the forced landing in the dark he was killed. On another occasion an aircraft landed at Burtonwood with major problems and was found to have been sabotaged, fortunately without serious consequences. These occurrences were very rare and thousands of aircraft got to their operational units without trauma. Burtonwood and Warton did not get all the aircraft from Speke. Many went to Hooton Park (No 7 AAU) and other to High Ercall, Shropshire, (No 29 MU) which also specialised in US-manufactured aircraft for the RAF.

Other losses involved a Curtiss Kittyhawk AR575 on 10th December 1941 which was on a ferry flight from Speke to Prestwick piloted by an ATA pilot, 1st Officer J S Wiley. The aircraft went missing during the flight presumably over the sea and his body was never found. A Mustang III crashed on 13th October 1943 killing a civilian test pilot, J P W Topham. The aircraft took off on what appeared to be a normal climb out but shortly after leaving the boundary of the airfield, in the direction of Garston, the engine appeared to cut out and the aircraft turned left towards the river as if doing a normal circuit. The cockpit hood was jettisoned into Garston Docks and the aircraft belly landed on a mud bank in the middle of the Mersey. Investigation showed that the landing was perfect but the sand bank caused the aircraft to break up and the pilot was thrown out; his straps were found to be undone. The subsequent inquiry determined that it took 30 minutes for rescuers to reach the aircraft as no boat was available and it was recommended

Group of civilian workers from Lockheeds in front of a P-51. (Brian Jones via Phil Butler)

that a suitable power-driven boat should be made available in case of future similar accidents.

With the run down of the war some aircraft were returned to Speke for return to the US but very few were taken back because they were surplus and therefore scrapped. The assembly of aircraft for the RAF and FAA continued until late 1945 including work on conversion of B-24 Liberator bombers into interim transport aircraft for RAF Transport Command squadrons. Lockheeds continued at Speke until well in 1946 but by the middle of that year all US units had withdrawn back home and the work came to an end.

When war broke out Speke was still a grass airfield. In mid 1941 a contract was awarded to Costain to build a hard perimeter track around the airfield and twelve twin-engine concrete dispersal pens on the Speke Hall side of the base. There were five marked runways which coped until 1942 but with the rapidly increasing utilisation of the airfield, plus the fact that Rootes were about to start Halifax production, hard runways became a necessity. In July 1942 work commenced on laying three hard runways as follows:

08/26	5,122 ft x 150 ft
04/22	4,299 ft x 150 ft
17/35	3,187 ft x 150 ft

The large concrete apron in front of the terminal building running from hangar No 1 to runway 17/35 was probably laid at the same time.

When Speke was requisitioned as a military airfield it was administered by No 12 Group, Fighter Command, who had commanded 611 Squadron before their departure to Duxford. RAF Speke was formed by a flight of 611 Squadron being known as No 6 Company (County of West Lancashire) WAAF. The first front line RAF units were bomber squadrons 'scattered' from their bases in the east of the country to westerly airfields to foil any pre-emptive strikes by the Luftwaffe. When Nos 44 and 50 Squadrons arrived with Hampden bombers these were mostly from Waddington, Lincolnshire. Then Nos 61 and 144 Squadrons from Hemswell, Lincolnshire moved in, also with Hampdens. These squadrons flew night bombing sorties from their home bases and then moved out to Speke at daylight for maintenance and to prevent damage from any 'revenge attack' These attacks did not occur so this scattering proved to be unnecessary and they all returned to their home stations later in September 1939. The space was immediately taken by Oxfords from 'C' Flight of No 5 FTS at Sealand

Ju88A shot down at Bromborough by 312 Squadron on 8th October 1940.
(Phil Butler collection)

whose circuit was extremely busy and used Speke as a relief landing ground (RLG) from March 1939 through to March 1940. The school undertook basic flying training in Masters and then Oxford twin-engined trainers. Their establishment in May 1940 was 45 Masters and 63 Oxfords. Other RLG's were used at Hawarden, Hooton Park, Ringway and Cranage as there was simply not enough room at Sealand and its low lying airfield was prone to waterlogging and rutting in heavy use.

Number 236 Squadron was the first to be permanently relocated to Speke, arriving from North Coates, Lincolnshire, on 23rd April 1940 with Blenheim IF fighter aircraft and commanded by Squadron Ldr Drew. These aircraft were operated by Coastal Command and had gun packs under the fuselage also operating as night fighters. They only stayed a few weeks, moving to Filton, Bristol, in May. From Filton they were to become one of the finest Torpedo bombing squadrons hitting enemy shipping from Narvik to the Bay of Biscay. The following month the Lysanders of No 13 (Army Co-operation) Squadron arrived from Hooton Park, just across the Mersey. This squadron had evacuated with difficulty from France and was tasked with anti-invasion and convoy patrols but moved back to Hooton Park after only four weeks.

No 9 Group, Fighter Command, reformed at Barton Hall, Preston, on 9th August 1940, covering the north of the country and created a sector station at Speke for local defence against the Luftwaffe. Number 308 (Polish) Squadron arrived without aircraft but moved to Baginton to receive them and the first fighter unit to move into Speke was No 312 (Czech) Squadron, which arrived from Duxford on 26th September 1940 with Squadron Ldr F H Tyson in command. Liverpool was being ravaged by the blitz and had scant protection, limited to Defiants from Cranage, Cheshire who provided night fighter coverage to Merseyside, and a few other fighters elsewhere in England.

Liverpool was without real fighter cover for the blitz. The bombing took place at night and there was virtually no radar coverage nor did the aircraft have any form of airborne radar or homing or detection devices to counter the attacking bombers. The main raids occurred on 12th and 13th March, 7th and 26th April and the infamous May Blitz on the nights 1st, 2nd, 3rd, 4th and 7th May. On the raid of 12th March alone 316 bombers attacked Merseyside with a total of 303 tons of bombs dropped in that one night. Cranage was well positioned on the southerly approach to Merseyside but relied on the Royal Observer Corps identifying the incoming bombers and then on the skill of the pilot and gunner to find and shoot at the enemy. In fact the Defiant had a top speed only very slightly higher than the attacking bombers which explains the pitifully low success rate.

The first real action at Speke involved Yellow Section of 312 Squadron who were scrambled on 8th October 1940 attacking a Ju88 approaching the airport. The Ju88 belonging to Kampfgruppe 806, had taken off from Caen-Carpiquet airfield in northern France with four 250 kg bombs with orders to attack the Rootes factory at Speke. It flew down the English Channel turning right at Land's End then flying up the Welsh coast before turning inland over North Wales to start its bombing run. It was as it commenced its bombing run that the readiness section at Speke was scrambled to intercept the enemy aircraft. The three Hurricanes caught the enemy raider over the Mersey and the last to take off, Sgt Stehlik, was the first to attack it actually over the airfield. Stehlik literally still had his wheels down! All three aircraft attacked and all received return fire and some damage before the gunner was killed. The Ju88 was now flying low towards Bromborough where it made a belly landing on an open piece of land, with both engines on fire. One engine was ripped out of its mountings and two bombs still hung in their wing bomb racks, fortunately not exploding on the impact. All three pilots received accurate and intense defensive fire from the Ju88 but were uninjured and jointly credited with the kill; Flt Lt D E Gillam (RAF liaison officer with 312 Squadron), Plt Off A Vasatko and Sgt J Stehlik. The German pilot and bomb aimer were unhurt but the WT operator was slightly injured and the Observer/Air Gunner was killed. He was buried with full military honours at Hooton churchyard but was later exhumed and laid to rest at the German cemetery at Cannock Chase. The aircraft was recovered and displayed outside St George's Hall, Liverpool.

This proved to be the only enemy aircraft shot down solely by a Speke-based fighter and created a record for take off to landing in a successful combat. The entire sortie took six minutes from take off to touch down.

The same squadron was also inevitably to suffer losses at Speke. Sgt Otto Hanzlicek was killed two days later when his Hurricane crashed into the River Mersey after an engine fire. Another very unfortunate incident occurred on 13th October when three Hurricanes from 312 Squadron attacked Blenheims of No 29 Squadron, over the Point of Ayr, misidentifying them as Ju88s. One Blenheim, L6637, was shot down and another, L7135 was damaged. The Blenheims were based at Tern Hill, Shropshire and after the first attack fired two red lights with a Very pistol, the recognition signal of the day, but it was too late. The Blenheim burst into flames and crashed into the sea at Hoyles Bank in the Dee estuary killing the three crew. The damaged Blenheim was then escorted back to Tern Hill by the Hurricanes. The resulting investigation determined that the incident was caused by a culmination of a succession of faults, each of minor character. Evidence disclosed a lack of team work and co-ordination between Sector and squadron; the deficiencies were subsequently eliminated, with special attention paid to aircraft recognition! Only two days later the squadron lost three aircraft when the pilots became lost. Squadron Ldr Ambrus led them northwards hoping to find somewhere suitable to land in the gathering gloom. He managed a belly landing near Carnforth, after running out of fuel. However his companions, Plt Off Vybiral and Flt Lt Comerford, had to bale out near Dalton-in-Furness when they ran out of fuel. Not a happy time at Speke!

The squadron saw many other incidents and eight Hurricanes detached to Penrhos in North Wales to extend their fighter coverage. Here they saw action with the Luftwaffe but the Headquarters at Speke did not see any further action and the squadron left for Valley on 3rd March 1941. President Benes of Czechoslovakia visited the squadron to decorate some of its members and also sympathise with local residents who had been bombed by the Germans, amazingly the airfield escaping any hits. Another visitor was Gp Cpt HRH The Duke of Kent, who later lost his life in service with the RAF.

312 Squadron pilots in posed rush to their Hurricanes, Flt Lt D Gillam DSO, DFC, AFC in dark suit, 1940. (Phil Butler collection via Alan Davie)

On 22nd December 1940 312 had been joined by 229 Squadron, which moved in from Wittering. They too had Hurricane Is providing a second day fighter squadron for the Speke sector. The squadron was commanded by Squadron Ldr F E Rosier. On 4th February 1941 a flight of three Hurricanes was ordered to fly to Ormskirk to escort a de Havilland DH89 with a VIP on board returning from Dublin. The number 3 aircraft flown by Sgt John Arbuthnott did not land with the other two and it was assumed the fog made it difficult and he landed elsewhere but his aircraft was found the next day on a sand bank and the pilot had perished. Unfortunately the squadron lost two more pilots and Hurricanes on 30th March when two collided on a standing patrol over Prestatyn at about 2.30 in the afternoon. Fg Off J M F Dewar and Plt Off R A L DuVivier were killed. The squadron did not have any success with interceptions at Speke and moved away to the Middle East in May 1941 to be replaced by No 315 (Polish) Squadron which arrived from Acklington on 13th March 1941 also with Hurricane Is and under the command of Squadron Ldr H D Cooke. Plt Off E Fiedorczuk, from 315, lost his life on 6th April 1941 when he crashed on landing in P2974. He is buried at Formby. It was two months before 315 saw any action with a combat with a Ju88 over Ruthin on 24th May but without result. In July the squadron moved to the main Polish fighter base at Northolt to rejoin the much fiercer fighting in the south-east to be replaced by 303 (Polish) Squadron on the same day. In July command of 303 Squadron was assumed by Squadron Ldr Pietraszkiewicz but still the squadron saw no real action but lost a Spitfire on 7th July 1941. Plt Off S J Juszczak, aged 23, took off in Spitfire II X4065 on a routine training flight. He lost control when his cockpit froze over in cloud, and dived into the Irish Sea some three miles from Prestatyn. His body was not recovered and he was posted as missing presumed drowned. The squadron rested for a while before moving back to Northolt, Middlesex, in October to be replaced by the Spitfire IIs of No 306 (Polish) Squadron moving north from Northolt.

Squadron Ldr D E Gillam AFC, DFC commanded and almost returned to Speke after his success shooting down the Ju88 at Bromborough whilst he was with 312 Squadron. However he was superseded by Squadron Ldr M Mczelik when the squadron left Northolt for Speke by rail on 7th October. The Spitfire II aircraft were flown up. Up to this point the squadron had been heavily involved in fighting including Rhubarbs over France, escorting bombers to St Omer and wing sweeps over St Omer. They achieved success shooting down two enemy aircraft on 14th August and another six two days later and an Me109 on the 19th. All aircraft and equipment arrived safely at Speke except the squadron Magister which remained at Northolt for use by 303 Squadron. Whilst at Speke they carried out a patrol over Southport on 13th October and during the month undertook convoy patrols, practised interceptions and formation flying, and generally recovered from intense fighting, getting ready to return.

Again there was no action at Speke but a pilot was lost on 5th December 1941 when Sgt Otton Pudrycki took off as part of A Flight in Spitfire IIa P7749, named *'The City of Bradford'*. It was a routine training flight to take place round the Ribble estuary. Cloud level was 2,000 ft but during the exercise the weather deteoriated and the cloud base descended to 200 ft. It is not certain what happened but he crashed near King Edward VII School at Lytham at 10.13. Sgt Pudrycki was 30 years old; having joined the Polish Air Force as a reservist he escaped from Poland to England to join the RAF. He travelled via Romania and joined the RAF in August 1939. He shot down a Bf109 near Boulogne in August 1941. A plaque with a carved Polish White Eagle along with a photo of Sgt Pudrycki was erected by the Old Lidunian's Association (School Old Boys) in the Hawkins Library on 6th December 1991. With no enemy activity 306 moved on to Church Stanton becoming the last fighter squadron at Speke as RAF Woodvale opened on 11th December 1941 and immediately assumed the role of Sector Station for No 9 Group.

Speke was, however, by no means devoid of military aircraft. The Speke Station Flight formed to provide 'hack' and communications facilities with a Miles Master and two Hurricanes. No 8 Radio Maintenance Flight formed in July 1940 and, with two name changes, was a secret unit utilised for calibrating the early radar installations on the coast of the Irish Sea. Liverpool University Air Squadron formed at Speke in January 1941 but had virtually no aircraft although a Hornet Moth and Tiger Moths were allotted. LUAS was to provide under-graduates with basic flying and officer skills whilst they were still at University prior to joining the RAF. The squadron still exists at Woodvale.

The Fleet Air Arm arrived in March 1941 in the form of No 776 Squadron which was a fleet requirement unit providing aircraft with and without towed targets to act as targets for gunnery from both ships and land-based establishments such as HMS *Queen Charlotte* at Ainsdale, Southport, a naval gunnery school. This unit operated a

Sea Hurricane Z4935 of the Merchant Ship Fighter Unit being loaded onto catapult.
(IWM CH15390)

variety of aircraft including Roc, Skua, Chesapeake, Hurricane, Oxford and Martinet. The squadron operated mostly out of Woodvale whilst retaining its HQ at Speke but moved to Woodvale when it became a Fleet Arm Base in 1945 named HMS *Ringtail II* (a tender of HMS *Ringtail*, Burscough).

Co-operation flying was also provided for the army when No 116 Squadron sent a detachment operating Lysanders for AA calibration, prediction and using drogues as targets. Except for a short break, this unit remained at Speke until November 1942 when it moved to Woodvale. Other FAA units included Nos 849 Squadron with Avengers; 1832 Squadron with Wildcats; 1834 Squadron with Corsairs, 787Y Squadron with Dominies and Seafires, 736B Fly with Seafires and 1820 Squadron with Helldivers. Most of the squadrons were only at

Speke for a few days when these units flew off aircraft carriers inward bound to Liverpool docks. They used Speke as the shore base until the ship sailed and then rejoined the ship outbound. Although they were spread over 1943 to 1945 the majority of these short stays were accommodated at Burscough or Inskip. The RAF closed its Station Flight down by November 1943 but No 15 Group Communications Flight moved across the river from Hooton Park for eight months in December 1942 with a variety of communications aircraft including de Havilland Dominie, Oxford and Proctors.

A very unusual unit formed on 5th May 1941 named the Merchant Ship Fighter Unit (MSFU). It was commanded by Wing Commander Moulton-Barrett. Convoys were vulnerable to attack from both U-boats and Luftwaffe air attack, primarily Fw-200 Condor, four-engined long-range reconnaissance aircraft operating from Northern France. By March 1941 these aircraft had been responsible for the sinking of 85 vessels, including five on 9th February alone. At this time there were insufficient aircraft carriers to protect convoys and also insufficient long-range maritime patrol aircraft, such as the Consolidated Liberator. To make up for the shortfall and help combat this threat merchant ships were equipped with a platform and catapult from which a Sea Hurricane could be catapulted, attack the enemy and, if within range, land at a friendly base. If too far out to sea the pilot would fly as close as possible to an Allied ship and bale out, leaving the aircraft to a watery grave. The unit comprised an HQ, practice flying unit, two mobile erection parties and 50 ship detachments with 60 Hurricanes made immediately available for catapult conversion. These ships were named 'CAM-ships', Catapult Aircraft Merchant Ships. The crew comprised a fighter pilot, a Fighter Direction Officer (FDO usually a Naval Officer) and RAF airframe and engine fitters for routine maintenance and to protect the aircraft as much as possible from the ravages of salt water on a metal aircraft. The pilots were volunteers from RAF Fighter Command under the control of No 9 Group based at Barton Hall, Preston. In addition there were radio-telephone operators and armourers plus radar operators and seamen-torpedomen who would service the catapults while Army volunteers manned the ships' anti-aircraft guns.

The catapult for training these pilots was established on a concrete base to the south of No 2 Hangar (which, much later, became a helicopter landing pad). The catapult had been used experimentally at the Royal Aircraft Establishment at Farnborough, Hampshire and came to Speke in May 1941. The first launch was made on 6th July 1941 with

Sea Hurricane V7253. The MSFU had 60 operational Hurricanes and Sea Hurricanes allotted to it, mainly due to them already being built for catapulting from carriers. Most Hurricanes were on board ship so they were never all at Speke at the same time but five were held at Speke for training plus a Tiger Moth for communications duties.

The CAM-ships were mostly on the Atlantic convoys with many sailing from Liverpool. In this case the Sea Hurricanes were loaded by crane onto the ship at either Liverpool, Birkenhead or Ellesmere Port docks. Other ports included Glasgow, Belfast, Barry and Avonmouth. In these cases the aircraft were flown to Abbotsinch, Sydenham, St Athan or Filton from where they were transported to the docks by road and lifted onto the ships. Initially the reverse procedure took place when the ship returned but this was time consuming so the aircraft were later catapulted from the ship and flown back to Speke for maintenance and inhibition. Similar arrangements were made in Canada for the other end of the convoy's journey. Dartmouth, Nova Scotia was used as the Canadian servicing base and a small reserve pool of three Sea Hurricanes was formed at North Front, Gibraltar. CAM-ships were also used on Arctic convoys and to the Mediterranean via Gibraltar. From October 1942 the availability of carriers and long range escort aircraft reduced the requirement for CAM-ships resulting in the establishment being reduced to ten Sea Hurricanes, nine Hurricanes and one Master II replacing the Tiger Moth.

The first trial launch from a merchant ship was made on 31st May 1941 when SS *Empire Rainbow* flew off a Sea Hurricane at Greenock, Scotland which later landed successfully at RAF Abbotsinch. After a very successful operational career the Air Ministry asked to be released from their commitment to the MSFU in March 1943, both at Speke and North front with the reason that it was equivalent to 'locking up' two complete fighter squadrons. MSFU finally closed on 15th July 1943. Between May 1941 and August 1943 170 CAM-ships made round journeys, eight operational launches were made resulting in six enemy aircraft being destroyed, two seriously damaged and three driven off from convoys. In total 401 catapult launches were made at Speke. Only one RAF pilot was lost in the entire operation. Several aircraft went down with their ships when attacked by U-boats including one on the first ships to be equipped, SS *Michael E*, which sank on 2nd June 1941. The first success was on 1st November 1941 when Plt Off G W Varley shot down a Condor in the Atlantic after launching from SS *Empire Foam*. In all 35 vessels were fitted out with catapults and eleven were sunk by enemy action plus one other by an accident at sea. Looking

The last Halifax Mk VII from the Rootes factory July 1945, surrounded by workforce. (D J Smith)

purely at statistics it was not the most successful unit but it kept enemy aircraft and U-boats away from convoys when they were at their most vulnerable.

The MSFU did not lose many aircraft in training but Hurricane V6843 took off at 15.10 on 15th April 1942 for an air test prior to embarkation. When over the River Dee between 6,000 and 8,000 ft the aircraft collided with a Tiger Moth from No 24 Elementary Flying Training School, Sydenham, Belfast, and was seen to turn onto its back and dive vertically crashing into the river near Parkgate, Wirral. The pilot of the Tiger Moth also perished. Plt Off R McIntyre crashed in Hurricane P3385 en route from the MSFU to RAF Valley, Anglesey on 9th August 1942 after getting lost and crashing into high ground near Blaenau Ffestiniog. Another Hurricane, P3868, was lost on 13th September 1942 spun into the ground near Babel, Holywell, North Wales killing Flt Lt T D H Davy DFC and Hurricane V6696 was lost on 13th November 1942 when Fg Off Fannon took off for a cine gun practice flight. Not long after take off his engine failed and he attempted a forced landing at Allerton Golf Club, Liverpool but hit some trees and died in the subsequent crash

Civil flying was stopped on the outbreak of war but routes over the Irish Sea were reinstated by the end of 1939 under National Air Communications control and flown by the former operators. In May 1940 West Coast Air Services joined Aer Lingus to operate the Liverpool–Dublin route and simultaneously Railway Air Services reopened a daily Glasgow–Belfast–Liverpool service with DH.86s. The Isle of Man Air Services' Liverpool–Isle of Man flights were reduced to two a day but from 6th May were restored to four a day. All passenger schedules were severely disrupted during May and June as the aircraft were required to assist with the evacuation from France. The extremely stylish art nouveau terminal building was now finished and many of the offices used by the military jointly with the civilian operators.

Airline operations became the responsibility of the Associated Airways Joint Committee comprising Railway Air Services, West Coast Air Services, Isle of Man Air Services, Scottish Airways, Great Western & Southern Airlines, Air Commerce and Olley Air Service. They had a total fleet of four DH.86s, fourteen Rapides and two Dragons. The Committee was administered from Railway Air Services' HQ in London but its engineering base was at Speke and employed about 75 personnel using the former Liverpool Aero Club hangar to the west of Chapel House Farm. From 5th August 1940 the Liverpool–Dublin route was moved to Barton near Manchester to prevent the aircraft overflying Liverpool Docks, as this was considered a security risk, and remained there until November 1942. The service was again suspended from April 1944, again for security reasons, until well after the Normandy invasion and was reinstated in September 1944. Although restricted by war, fuel rationing and operational requirements, the wartime civil flying from Speke carried more passengers from Speke than in any pre-war year. The Liverpool–Isle of Man route was the most popular, operating at 87% capacity in 1941. Towards the end of the war routes were expanded by introducing one of the Belfast–Liverpool DH.86 services to London (Croydon) from November 1944 and then the introduction of a daily Glasgow–Liverpool–Croydon Rapide flight from April 1945. Aer Lingus, operating from the officially neutral Eire, started operating the new DC-3 in 1940 much to the chagrin of the British operators who became very aware of their dated bi-plane equipment.

Post-war, Speke had mixed fortunes missing out to Manchester, Ringway as the premier regional airport. However the building of a new runway on land owned by Liverpool Corporation between the River Mersey and Hale Road kept it very much alive. The runway is 2,169 metres long and orientated 09/27 exactly east-west. It was opened by HRH The Duke of Edinburgh on 7th May 1966. Terminal operations continued at the old terminal with Hangar No 2 converted into an international terminal to cater for the increasing holiday trade from the 1960s onwards. The taxi distance was considerable and tortuous until a new terminal was built parallel to the runway in 1986. A new general aviation parking apron was opened in September 1999 with a new hangar completed in August 2000 allowing the facilities on the old airfield to be completely closed down on 29th August that year.

Today Liverpool John Lennon Airport is wholly owned by Peel Holdings plc from Manchester which has invested heavily in the airport. Passenger figures rose to around two million in 2002 and are now considerably more. EasyJet signed a 20 year agreement with the airport in 1997 using it as their second UK base after Luton. The airport handles significant volumes of freight and mail. The Royal Mail have operated their night-time hub through Liverpool since 1979 with a sorting office on site, whilst express parcels, newspapers, car parts and general freight movements also combine to provide extremely busy night-time operations.

Over £10 million was invested in a range of infrastructure works at the airport over the past three years and a further £42.5 million has now been invested with European Objective One support. A new terminal building and control tower were opened on 25th July 2002 by HM The Queen.

The original airport is now being slowly redeveloped into a business park. The terminal is listed as being of historic and architectural interest and has been converted into a first class luxury hotel retaining the control tower and many original features. Hangars No 1 and 2 were similarly listed and are retained with one of them now housing a substantial sports centre.

Speke has grown from one of the first municipal aerodromes through its vibrant and vitally important war-time role to a major regional airport. Its role in the support of Britain and the Allies throughout the Second World War cannot be overstated.

12
SQUIRES GATE

On southern edge of Blackpool
SD 320315

Blackpool's Airport at Squires Gate has associations with aviation history unmatched by any other UK airport. The first link to flying goes back to a famous meeting in October 1909. That meeting was organised by Lord Northcliffe of the *Daily Mail* and saw the very first flying in the county of Lancashire (see Setting the Scene for more information). The site originally formed part of the Clifton Estate and since the turn of the twentieth century had been utilised for many purposes in addition to aviation including farming, a golf course, race course, First World War Army camp, and an agricultural and circus showground.

Until 1935, Stanley Park was the established Blackpool Airport (see separate chapter on Stanley Park) but that year Blackpool Corporation acquired 461 acres of the Squires Gate site to develop a much larger and more modern airport in a location which had expansion space and much more potential. Limited scheduled and charter services operated from the grass airfield. With the outbreak of war with Germany looming, the Air Ministry took a close look at all airfields throughout the UK and sent 'F' Flight of No 1 Anti-Aircraft Co-Operation Unit up to Squires Gate from Farnborough on 28th April 1939. This unit operated a mixture of Tiger Moth, Hawker Henley, Westland Lysander and Miles Magister aircraft. These aircraft towed red and white banned targets for army anti-aircraft training units, several of which were located around the Lancashire coastline, firing over the sea. This particular unit was allocated to work with No 9 Light Anti-Aircraft Practice Camp at Flookburgh, near Cark on the southern edge of Morecambe Bay. The army unit was located alongside what was to

The control tower as seen on 22 August 1979, but the basic building is a standard RAF wartime tower.

become Cark airfield and once this new base was opened (March 1942) the Flight moved to Cark to continue the same role. No proper hangar accommodation was available so they had to use a canvas Bessonneaux hangar on the east boundary of the airfield.

In the meantime No 42 Elementary and Reserve Flying Training School was formed at Squires Gate on 1st August 1939, at a time when war was inevitable. Operated by civilian firm Reid & Sigrist Ltd the idea was to train civilians to fly military trainers so as to form a cadre of partly-trained pilots in the event of war. The unit was one of 59 either planned or actually opened and the one at Squires Gate operated de Havilland Tiger Moth, Hawker Audax and Hawker Hind two-seat trainer versions. The instructors were civilians but working to RAF standards. This school really opened too late and immediately war broke out they were all disbanded. The earlier units reformed into RAF Elementary Flying Training Schools but not so for No 42 because Squires Gate was destined for other uses.

The outbreak of war on 3rd September 1939 saw all airfields requisitioned by the Air Ministry for the RAF or other use. Squires Gate was earmarked for Coastal Command training but was to see an amazing variety of units using its facilities. A building programme was immediately instigated to provide suitable living, training, technical and support use. The grandstand for the racecourse was still extant on

212

the north-west corner of the site, adjacent to Squires Gate Lane, and was put to use as the photographic section, dining room and Institute, workshops, armoury and stores. The first hangars were adjacent to the northerly boundary, known as VR type and built to design W/431/39, orientated east–west, whilst later four Bellman hangars (steel frame and corrugated steel cladding) were erected south of the grandstand in two pairs of two, all orientated north–south. This corner saw considerable development with the main entrance being on the corner of Lytham Road and Squires Gate Lane, on the extreme north-west edge of the airfield. Stores, offices, blast shelters and air-raid shelters, NAAFI, MT section and a works section were constructed close by. The school, instructional centre and classrooms were constructed along the northern edge together with the Sergeants' Mess and SNCOs' quarters. A Battle Headquarters was located on the south-east side, from where the defence from any enemy attack would be directed. Three runways were constructed in late 1940 at the usual 60 degree angle, 02/20, 08/26 and 14/32 being 3,300 ft, 4,200 feet and 3,300 feet long respectively, all 150 feet wide and connected together by a taxiway. Outside the taxiway 15 'frying pan' type hardstandings were constructed to accommodate one aircraft each with five dispersal areas, numbered 1 to 5, to accommodate squadrons or flights of aircraft dispersed around the perimeter. To the east, on the east of Blackpool Road, a substantial surfaced hardstanding area was laid down outside the original boundary and a bomb dump with four bomb enclosures was erected to the extreme south, at maximum distance from any buildings or aircraft dispersals. The RAF control tower sits in the centre of the runway pattern and was built to design standard W/943/41. Heavily modified, it still stands and is in use today.

On the outbreak of war there was a fear that the Luftwaffe would make immediate surprise attacks on our airfields. A 'scatter' programme was immediately put in place with the bomber squadrons moving west, away from their bases, and dispersing to places like Squires Gate to avoid such attacks. The unit would fly from its home base for operations and then retire west for maintenance and training. No 63 Squadron sent its 'C' Flight from Benson, Oxfordshire, with Fairey Battles as soon as war broke out and this unit dispersed to a corner of the airfield for a couple of weeks until it was realised that the Luftwaffe were not coming and it relocated back to its home base. A month later 75 Squadron sent 'A' Flight from Harwell, Oxfordshire with Vickers Wellington twin-engine bombers. This squadron returned south in November.

On 25th September 1939 No 9 Civilian Air Navigation School (CANS) formed at Squires Gate. It was one of ten to form around the country. Like the E&RFTS, it was civilian manned but this time by Brooklands Aviation Ltd and flew Anson I aircraft which were flown up from Shoreham, Sussex. The school was staffed by civilian instructors and pilots to give basic navigation training to RAF navigators under training. The school slowly developed but was redesignated No 9 Air Observer & Navigation School on 1st November 1939 with 12 Anson aircraft. On 25th November it absorbed No 8 AO&NS from Sywell adding another 12 Ansons to its fleet. Now its role was to teach RAF observers and navigators prior to them graduating and moving on to an OTU where they would be integrated into a bomber crew and continue training onto the specific type as a complete crew. Living accommodation was not adequate on the airfield and boarding houses were used for sleeping accommodation with all meals and training being undertaken on base.

About this time a gunnery range was formed on the western side of the original aerodrome. Target tugs were Fairey Battles and the gunnery aircraft were Bristol Blenheim Mk I. A Battle suffered a fatal accident, when after slipping the drogue it lost speed on turning and caught the old railway bridge south of the railway station killing all three crew.

The Ansons of No 8 AO&NS were seen all over the north of the country and many cross-country flights put the theories that were taught in the classroom to the test. However, in wartime things never stay still for long and the school disbanded to make way for No 2 School of General Reconnaissance, a Coastal Command unit. The Ansons of No 8 AO&NS were taken over by the new school. This school also took over the new accommodation on base, now ready for occupation and grew with both Ansons and Blackburn Botha aircraft. Later, in February 1942, a Photographic Reconnaissance Unit was formed as part of the school with ten Spitfires. This unit left in May 1942 to form the nucleus of No 8 OTU at Fraserburgh, Scotland, but by August 1942 the school had a strength of 54 Bothas and 10 Ansons with 18 and 3 reserve respectively. The sky around Squires Gate was extremely busy and at this time Warton was looked at as a possible satellite to Squires Gate.

Squires Gate was called on to supplement the fighter squadrons at Speke in the defence of Merseyside. Woodvale was not yet built and the Nazi bombers were wreaking havoc over the cities of Liverpool and Manchester and the surrounding area. On 21st December 1940, 96

214

Squadron based at Cranage, Cheshire with Hurricanes, sent 'A' Flight as a detachment of four aircraft to Squires Gate to enable a greater area to be covered. The next night Fg Off P W Rabone was flying Hurricane V6887 ZJ-A on a night patrol between Blackpool and Formby at 14,000 ft when he spotted an enemy bomber close by. He closed to within 50 yards and attacked and the bomber dived away on fire. Rabone claimed it as 'probably destroyed'. It was 96's first blood. The remainder of 'A' Flight joined the detachment at Squires Gate in January leaving 'B' Flight at Cranage. The squadron slowly converted to Defiants and saw moderate success. Sgt MacNair shot down an He111 near Widnes but he almost crashed due to the balloon barrage. On the same night there were two more inconclusive attacks on German bombers with one Hurricane damaged by return fire. Just before midnight on 3rd May, Fg Off Verity and his gunner engaged a Ju88 over Liverpool, lost contact but shortly afterwards attacked another Ju88 which later crashed. This was 96's first victory with Defiants. Three nights later Verity made two sorties and destroyed an He111 and claimed a Ju88 as 'probable'. 'A' Flight was recalled to Cranage and the squadron moved to Wrexham in October.

Although No 3 S of GR virtually filled Squires Gate, other units still came and went. No 3 School of Technical Training had reformed in Blackpool using small parts of the airfield while undertaking most work elsewhere. No 215 Squadron detached from Bassingbourne, Cambridgeshire, with Wellingtons for two months from November 1939. Number 2 School of General Reconnaissance had formed at Squires Gate on 28th May 1940 with Ansons and a Botha but moved on to Canada in December. All instructors and pilots were RAF. Pupils were observers and pilots and after completion of the course were sent to Coastal OTU or, if exceptional, to squadrons in Coastal Command. The first Chief Instructor was Sqn Ldr T L Mosley who later became a Wg Cdr and was posted away. Later he was the Captain of the Sunderland in which the Duke of Kent was killed in Scotland.

Number 2 was rapidly followed by No 1 S of GR moving in from Hooton Park, Wirral, on 11th July 1940 with 28 Ansons. This unit had been in Jersey but evacuated after threat of German invasion. No 1 and No 2 S of GR ran separately but the aircraft were maintained by civilians. After two months this unit disbanded and the personnel embarked on SS *Lepoldville* for Canada under the British Commonwealth Air Training Programme. On 5th September 1940 308 (Polish) Squadron formed at Squires Gate but had not received its Hurricanes

The presentation of Spitfires to the RAF financed by local fundraising.
(Crown PRO Air 28 724 via D J Smith)

before moving on to Speke one week later. Rather late and well after being in full use, RAF Squires Gate was officially established and opened on 1st December 1940.

Squires Gate was bombed on several occasions. In one attack a German raider dropped a stick of six bombs between Squires Gate Lane and the VR hangars, the last of the stick making a direct hit on the new Sergeants' Mess which was to open two nights later. On another occasion a German followed a night fighter in and dropped a stick alongside the main runway. Two did not explode so the bomb disposal squad came but the bombs had sunk into the sand and water. The craters were marked with red flags as a warning of soft ground, but some days later three Halifax aircraft on a training flight landed in bad weather. One taxied his undercarriage into one of the soft spots but the bombs did not go off. On a third occasion three bombs were dropped on the west end of the factory, one hitting a hangar and blowing out both sets of doors, one covering a Liberator on delivery with sand and soil (see below).

The south-east corner of the field became home to 307 (Polish) Squadron which flew into Squires Gate from Jurby, Isle of Man on 23rd January 1941 with Defiant fighters. These two-seater fighters had been used in the very early part of the Battle of Britain but immediately withdrawn because they were too slow to compete with the German Bf109 and had no forward facing guns. A powered turret behind the pilot carried four machine guns but the crew had to manoeuvre very carefully to allow the gunner to get a bearing on an enemy aircraft. The Defiant was vulnerable to a head-on attack or below and saw no more front line service. However one of their new duties was night flying to try and stem the Luftwaffe onslaught against British cities. The first Polish night fighter unit, 307 had formed at Kirton-in-Lindsey with Defiants. It had moved to Jurby in November 1940 and on to Blackpool in January. On 12th March the squadron managed to damage an He111 over Ruthin, North Wales but did not score its first 'kill' until shortly after leaving for Colerne, Wiltshire. One unfortunate incident occurred with 307 Squadron one evening. The runway was being laid with goose-neck flares for night flying when one of 307's Defiants took off but failed to clear the Austin lorry which was laying the flares. The propeller cut off the driving cab killing the driver.

This left room for No 3 S of GR to literally spread its wings and saw huge intakes of new recruits from around the world to train ready for service with Coastal Command. The fleet was predominantly Bothas with Ansons only forming one flight (No 6 Flight) but grew to include

Dragon, Oxford, Blenheim, Master, Lysander and Battle aircraft plus the Spitfires for PR training as mentioned above. The Ansons were mainly used for night flying and for astral navigation. All maintenance was undertaken by civilians from Brooklands Aviation Ltd under manager Captain Davies whilst the technical side was run by Bill Williams.

With this number of aircraft, accidents were inevitable and a particularly bad one occurred on 27th August 1941. On 26th March Squires Gate welcomed 256 Squadron from Colerne, Wiltshire with Defiants, to help with night defence against enemy bombers in the Merseyside area. A flight of four Defiants took off from Squires Gate for practice formation flying. The leader was recalled and the remaining three spotted a Botha from No 3 S of GR flying 500 feet below them, over the sea just off Blackpool Tower. The Defiants took it in turns to execute practice attacks on the Botha (L6509), with two making successful passes. When the last one dived to attack, the Botha turned to the right and the Defiant (N1745) could not avoid a collision. Unfortunately the Defiant cut the tail off the Botha which dropped like a stone crashing through the roof of the entrance hall to Central Station, spilling aviation fuel which immediately caught fire causing carnage. There were 13 people killed instantly with 39 others injured, out of which five later died. The Defiant crew, New Zealanders Sgt L J Ellmers and Sgt N A Clifford, were buried at Lytham. The Botha had a crew of three, Sgt N A Clifford, Plt Off A A Horne and Plt Off K J A Sale, all of whom also perished.

The Botha had a troublesome career with the RAF. Underpowered, it was very difficult to control if one engine failed. At least ten other Bothas from 3 S of GR crashed, L6141 crashed into the sea on 6th May 1942; L6210 force landed on the shore at Blackpool on 24th April 1942; L6249 crashed into the River Mersey on 7th February 1942; L6265 crashed into the sea off Puffin Island, North Wales; L6314 near Port Erin, Isle of Man on 12th March 1942; L6315 was wrecked on 31st August 1941; L6326 crashed in the sea off Ronaldsway, Isle of Man on 2nd May 1941; L6330 was a total wreck on the same date; L6512 was a total wreck on 16th May 1942 and W5141 was struck at dispersal by Botha L6192 which was landing. The Botha was originally designed as a general reconnaissance and torpedo bomber. Two prototypes were built – L6104 which first flew on 28th November 1938 and L6105 which flew on 7th June 1939. The production aircraft were built at Brough, Yorks and Dumbarton, Scotland, the latter aircraft being test-flown from Abbotsinch. The only operational units to operate the aircraft

Wellington production in the Vickers factory. (IWM photo via D J Smith)

were Nos 608 and 502 squadrons but by April 1941 it reverted to a training role and a few aircraft had target towing gear in place of the dorsal turret. The Botha was never a popular aircraft with its crew mainly because it was seriously underpowered. The loss of an engine on take-off required immediate and careful handling to avoid a stall and incipient spin. Even though 580 were built, the Botha was declared obsolete in August 1943 with a few remaining in service until September 1944.

Back in 1939 the Air Ministry inspected Squires Gate as a possible site for a 'shadow factory' for Vickers-Armstrong (Aircraft) Ltd at Weybridge. On 30th December 1939 it was selected as a site to manufacture the Vickers-Armstrong Wellington twin-engined bomber. Construction of the factory commenced immediately in January 1940 and the proposal was for aircraft to be manufactured on site rather than be assembled from components made elsewhere. Parts were initially brought in from Weybridge and Vickers' other factory at Broughton, Chester and other subcontractors. Assembly commenced before the factory was ready, utilising two Bellman hangars by the main entrance, with the first three aircraft completed there. During construction of the factory, a section of the south side collapsed, killing some of the erection crew. This bay was never rebuilt.

The first aircraft flew in September 1940 and the last on 13th October 1945 with the factory closing down almost immediately. Several were also assembled at Stanley Park and then test-flown from Squires Gate. In all some 3,406 Wellingtons were constructed, flown and delivered from Squires Gate comprising 180 Mk XI (commencing with HF720); 843 Mk XIII (commencing with HZ551) and 400+ Mk XIV.

Squires Gate acted as a ferry terminal for some aircraft being ferried in from the US. Consolidated Liberator AM259 had departed the US on 5th March 1941 flying to Gander, Newfoundland where it was held up by bad weather. It took off on 13th March reaching Squires Gate the next day having completed the Gander to UK leg in 9 hours 45 minutes. Shortly after the aircraft landed there was an air raid during which the Liberator was slightly damaged by bomb blast. The report on this, the first Liberator to reach England, stated that it used the whole of the 1,400 yard runway available for landing! Two more Liberators followed on 6th and 7th April but after that Prestwick, Scotland was to become the main ferry terminal with Valley, Anglesey also being well used.

'A' Flight of 256 Squadron were on a night standing patrol with Defiants on 8th May 1941 when, at 01.10, they spotted a Ju88 on their left flying on a converging course. The pilot, Sqn Ldr Gatheral, and gunner Fg Off Wallen turned to the right and dived until the enemy aircraft was 300 feet above them and 100 yards in front. The gunner waited for the pilot to manoeuvre to a more favourable position where he could open fire when the enemy gunner opened fire and Wallen was forced to reply. All of a sudden the Defiant's turret filled with fumes completely obliterating all external vision. Wallen fired again at where he thought the enemy was but was ordered to bale out as their aircraft had been hit. They claimed the Ju88 as 'damaged'.

Flt Lt D R West of 256 Squadron destroyed a Ju88 off Southport on 7th April 1941 but on 10th April he was shot down by an He111 over Smethwick. The Defiants suffered a high accident rate and were barely faster than the enemy bombers they were attempting to intercept. With little radar coverage on the west side of England they had little help in finding the enemy and had to hope to see one silhouetted against the moon or by fires from bombing below. Hurricanes were allotted to the squadron to try and improve the interception success and on 7th May 1941 three He111s were destroyed, two damaged and two Ju88s were damaged during an attack on an air raid on Liverpool and Manchester.

256 Squadron with a trophy formed from a German aircraft shot down by the squadron. (Via Mark Gaskell)

With space at Squires Gate being at a premium, and Woodvale becoming the Sector Station for No 9 Group, 256 moved there on 1st June 1942. This was the last fighter squadron to be based at Squires Gate with Woodvale now assuming the role.

'R' Flight of No 1 AACU arrived from Farnborough, Hampshire in September 1941 with Hawker Henley and Hawker Hurricane aircraft. AACUs provided services to anti-aircraft practice camps and any other unit needing targets, normally towing a sleeve target about half a mile behind the tug aircraft. This unit worked with No 14 Light Anti-Aircraft Practice Camp at Nethertown on the Cumbrian coast near Workington. With Millom opening and being nearer to the operating area, this unit moved north to Millom on 13th September.

On the night of 17th–18th August 1942, 44 (Rhodesia) Squadron attacked the MAN diesel factory at Augsburg in Southern Bavaria, Germany. This was an unescorted low-level raid leading to many casualties. Sqn Ldr J D Nettleton led six aircraft and his was the sole survivor. On return he landed his Lancaster at Squires Gate at 01.00 hrs on diversion rather than his base at Waddington. He was awarded the VC for his heroic actions on this raid. Another famous personality was Amy Johnson (married name Mollison) who was an ATA pilot ferrying aircraft around the country for the RAF and FAA. She took off from Squires Gate on 7th January 1941 in an Oxford bound for Kidlington, Oxford. Although she had flown solo to Australia, she somehow got lost on that dreary January day. Her aircraft was seen to crash into the Thames estuary and her body was never recovered.

With a growing requirement for air-sea rescue around our coasts a School of Air-Sea Rescue was formed at Blackpool on 3rd May 1943 using the flying facilities at Squires Gate with three Ansons allotted specifically for its use. The main aim was to train pilots, observers and navigators to home into beacons set off by downed airmen, fly a search pattern in an area where the aircraft was thought to have crashed, be able to guide amphibious aircraft to aircrew in the sea, drop dinghy and similar equipment etc. It was an exacting task over a cold, grey sea. This unit remained until February 1945 when it relocated to Calshot with flying facilities at Gosport. It is possible the unit also flew the amphibious Sea Otter, Walrus and Catalina from Squires Gate.

The final military unit to arrive at Squires Gate, on 15th August 1944, was No 1510 Flight, formed at Leuchars, Fife. This flight was originally known as No 10 Blind Approach Training Flight and was equipped with Oxfords which were replaced with Ansons in 1942. These Ansons

The last Wellington manufactured at Squires Gate RP590 T Mk 10 flies overhead on 25th October 1945. (Chas E Brown via D J Smith)

were fitted with air-to-surface vessel radar and blind approach equipment. They trained bomber crews in beam landing techniques. Beam approach equipment must have been available at Squires Gate at this time and was probably extensively used by No 3 S of GR. In June 1943 the unit was renumbered 1510 Flight for security reasons and it was with this designation that it arrived here. Whilst at Squires Gate it trained many pilots on beam techniques before moving to Melbourne, Yorks on 21st August 1945 and was the last RAF unit to operate at Squires Gate. The site was now devoid of all military aircraft except the very last Wellingtons being produced by Vickers-Armstrong.

At the end of the war the RAF moved out. The RAF pennant was lowered for the very last time and in August 1946 the Air Ministry transferred the site to the newly-formed Ministry of Civil Aviation which took over control of most former municipal aerodromes. The former RAF buildings were adapted for civil aviation use, the factory was taken over by the Ministry of Supply and by the next month all ground and technical services were established allowing the airfield to become available for civil flying. It formally re-opened on 6th September. The first schedules were the BEA Isle of Man–Blackpool–Manchester route and Lancashire Aircraft Corporation operated a Rapide for pleasure flights. This fleet was expanded to include four Rapides and two Austers. Other companies operating here included Pine's Airways, Thorne Aviation, Skyways, Westair Flying Services, Air Navigation and Trading Co and Loxhams. By 1950 routes were extended to include Blackpool–Manchester–London, Leeds–Manchester–Blackpool–Isle of Man plus routes to Glasgow and Birmingham.

With the outbreak of the Korean War in 1950 there was renewed interest in aircraft production and Hawker Aircraft Company took over the former Vickers-Armstrong factory for production of the new Hunter jet fighter. Hunters could not operate from the short runways so a fourth runway was constructed in 1951 orientated 10/28 and 6,132 feet long. The Ministry of Supply paid for the runway extension onto land acquired from the Clifton Estate. Between 1953 and 1958 a total of 374 Hunters were produced here, the first being flight-tested in April 1954. Additionally Hawkers refurbished Sea Furies in the factory which had a work force in the region of 5,000. The factory closed in 1958 and was sold to private developers.

Squires Gate is now known as Blackpool Airport, has several scheduled services and an active general aviation section for executive and private flying plus several flying clubs.

13

BLACKPOOL (STANLEY PARK)

1½ miles east of Blackpool Tower
SD 325360

Stanley Park has a comparatively dull and uninteresting history when put alongside other Lancashire airfields. Opened in controversy and unwanted by many, it was never big enough to develop into a commercial success. It played a background support role in the Second World War so many locals will be surprised to know that an airfield even existed in this location. Historical facts and information are not easy to find but Blackpool played a very important part in pre-war aviation history and development and the two local airfields played an important part in the success of the Second World War.

Blackpool (Stanley Park) Landing Ground was located to the east of the town on open ground and on the opposite side of the road to the Park after which it took its name. According to the 1931 edition of *Air Pilot* the airfield was controlled by Blackpool Corporation. It was 45 feet (14 metres) above sea level with a clay soil, well drained and grass covered, and with a slight slope down towards the south. The four landing strips were N–S 400 yards; NE–SW 540 yards; E–W 650 yards and SE–NW 400 yards. There was no ground control, no hangars, and no handling or repair facilities. Fuel was available. There was no radio but a phone was available. Flying hours were restricted to daylight only and meteorological information had to be obtained from RAF Sealand because, even though it was open, Blackpool (Squires Gate) could not provide this facility. In spite of its basic facilities, Prime Minister J Ramsey MacDonald and Miss Ishbel

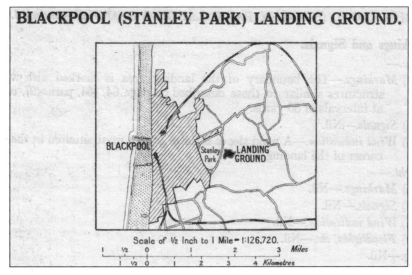

The plan of Stanley Park, Air Pilot *1931.*

MacDonald officially opened the airfield on 2nd June 1931.

Allegedly Amy Johnson used to land her aircraft at the far end of the aerodrome, away from the buildings, drop off whoever was her passenger, and take off again to avoid paying airport fees! (Her married sister Molly Jones, lived nearby on Newton Drive, Blackpool.) Amy Johnson gave lectures in Blackpool on 27th September 1932 on her epic flight to Australia. The first Air Pageant took place at Stanley Park Aerodrome on 26th June 1932 and on the following week the giant German airship *Graf Zeppelin* flew over the town.

When Amelia Earhart successfully crossed the Atlantic in May 1932, after landing in Ireland, she was shuttled in another aircraft across the Irish Sea to Stanley Park, and changed planes there for a flight to London for a banquet/civic reception. The local newspapers got a scoop when they got an interview with her and a photograph at Stanley Park in between planes.

In 1927 Alan Cobham was commissioned by Blackpool council to recommend a site for Blackpool's Municipal Aerodrome. He produced a report with alternatives listed in order of preference. His preference was Stanley Park so it was picked as the site. It was owned by Sir John Bickerstaff who was prepared to sell it at a very reasonable figure. The much better Squires Gate site was actually outside the Blackpool borough boundary, in Lytham St Anne's. The council there was definitely NOT air-minded, and purchasing the land from the owners, the Clifton family at Lytham Hall, would have cost considerably more. The levelling and draining was commenced and a hangar was built for 20 light aircraft together with a club house with observation room, bar and dining room. The hangar was very substantial looking, similar to First World War Belfast truss aircraft sheds with a curved roof and full-width opening doors at one end. The word 'BLACKPOOL' was written in very large letters over the doors. Interestingly, both these buildings still survive in 2004 as part of Blackpool Zoo. The intended passenger traffic was slow to materialize and much of the early flying comprised trips around Blackpool Tower for five shillings (25p)! Railway Air Services, jointly owned by LMS Railway and the Isle of Man Steam Packet Company, did operate some de Havilland Rapides from Stanley Park to and from the Isle of Man but these services moved to Squires Gate around 1933. Other companies filled the gap but not for long. Midland & Scottish Air Ferries promised many routes in 1934, but failed to deliver and United Airways took over in 1935 and flew restricted services linking London, Blackpool and the Isle of Man. United's lease expired in April 1937 and was not renewed. The occupiers of Squires Gate were asked to move temporarily to Stanley Park whilst the former was being rebuilt.

Alan Cobham's flying circus returned to Blackpool in 1935 and two of his aircraft collided over Blackpool with wreckage falling in Cedar Street and Swainson Square. One pilot and two female passengers were killed. Another tragedy occurred in 1936 when an aircraft flying in from the Isle of Man hit the hangar in dense fog killing the pilot and one female passenger.

British Amphibious Airlines Ltd operated from Stanley Park, flying a single Saro Cutty Sark flying boat and owned by Wing Commander R C H Monk. A propeller from his Saro Cutty Sark flying boat still hangs in Ronaldsway Airport, Isle of Man, in his memory.

Once Squires Gate became established Blackpool Council gave up Stanley Park as the Municipal Airport and commenced developing the new site which was far better in terms of flat, unobstructed land linked to the town by the tramway. Squires Gate was requisitioned by the Air Ministry in September 1938 due to the worsening relations with Nazi Germany and in 1939 the RAF staged an Empire Air Day at Stanley Park showing off all their latest aircraft including a Spitfire and a Whitley together with a very old-fashioned Handley Page Heyford bi-plane bomber.

Club hangar 1990s. (D J Smith)

Oblique of hangar in perfect condition in 1938, note club house beyond. (D J Smith)

The local branch of the Civil Air Guard formed at Stanley Park in August 1938. It was subsidised by the Air Ministry and founded to foster interest in flying. Flying lessons were made available at a low cost with the idea that if the country went to war there would be a cadre of civilians who already knew how to fly, which would reduce their training time and encourage them to join the RAF. The unit had 248 members and at the outbreak of war there were 88 flying members. Of those 30 had received their 'A' licences and 62 were well advanced with their training. The unit was commanded by Stephen Wilkinson, with Fred Berry the secretary. They managed to acquire three aircraft, one being an ancient Avro Avion bought for £100 from a private owner in Morecambe. Another was probably a Miles Monospar G-AEPA, which was once owned by Wally Westoby, director and instructor of Blackpool Flying Schools Ltd. The Monospar was given the RAF serial X9372 and was used by Rootes Securities at Speke (see separate chapter). With the outbreak of war the unit was immediately disbanded, all civil flying was prohibited and the three aircraft were flown away and impressed into the RAF.

On the outbreak of war Stanley Park was requisitioned by the Air Ministry and all civil flying ceased immediately. Initially it may have been intended as a parachute training centre but this did not happen. Blackpool rapidly filled with new recruits for the massively expanding RAF. They were kitted out, and did their initial drill and discipline training in all weathers on the promenade. The plentiful supply of accommodation, in the form of Blackpool's boarding houses, was put to use when No 3 School of Technical Training was formed at Deacons Bank Chambers, Talbot Square, Blackpool on 20th October 1939. The school undertook courses for Flight Mechanics, Flight Riggers and drivers (petrol) using local buildings, Squires Gate and Stanley Park. The airfield at Stanley Park had various instructional airframes such as Whitleys, in differing states of disrepair, dotted around the aerodrome.

Vickers Armstrong had selected Squires Gate as a site for a 'shadow' factory, far away from Brooklands and Weybridge, which were a prime Luftwaffe target. The special factory was built at Squires Gate but even this factory dispersal needed protection against possible enemy air attack. Stanley Park was selected as a satellite assembly line for the construction of Wellington bombers. Five Bellman hangars were erected and the component parts of aircraft brought in from factories including Squires Gate, Broughton at Chester and small local firms were contracted to manufacture aircraft parts. The first Wellington took off from Stanley Park on 26th October 1941 landing at Squires Gate where all test-flying took place. Production grew to five per week and a special celebration took place when the 100th Wellington was produced here. Stanley Park's runway was strengthened by Sommerfeld tracking, a form of steel mesh designed to be rolled over grass, staked down and thus spread the weight of the aircraft to prevent it sinking into the ground. It was too short to safely allow the new Wellingtons to land, hence only delivery flights were undertaken from this short runway with light aircraft carrying minimum fuel.

Stanley Park was also home at weekends to No 181 Gliding School, ATC, which formed in August 1943, with Kirby Cadet I and II gliders, and at least one Slingsby, under the command of F/Lt Jack Aked. The school moved to Warton in January 1947 only to be disbanded on 1st June 1948.

Also, from summer 1944, tented summer camps were held there for cadets of all three services until at least 1947. The Lancashire Aircraft Corporation moved from Samlesbury to Stanley Park towards the very end of the war, (after its owner, Eric Rylands, allegedly fell out with English Electric) repairing Beaufighters for the Bristol Aircraft Corporation, which apparently were brought in on Queen Mary trailers, and flown out after repair.

Finally, approximately 40 Hurricanes were flown into Stanley Park at the end of the war (September 1945) and scrapped there. A Mr Norman Riddle of Blackpool remembers that when they arrived at Stanley Park late in the war 'they had a building full of [aircraft] engines, there was talk of dumping them at sea!' The Hurricanes had been superseded by the Spitfire later in the war and became surplus, also production eventually overtook losses and demands from new units. Surplus aircraft were stored at bases all over the country and eventually scrapped. Mr Riddle continued: 'It broke your heart to see these aircraft but, the same time, everyone was feeling pretty good because the war was ending.' He was a keen photographer and took some photographs, strictly against the rules in war-time. He also used parts of the Hurricanes to make Christmas presents, 'We cut up the aluminium from inside the Hurricanes and made a little set of tubular bells out of them different lengths hung on a string – it worked a treat!'

By 1946 all aircraft repair and manufacturing had ceased at Stanley Park and, except for No 181 Gliding School, the site never saw any aviation again. It became the site of the Royal Lancashire Agricultural Show until 1971 when it was taken over by Blackpool Zoo, the role it continues today with the main pre-war hangar, war-time 'temporary' Bellman hangars and the club house in use by the zoo.

14
WARTON

4 miles east of Lytham St Anne's
and 7 miles west of Preston, south of A548
SD 415280

During a visit by General Doolittle of the USAAF's 8th Air Force, Warton was named 'The World's Greatest Air Depot', a label of which all members of Base Air Depot No 2 were justifiably proud. Warton had humble beginnings; a piece of marsh land immediately north of the Ribble estuary was looked at in 1936 by the Air Ministry as a possible site for an airfield, but was not considered suitable. However land slightly west of Grange Farm was looked at again and requisitioned by the Air Ministry. Initially it was to be a satellite to Squires Gate and work started in 1940 but it was not available until at least 1941. After minimal use by Squires Gate, in March 1942 further building works started seriously and with great urgency because Warton had been offered to the USAAF in October 1941 and the first units were due to arrive in August 1942.

The airfield was laid out in the normal RAF three runway pattern with the runways at 60 degrees to each other with the longest being orientated east–west into the prevailing wind. The runways were constructed of concrete being 08/26 5,631 feet; 02/20 4,182 feet and 15/33 3,960 feet long, all connected by a concrete taxiway. Beyond that it was anything but a standard RAF pattern, from the control tower to the hangarage. There were 50 dispersals arranged off the taxiway around the airfield and seven hangars were grouped together on the north side with two hangars on the river (south) side, all of which were complete by August 1944. The repair shops had a total area of 623,005 sq feet plus an additional 137,363 sq feet of storage space. Initially accommodation was limited to tents (known as tent city!), which was extremely damp and uncomfortable for the arriving Americans. Eventually ten living sites were constructed with

Aerial shot of B-17 turning finals over Ribble mud flats. (Geo Gosney)

accommodation for 15,902 personnel. George Wimpey Construction Ltd undertook the first building phase, and it was completed by Sir Alfred McAlpine & Son Ltd.

Warton Air Depot was established from 5th September 1942 within 8th Air Force Service Command and was redesignated Base Air Depot No 2 on 21st October 1943, also known for security reasons as AAF Station 582.

With the US entry into the Second World War four UK airfields were allocated to the USAAC for maintenance purposes – Little Straughton, Bedfordshire; Langford Lodge, Northern Ireland; Warton and Burton-wood, both in Lancashire. Burtonwood was already handling US aircraft in RAF service and was strategically located close to Liverpool and the docks. These bases were earmarked for the overhaul and repair, modification, acceptance, conversion and support of all USAAC aircraft in the 8th Air Force in the UK. This was a tall order considering the USAAC planned to have 1,000 aircraft operating from Britain by August 1942 and over 3,500 by mid 1943. Burtonwood took the major initial brunt of the workload because it was already established and up and running. Slow development meant that the Lancashire bases would concentrate on heavy maintenance. Little Straughton would become a Strategic Air Depot (SAD) being located nearer to the operational squadrons in the east of the country and Langford Lodge would remain smaller and specialise in modifications and engineering, although all bases did their fair share of this. The SADs are often considered more important than the BADs but this is far from the truth as they were minute in size in comparison.

The first Americans arrived at Warton, via Lytham St Anne's railway station, on 18th August 1942 and Warton Air Depot was formally established on 5th September. Building work prevented a quick build up of production even though new units of personnel continued to arrive. A ferry unit, 87th Air Transport Squadron, was established to ferry aircraft to and from the BADs and the operational units. This unit also had detachments at both Burtonwood and Langford Lodge, but this was to prove inadequate so a dedicated ferry squadron, 310th was formed specifically for this purpose. The title Warton Air Dept was changed to Army Air Force (AAF) Station 582 on 12th February 1943 for secrecy and the name Warton was not used thereafter so the base could not be pin-pointed by the Germans. Burtonwood became AAF 590. RAF Warton was formally handed over to the 8th AFASC at a parade on 17th July 1943.

Production was about to start. A detachment from 7th Air Depot Group arrived to man the control tower after training at an RAF base in England. Burtonwood was in full flow and Warton was anxious to join in and its contribution was urgently needed. Aircraft were beginning to arrive. At first it was just new aircraft flown from the US requiring only checks and tests prior to being delivered to their units. B-24 Liberators and B-17 Flying Fortresses could fly the Atlantic but the smaller aircraft (especially single-engined) could not. Some B-17s arrived for modifications in August 1943 for the installation of external release switches for the life raft compartment, modifications to radio and intercom equipment and the enlargement of ammunition boxes. Specialisation was to speed production so it was decided that Warton would specialise in B-24 Liberator aircraft and the new P-51 Mustang plus, from December 1943, the Engine Division would specialise in in-line engines. Burtonwood, meanwhile, would specialise in B-14, P-38 and P-47 aircraft and radial engines, although, in reality the two bases would work on both sometimes.

In October 1943 the USAAF re-organised its maintenance by forming a Base Air Depot Area (BADA) located at Southport with Burtonwood, Warton and Langford Lodge becoming Base Air Depots Nos 1, 2 and 3 respectively. A new CO arrived, Colonel J G Moore, and morale improved with accommodation slowly coming on line, real aircraft to work on and a sense of purpose amongst the men. It was at this time the motto 'It can be done' was coined and retained until the end of hostilities. As will be seen, 'It WAS done'!

The inflow of aircraft and engines for maintenance rapidly grew creating the need for 24-hour operation and a shift system was established to achieve this. New aircraft were flying in from the US plus huge numbers of smaller aircraft from Speke and Renfrew, Glasgow. These aircraft had crossed the Atlantic as deck cargo on all types of ships from small freighter to aircraft carriers. Small fighters and communications aircraft were prepared by removing their propellers, tails and other protruding items which were separately boxed. Most were landed ashore at Liverpool with many more at Glasgow docks and they were transferred to Speke or Renfrew respectively by road. Here they were reassembled and test-flown and then delivered to either BAD No 1 or 2 for inspection, modification, test and delivery.

By February 1943 the two Lancashire bases, BADs 1 and 2, were able to take on the full load of maintenance and support of all USAAF aircraft and their equipment with the two bases eventually employing

Aerial view of sheds and flight line. (Geo Gosney)

a total of over 33,000 men and WAC. Accordingly Army Air Force HQ was advised that the contract with the Lockheed Overseas Corporation for the operation of Langford Lodge could be terminated as from 3rd July 1943.

It was now possible to introduce assembly line methods, which permitted maximum utilisation of the large number of unskilled soldiers who now helped at Warton. Specialisation and the assembly lines explain in large parts the great productivity of the base beginning in late 1943. Helpful too was the reorganisation of the BADs along the functional lines suggested in the Bradley Plan. All of the personnel at Warton, with the exception of some specialised units, were assigned to one of three maintenance divisions: military administration, supply and maintenance. The former units to which they belonged were closed down. The maintenance division was by far the largest with more than 8,000 men at Warton by the middle of 1944. The Strategic Air Depots were not expanded as greatly as Warton which had to receive, organise and train thousands of men whilst at the same time constantly expanding its services to the Air Force. Warton was short of heavy equipment needed for fourth echelon repair and overhaul throughout the summer and autumn of 1943 with a consequent frustrating limitation on operations.

The pressing need for long-range escort fighters in November and December 1943 focused attention on increasing the production of assembled aircraft at Speke and Renfrew with increasing numbers of P-51s arriving at Warton for work and delivery. Prior to the demands of 1943, Warton was also modifying aircraft in addition to production of new heavy bombers, fighters, B-26 Marauders and C-47s.

The ten living sites spread around the base dwarfed the population of Warton and Freckleton villages. Number 1 site was the main technical area hosting the five production hangars that remain in use today by BAE Systems and were used for 'production' work on aircraft. Engine overhaul was immediately to the north with the propeller and machine shops on the east side. To the west were two more hangars used by Flight Test and the Ferrying Squadrons for final flight test and rectification of minor faults. After a 'test hop' the aircraft would be handed over from Flight Test to the ferry unit for ferrying out. The control tower was a two storey brick structure, and is still extant today, plus a steel lattice tower added to the side for local control to give a clear view across the whole airfield and see aircraft on approach and departure.

Hangars 31 and 32 were to the south-east by the river near the

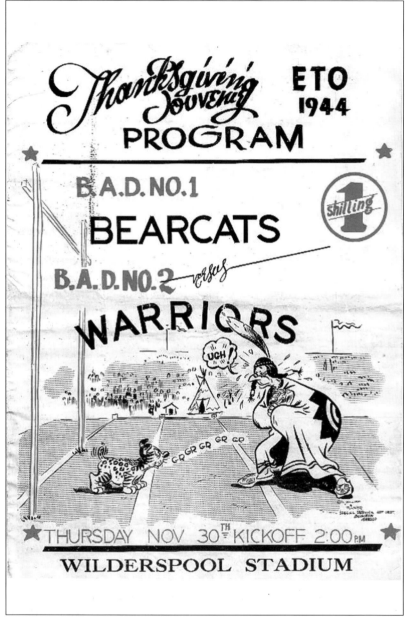

Cover of the football programme for the American football battle between Burtonwood Bearcats and Warton Warriors, November 30th, 1944.

ammunition store. The base hospital was to the west of Warton village just north of the A584. Sites No 2 and 2A were just across the main road from the main gate on a small road going north. Other identifiable sites in this area were Sites 3, 3A, 4, 4A (around Lime Tree House), 5, 7 and 7A to the north of Freckleton around Raker House Farm and Strike Farm. Site 8 was west of the Sick Quarters and Site 9 was just south of the A584, just west of the airfield boundary. Site 10 adjoined the A584 in the centre of Freckleton village (now built over) and was linked to the main site by a track known as 'The Burma Road'. Site 11 was around Grange Farm to the east of the airfield and Site 12 adjoins Trinity School and is now also totally redeveloped. The unit HQ was on the airfield west of the technical site close to the threshold of runway 20. The main gate was where it remains today, leading directly onto the main road in the centre of Warton village with the Motor Pool close by to the east.

Supply warehouses were built between the Preston to Lytham road and runway 26 with the Base Theatre in the same area. The engine test cells were on the airfield just west of the threshold of runway 02 to keep them as far away from houses and living accommodation as possible. These test cells worked 24 hours a day 365 days a year test running engines that had just passed through overhaul. They were very noisy and could be heard several miles away. When the war was over and they were closed down, a deathly hush passed over the area, a new experience for everyone who had grown so used to hearing the noise. The 494th Anti-Aircraft Artillery Battalion (Mobile) operated the anti-aircraft gun site located on Grange Farm, along the North Training Wall which was a sea defence structure on the Ribble. With the lack of Luftwaffe threat this unit moved away on 4th July 1944. A short distance west of the airfield, located on the north side of the A584, was a substantial railway goods yard formed by a spur of the Preston, Lytham, Blackpool railway line. Vast amounts of material were transported around the UK by train but were supplemented by US Transport units using road transport to convey engines and other components to and from the active units to the east of the country. This goods yard lay empty and disused for many years after the war before being redeveloped with housing. Aircraft dispersals were spread over a large area as there were often in excess of 500 aircraft on the base awaiting attention or delivery. Although they were turned round at a very rapid rate they also came in at an amazing rate. The dispersals comprised No 1 to the north-west side between runways 08 and 15, crossing the road to Warton Bank, surrounding Site 9 and running even

P-51 in main workshops. (Geo E Knowles)

further west across Lodge Farm to Lytham Dock. No 2 was to the south-west between runways 02 and 08 running across to Warton Brows onto the marshy area; No 3 lay between runways 02 and 33 to the extreme south, straddling the taxiway by the river; No 4 was extensive and surrounded hangars 31 and 32 between runways 26 and 3 to the south-east leaving a very small No 5 north of runway 26 close to the supply warehouses.

By November 1943 a total of 1,216 aircraft had been delivered to Warton, most being new aircraft delivered from the USA. By the end of 1943 the P-51 was arriving in large numbers and as with any new aircraft problems showed up almost immediately. The first was a shortage of radiator gaskets and the BAD2 engineers soon had a substituted one manufactured on site. Engine overhaul changed with the rationalisation to in-line engines although Warton had already overhauled 126 radials before passing the task to Burtonwood. Representatives from Allison Engines and Rolls-Royce arrived to teach the mechanics how to maintain and overhaul their engines which powered the P-51. In addition to the B-24 and P-51 aircraft,Warton was to receive A-26 Invader medium bombers plus a large number of C-47s.

The engine overhaul facility ran its first Merlin engine on the test blocks on 16th January 1944 and continued to work flat out until the end of the war in Europe. Modifications were made to the tails of P-51s with 300 being processed in three months from 9th January. Personnel numbers rose to 10,408 by the beginning of March and it was May when Lt Gen James H Doolittle visited the base and christened it 'The World's Greatest Air Depot'.

Warton had a famous P-51 which carried the name *Spare Parts*. It was being unloaded at Liverpool in February 1944 when it was dropped and declared a write off. The remains were transported to Warton to be broken down as spares but the BAD2 engineers had other ideas. They suggested they should rebuild it in their own time and they were granted permission to do so. It was slowly rebuilt and was ready for flying by the end of May. Permission was received to fly it and the radio was removed from behind the pilot's seat to allow a passenger. Hence many of the mechanics who worked on it were able to enjoy the fruits of their labour and fly. The idea was it would remain at Warton as a 'hack' aircraft and not fly operationally. *Spare Parts* also filled another role. The guns were removed and it was flown regularly to Scotland where friends had been established at a whisky distillery. It was a popular aircraft for two very good reasons but was unfortunately written off in an accident in late 1944.

During May the base had a War Bond drive, the object of which was to sell enough to buy two Mustangs. The aircraft were to be modified and presented to pilots in a ceremony here. One plane was to be named *Too Bad* from the BAD2 designation and the other named by an enlisted man. For every $25 bond bought each enlisted man received one chance to name the aircraft. The goal was $114,000 and it was oversubscribed by $5,000. Eventually enough money was obtained to buy three Mustangs. The draw was held and the two other Mustangs were named *Mazie R* by Private Stanley Ruggles after his mother and *Pride of the Yanks* by Private Samuel Silverman. The unveiling took place on Memorial Day, 30th May, with Maj Gen Hugh J Knerr, Commanding General ASC and Brig Gen Isaac W Ott, Commanding General BADA in attendance. At the ceremony the CO was also able to announce record production figures for that month, 606 aircraft delivered including 492 B-24, 206 P-51, 59 P-47 and 18 miscellaneous. It was later learned that *Mazie R* had destroyed a Bf109 whilst with the 357th Fighter Group and *Pride of the Yanks* had destroyed two enemy aircraft whilst *Too Bad* was yet to score.

Doolittle had visited to push for even greater productivity without telling anyone that D-Day was close by. The 9th Air Force had formed in the UK ready to move to Europe once a foothold had been established. Warton did its part providing aircraft, engines, spare parts, safety equipment and everything needed to keep both the 8th and 9th Air Forces flying. Productivity did increase with over 800 aircraft test-flown during June. With up to 800 aircraft now on the airfield and 300 ready for delivery there was huge pressure in getting the job done and many problems finding safe parking for all the planes.

Warton suffered many accidents and needed extreme ingenuity to solve one problem. On 12th June 1944 a new P-51D lost a wing on a test flight and crashed on the south bank of the Ribble killing the pilot, Lt Clearwater. The wreckage was recovered and taken back to Warton for investigation. The aircraft had been seen flying straight and level when the wing folded off so there was great cause for concern in case it was a design or maintenance fault. On 27th June another P-51D Mustang was flying at approximately 7,000 feet on a clear day when its right wing folded off in a carbon copy incident. Again the remains of the aircraft were recovered and brought back to Warton for investigation. Suspicion fell onto the undercarriage and an aircraft was put onto jacks and tested. It was found that the undercarriage on the two crashed aircraft had dropped in flight, twisted round and with the drag caused, pulled the wing off from the root. It was then discovered that the 'D' version of the Mustang had an extra machine gun in each wing together with other changes putting an extra stress onto the wing. To save weight the undercarriage uplocks were omitted allowing the wheel to bounce in its well when retracted but only held in place by hydraulic pressure. If the pressure dropped, the wheel dropped and was dragged down in the slipstream, twisted on its mounting and pulled the already overstressed wing from its root. The immediate modification was to retrospectively fit the earlier lock to all 'D' models which solved the problem. Unfortunately it was solved at a price, with the loss of two test pilots.

Jack Knight and John Bloemendal had taken two P-51s airborne to try and replicate the problem causing the disaster without success. Bloemendal was airborne with another test pilot, Major C Himes, in a Mosquito to test single engine performance. Unfortunately a problem resulted in insufficient power in the remaining engine and the aircraft crash landed on the airfield between sites 10 and 11 much to the embarrassment of the crew who were unhurt. A more serious accident on 27th June killed test pilot 2nd Lt Burtie L Orth when P-51 40-805666 crashed three miles north of Preston whilst on a test flight. He is buried at the Cambridge American Cemetery at Madingley.

Douglas A-20 K44-560 over Blackpool's central pier. (BAD No 2 Association)

Although the men and women at Warton worked very hard they also had time to play. They were lucky that Warton was, for some reason, never bombed by the Luftwaffe although it presented a wonderful target opportunity. Any bombs hitting the base would be likely to hit something as P-51s and B-24s were covering every spare inch and the workshops were very densely packed with men and machines. Blackpool was very close by and many of the Americans would catch the train from Lytham station for a night out on the town. Blackpool was full of airmen and women from the RAF recruiting base in Blackpool itself, No 3 School of Technical Training in Blackpool, the personnel of RAF Squires Gate, RAF Kirkham and RAF Weeton plus the navy personnel from HMS *Nightjar* at Inskip. Blackpool must have been a sea of uniforms and had just the ingredients to allow a good time during non-working hours. In addition to the bars there was the beach and the world famous Blackpool Pleasure Beach fairground.

There was also entertainment on the base, the British ENSA travelling theatre called many times, local plays and variety shows were presented and famous US stars came to boost morale. In July the famous boxers S/Sgt Joseph L Barrow, better known as Joe Louis, and Cpl Billy Conn arrived as part of a large tour of the UK to give

James Cagney christening B-17 'Yankee Doodle Dandy'. (Geo Gosney)

Joe Louis and Billy Conn entertaining the troops.

exhibition boxing matches to the troops. Lt Col Robert Trent Jones Jr (Bobby Jones) was a famous American professional golfer and visited Warton on 6th August to give a demonstration at Royal Lytham St Anne's Golf Club. Bing Crosby visited on 1st September with a troupe consisting of Earl Baxter, Buck Harris, Darleen Garner, Jean Darnel, Joe Doretta and Raymond Ratford. They sang, danced, joked and signed autographs for 65 minutes in Hangar 7.

Bob Hope also entertained the troops there and on 14th August 1944 the famous Glenn Miller arrived with his band. They 'gave out' with an hour of music in the Technical Area. The bandstand was set up on the apron, in front of the main hangars. Now and then the band had to indulge in a duel with a passing P-47 or P-51, but the aircraft went unnoticed by the majority of the audience. Section 30, Squadron H held a party in Blackpool that evening and Major Miller and a few of the boys from the band dropped in to the party and treated the guests to a real jam session. When the party was over they considered themselves the luckiest people in the ETO that day, and not without good reason!

On 23rd August 1944, a tragedy occurred which was by far the worst ever experienced at Warton. At approximately 10.42 B-24H 42-50291, up on a flight test from Warton, was caught in a severe storm. Evidently coming in to land after an urgent recall to base, the aircraft was caught in a violent down-draught, was forced down and crashed in the village of Freckleton. The aircraft hit both the village school, part of which was occupied by children at the time, and a snack bar across the road. The plane crashed onto the infants' department of the school setting it on fire and demolishing it. The snack bar, which had been given the name 'The Sad Sack' by the men at the station, was also totally demolished. The fuel tanks of the aircraft burst, and the school buildings and the village street were immediately a sea of flames. The sound of the crash brought a rush of soldiers, police and villagers. Calls were sent out to the Depot fire station and the local stations of the National Fire Service.

Rescue work was started immediately. As the children were freed from the debris which covered them, they were taken to the station hospital for treatment. But a great many were beyond treatment and they had to be put into a temporary mortuary pending identification by their bereaved parents. During the day the bodies of 34 children were removed from the school and sixteen bodies were removed from the snack bar. The rescue work went on into the night, with the aid of searchlights. By 25th the death toll had been established as 61, made up of 38 children, nine civilians, four members of the RAF and ten

Burial of children after B-24 tragedy. (Ralph Scott)

members of the US Forces, including the crew of the plane which had been piloted by 1st Lt John A Bloemendal.

On Saturday, 26th August, the child victims of the crash and one of their teachers, 20-year-old Miss Jenny Hall, were buried in the churchyard of Holy Trinity Church in Freckleton. The grave was dug by US soldiers and behind it were banked more than 500 floral tributes. General HH (Hap) Arnold, Commanding General, Army Air Forces, cabled from Washington that he desired to be represented at the funeral. Brig Gen Isaac W Ott, Commanding General, Base Air Depot Area, ASC, US Strategic Air Forces in Europe, was Gen Arnold's representative.

In June the total airframe production was 477 comprising 234 B-24, 182 P-51, 29 P-47, 13 B-17 and 19 miscellaneous whilst engine production was 564 V-1710 engines and 211 V-1650 shipped out of the Depot. In August this increased to 636 including 290 B-24s and 298 P-51s.

The 40th Air Depot Group arrived on 20th September, a huge number of men who were accommodated on Site 5. Initially it was not understood why they arrived as they were not to be integrated into the Depot. However all was revealed when they moved on to AAF Station 169 at Stansted, Essex on 5th October.

Warton had its own American football team, the 'Warriors', who were probably the best in Britain. They played the Burtonwood 'Bearcats' at Bloomfield Road Stadium, Blackpool on 15th October and won. By December they remained, as recorded in the Station records, 'untied, undefeated and unscored upon'. On 10th December they defeated 'Burger's Bouncers', a troop carrier football team at Blackpool 40–0 in snow! On 31st December the team travelled to White City Stadium, London for the ETO championship against the 8th Air Force 'Shuttle-Raiders'. There was no score until the fourth quarter but the 'Warriors' won 13-0.

On 5th October Warton was brought to a standstill by three accidents in fifteen minutes of each other. A strong wind was blowing necessitating the use of runway 15/33 which was very short at 3,960 feet and rarely used for landing but just for parking. The runway also had a slight depression resulting in many landing aircraft becoming airborne again for a moment, creating problems for the pilot. First to arrive was a B-24 from Attlebridge, Norfolk which became airborne again and ran off the runway onto the soft grass ripping off the nose wheel and coming to a rapid stop. Twelve minutes later an A-20 arrived and although the pilot had been warned, the same thing happened and he managed to steer around the Liberator which was sitting tail high on the grass. The second pilot just managed to totally miss the B-24. Despite two aircraft stuck at the end of the runway air traffic decided to allow a P-51 from Speke to use the same runway. Once again he became airborne, dropped back onto the runway but far too fast and raced towards the two bombers. He applied full power and the torque of the Merlin engine pulled him off the runway onto the grass where he ground looped. The pilot was able to climb out, no-one was hurt but a lot of pride was lost that day, three damaged aircraft in 15 minutes!

The 56th Field Hospital had been based at Warton and it was to move to Le Bescat, France on 28th October 1944. To do this, forty-six C-47s were required to ferry the personnel and equipment. With an airfield already grossly overloaded with aircraft these 46 had to be brought in, parked, loaded and flown off. It all happened with no incident. On 20th November all personnel of the Instrument Department were present at a ceremony when the 200,000th instrument repaired was presented to the Supply Division. The Commander of the Department, Capt Hacker, presented Col Jackson, Base Commander, with the gyro compass and the names of 36 enlisted men responsible for the record were read out. Col Moore pinned Major's leaves onto the chest of a very surprised ex-Capt Hacker.

B-24 literally covered with ground crew, 1944. (Geo E Knowles)

Another serious flying accident happened on 29th November 1944. Two A-26 Invaders collided shortly after take-off for their new base in France. They had been collected by their Group and both aircraft fell into the River Ribble estuary. The Lytham lifeboat and small boats from the base tried to get to the stricken aircraft but the crews had died on impact. The remains of one of the aircraft can still be seen and many attempts have been made to salvage parts by aviation archaeologists but the soft sand has thwarted all attempts.

Also in November a war-weary C-47 named *Chukky*, arrived for scrapping but the BAD2 mechanics had a close look at it and thought otherwise. With previous permission to use *Spare Parts* they success-fully tried again. It was stripped down and everything replaced and polished a gleaming silver finish; on rollout it was renamed *Jackpot*. It served Warton and its engineers flying many 'supply' trips around Britain and into France. It was sold after the war to a French airline and remained in use for many years.

During December a large number of German prisoners were placed in a mill in Kirkham and there was concern that if any escaped they would head for Warton and try and steal an aircraft for escape. Plans were drawn up to advise Warton immediately if such a break happened and Warton had to provide adequate guards to prevent

Engineers pose with C-47 Jackpot *after refurbishment.*

this happening. Around Christmas there were strong rumours that there was to be a mass break-out by German prisoners in the area and special guards were put in place just in case. It did not happen.

Work continued to support the Allied troops in their push across France and Germany. One project was to convert B-24s into 'Carpetbagger' aircraft for dropping leaflets and other clandestine operations. Another project was named 'Firefly Big' for dropping flares and a similar project involved A-20 Havocs converted in a programme named 'Firefly Little'.

At the end of 1944 there were 838 aircraft on the base and it was calculated that it had dispatched an average of 293 trucks each week to all parts of Britain; whilst 140 railway wagons were dispatched, 302,482 items of varying quantities were requested and 61,000 teletypes received. In 1945 the Allies advanced across Europe but the German counter-offensive in the Ardennes, the Battle of the Bulge, put unexpected strain on the infantry. Calls went out for reinforcements and the engineers who had been well away from the front line were now suddenly being called for emergency infantry training before being sent into battle. Many sections at Warton were to lose men for this emergency and several were lost in combat. In January 395 men were dispatched with a call for 450 more in February. Fortunately regular Air Force men were exempt and none volunteered.

Work continued helping with the push although the loss of these men was keenly felt as all sections worked at maximum capacity. Programmes included assembling gliders for more airborne assaults. There were 1,600 gliders scheduled for delivery to be uncrated and prepared for flight but the loss of another 106 men to the infantry in February made it impossible for the limited resources to be stretched further, so the work was passed to men from BAD1 at Burtonwood who were detached to Warton to do this work. Some B-17s were being prepared to be flown back to the States so they could be used in the Pacific war and various modifications and checks had to be made to ensure everything worked properly before the long transatlantic flights. Another programme called for P-51 guns to be harmonised at Warton and then the aircraft to be delivered to their units with ammunition already loaded so they could go into battle immediately. C-47s were arriving in very poor condition, having flown continuously with little maintenance, and thus took up a lot of time at Warton. For instance, A-26 Invaders needed under-wing gun packs installing. The C-47s required engine changes, replacement fuel tanks, updated electrical circuits, blind-landing equipment, battle damage repairs plus a full set of new de-icer boots for each aircraft.

A B-24 crashed en route to Warton on 3rd January 1945. The Liberator had 17 men on board flying a ferry mission bringing crews to fly away new planes. Four fatalities were recorded. On the same day Fg Off Edward Jackson, for 310th Ferry Squadron at Warton, lost his life in a P-51 crashing at Little Walden, Cambridgshire on a ferry flight. Eight days later 1st Lt Leonard D Johnson, from the Delivery Section at Warton, died in a crash in a P-51 at Calveley, Cheshire.

The Mayor of Preston, Councillor James G Gee, was invited to christen a new P-51 *Winged Victory* on 23rd March 1945 and a delegation from the Air Ministry visited Warton in April to look at the facilities and assess the suitability of the site as a possible municipal airport in the post-war period. The 1,000th B-24 was rolled out of Hangar No 4 on 15 December 1944 with a large celebration and figures showing that 92 men had worked on the aircraft whilst it was at Warton. Engine overhaul saw the 2,500th engine successfully over-hauled in April 1945, mostly for P-51 aircraft. Production efficiency had increased to almost halving the 500 hours per engine originally allocated. Early in May forty C-47s were due to arrive and were to have priority over the B-24 programme but none had arrived by the time war in Europe came to an end. On 7th May 1945 unofficial reports were coming in and on 8th May work stopped whilst the whole base celebrated the end to the conflict. After two days of celebrations the B-24 programme continued with 59 arriving from storage at Stansted, Essex plus 53 from Langford Lodge and one from Burtonwood. The order was that these aircraft were to be redeployed via the US and that 12 aircraft would be required to be issued per day.

In February a plane loaded with rations contributed by men of BAD2 was flown to Ford near Worthing for about 1,000 Russian ex-prisoners of war. It included 6,000 packages of cigarettes, as many candy bars and gum, and several thousand packages of cookies. The national press and the *Stars and Stripes* newspaper covered the event with photos of the Russians tucking into chocolate bars. The paper said 'there were enough cookies to keep a thousand samovars busy producing the tea in which to dunk them'! Under a large red Russian banner proclaiming 'Long live the friendship of the American, British and Soviet peoples' Test Pilot Lt Jack Knight was told by a grateful Russian Lt, 'May I give you the deepest of thanks for the wonderful gifts and more important the spirit behind them'.

By the end of May, 120 B-24s had arrived for redeployment and the promised C-47s began to appear. During May fifty-one P-51s were

B-24 in front of control tower. (Ralph Scott)

B-24 being towed into Hangar 4. (Geo Gosney)

Last Packard Rolls-Royce engine through the Engine Test Department, 20th June 1945.

processed for delivery to Speke for packing and shipping back to the US by sea. However the rundown was inevitable, spark plug production ceased on 31st May and the glider programme immediately suspended with all gliders to be scrapped! However these orders were overturned and 103 CG-4As and CG-15s were towed away by Dakotas.

Victory in Europe was celebrated on 8th May with a Tannoy message from Col Tom Scott confirming official notification that Germany had surrendered. He said all but essential work would cease at 12.30 for a period of 35½ hours during which passes would be available, a celebration was scheduled for the evening and a huge party was held in the Technical Area Mess Hall that night with a large bonfire lit later.

During June the run down accelerated with items being prepared for dispatch to the USAAF in Germany, back to the US, or scrapping. There were 22 B-24s which had landed in neutral Sweden. They were made flyable and returned to Warton although most were scrapped on return. The return-to-the-States project saw 133 B-24s delivered by the middle of June and another 57 undergoing flight tests. The Engine Test Department had been working on in-line engines continuously and was not to close down. On 20th June 1945 the last of 6,164 came off the assembly line. The last Packard Merlin V-1650 was put through the normal tests and ran perfectly. It was decided that the last engine would be immediately put into a P-51 and flown away as a fitting tribute to the work undertaken by the section.

A rapid run down was in place with HQ BADA calling for a 38 per cent reduction in production in June and July and 50 per cent in August. With so many B-24s flying back to the US, troops were arriving at Warton to fly home in the aircraft which could carry 10 each. The propeller section closed on 22nd June and most sections were slowly coming to a standstill. Men were being posted home or on to Germany although 145 aircraft were flown out in July. On 2nd August the last aircraft to be flown out was a B-24 taking off at 09.00 with the appropriate celebration and not a little sadness. With the official surrender of the Japanese and the end of the Pacific War on 15th August there was no more need for BAD2 or Warton. However an important event took place on 20th August when over 2,000 people and the personnel from Warton took part in the dedication of the memorial playground and memory stone built to commemorate those killed in the horrific B-24 crash a year earlier. Over 600 men from the base took an active part in its construction and it is still in use today. The BAD2 Association makes sure it is maintained and regular ceremonies take place there.

On 24th August over 300 US servicemen left Lytham station for Southampton and the sail home. All had gone by the end of the month and BAD2 officially closed down on 1st September 1945. Two days later the station was turned over to the new personnel of the Warton American Technical School who used the warehouses and much of the equipment left behind. This school taught trades with 18 being available including building and electrical but not aeronautical engineering. A B-17 and a B-24 were available to work on together with many aero engines. Classes commenced on 16th September but the school was to close down on 11th January 1946 after 4,000 servicemen had taken advantage of the courses. This time the US forces had gone forever and the base was handed back to the RAF who immediately took advantage of part of the base for Maintenance Units, mostly disposing of surplus wartime RAF equipment.

BAD2 had been very successful after a slow and difficult beginning. It had processed 10,068 aircraft, including 4,372 P-47 Mustangs and 2,894 B-24 Liberators plus numerous other types including C-47, light communications aircraft, many P-47s and B-17s. There were 45,000 aircraft movements recorded and over 6,000 engines received overhauls plus the other sections dealing with magnetos, instruments, life rafts, guns, turrets, spark plugs, radios, parachutes etc. The motto was met. 'It could be done' and those who served there are rightfully extremely proud of their record.

The RAF took over control but flying ceased for a period. No 55 Maintenance Unit reformed here in December 1945 followed very shortly on 1st January 1946 by No 90 Maintenance Unit which was a barrack and clothing depot with a sub site at Ludford Magna, Lincolnshire. Of the MUs, 55 was absorbed by English Electric Co and 90 was disbanded on 28th February 1958 into a sub site of 35 MU at Heywood, Manchester, which had utilised this base as a sub site from January 1957, eventually to disband on 1st December 1963. Other units included No 2 MT Company, an organisation for moving RAF equipment around the country by road; No 21 Personnel Transit Camp for airmen moving to and from other countries and awaiting demobilisation; No 101 Personnel Dispatch Centre with a similar role plus a detachment of the RAF Regiment for defending the early Canberra bombers. The only flying was No 180 Gliding School for Air Cadets, which formed in November 1951 but disbanded on 1st September 1955.

Post Second World War English Electric commenced development of the advanced Canberra twin jet bomber. Production was at Strand Road, Preston and Samlesbury but the runways at Samlesbury were now too short for prototype testing and they set their sights on the now deserted airfield at Warton. The site was flat, not too close to major centres of population, was extendable and had a vast array of hangars and workshops. In 1947 English Electric won a contract from the Ministry of Supply to investigate the behaviour of high-speed aircraft during manoeuvres at high altitude. The aircraft used was a Meteor Mk IV and all flying was done from Warton. Slowly English Electric moved their flight testing from Samlesbury to here and all flight testing of the Canberra, Lightning, TSR-2, Jaguar, Tornado and more recently the Typhoon were completed here. A wind tunnel was built on Dispersal 2 near the old engine test cells. Runway 08/25 was lengthened to 7,946 feet and this, and 14/32 are both still in use but with full lighting, ILS and approach and area radar. A new Aircraft Assembly Hall was constructed on the Technical Site and Warton remains extremely busy as the centre of British military aviation and a major employer and innovator in military technology.

15
WOODVALE

1 mile north of Formby, on A565
SD 305100

Woodvale is located close to the coast, between Formby and Southport. The site is bounded by the A565 trunk road linking Southport with Liverpool to the east and the Southport to Liverpool electric railway to the west. To the south lies Freshfield with Ainsdale to the north. When it was built in 1941, the A565 was the extension of the new Formby by-pass, which was constructed just prior to the Second World War. To the north was the Cheshire Lines Railway running to Southport Lord Street station via Ainsdale Beach and Birkdale Palace Hotel stations, now long gone. Woodvale railway station was adjacent with a bridge spanning the A565 and the station and its associated goods yard were well utilized by Woodvale.

The chosen site was half occupied (south end) by the Liverpool Merchant Banking and Insurance Golf Course and the north was two farms. Several of the farm buildings were pressed into use and one farmhouse, adjacent to the control tower, remained until well after the end of the Second World War. Similarly barns and other buildings remained by the railway until the 1970s. The golf club house was pressed into use as the first Officers' Mess prior to the completion of the purpose-built one on the Old Southport Road communal site.

Woodvale was designed and built as a fighter station to defend Merseyside. It was far too late to help Liverpool in the 1940 May Blitz but it served as a deterrent to any Luftwaffe aircraft venturing this far west again. The site was very sandy and only 37 feet above sea level. It was cleared and drained and laid out with three runways, 22/04, 17/35 and 09/27 being 4,816, 3,287 and 3,505 feet long respectively. The airfield had a brick control tower and one of the farm barns was converted into the crash crew garage.

Three Bellman hangars were erected, two on the main site by the main entrance from the A565 and another dispersed on the Formby side (north) of the airfield. Access round the airfield was easy as it had a hard perimeter track 50 feet wide linking all parts together and nine extra-over steel blister hangars were erected around this track for covered aircraft dispersal. A further 22 open dispersals were provided with sand bagged revetments surrounding them to provide some protection in case of enemy air attack. There were 12 double hardstandings, each able to accommodate two twin-engined aircraft, and the remaining ten were for single-engined aircraft. The concept forming part of the design was that up to three squadrons or smaller units could operate simultaneously from the base. Normally Woodvale housed two squadrons with a smaller flight or detachment at any one time. Buildings were constructed to house the squadron HQ and admin facilities plus engineering and armament back up, because the entire squadron would move as a single unit. The main site and its hangars were normally only used for major servicing and for permanently based aircraft at the specific station. Each station had a Station Flight with up to three aircraft for use by the CO and senior officers. Woodvale had buildings constructed around the perimeter track for this purpose. Two units could be accommodated along the side of the Southport to Liverpool railway and one on the loop dispersal on the south-eastern side. Buildings were temporary brick being single skin brick with piers every 10 feet to strengthen the walls and support the steel roof trusses. Some farm buildings were also used and each site had brick air-raid shelters with open tops and brick and reinforced concrete roof accommodation blocks for readiness times or night use.

Woodvale had its domestic sites spread along the Old Southport Road to the east of the airfield giving them road access but putting them at a safe distance from attack on the airfield. There were seven airmen's living sites, one WAAF living site, defence site, communal site for airmen and NCOs, sick quarters site, RAF officers' communal site with officers' mess and living accommodation, WAAF site, operations block and two W/T sites. All that remains now are the WAAF communal site, sick quarters and operations block, all in very poor condition.

The airmen walked to their place of work but the WAAF quarters were so remote that they were carried by truck. The base was not finished and no water was connected but the opening up party arrived in early October ready to formally open it on 25th October 1941 under command of Group Captain J A McDonald. The guard room and one squadron office were completed when the advance party of No 308 (Polish) Squadron arrived from Northolt on 10th December ready for the first aircraft to arrive on 13th December. The airmen could be accommodated in No 3 Site whilst the officers were accommodated in the now defunct golf club house at the Freshfield end of the airfield. The squadron rebelled and said the facilities were worse than Tobruk! Sand was everywhere, there was virtually no heating and there was still no water. The squadron had been involved in bitter fighting in their Spitfires in the south-east and deserved better. The runways at Woodvale were not finished and not safe so the less experienced pilots were sent to Squires Gate for practice circuits. Things became more settled as the sites were completed but the cold winter weather did not help.

The squadron was commanded by Squadron Ldr M J Wesolowski and was made up of predominantly Polish aircrew. Several accidents marred their stay. The CO and Plt Off E Krawczynski died in flying accidents and three Polish airmen died in a road accident. The officers are buried at Our Lady of Compassion Church in Formby.

The plan was that each fighter squadron would rotate through Woodvale to rest from the fierce battles raging in the south-east, re-equip and retrain for a few months before resuming the bitter fighting in the south. Although there was not much enemy air activity in Lancashire by this time they were often scrambled and the main role was the defence of the north-west. Fg Off Dolicher and Sgt Marek were scrambled on 11th February 1942 and intercepted a Ju88 over Lancaster, found it and attacked but it escaped into cloud and was claimed as a 'Probable'. A second interception over Lancaster on 21st February had a similar result when Sgts Ziellinski and Marecki intercepted a Ju88 over Lancaster and after a fierce fight only managed to claim a 'Damaged' result.

By March 1942 Woodvale was complete, the WAAF contingent had arrived, and roads, runways, taxiways and buildings were complete. Woodvale was in No 9 Group Fighter Command, with its HQ at Barton Hall near Preston. This group was responsible for air defence in the north of the country and the area was split into sectors. Woodvale had its own Operations Room (just as seen on the war-time RAF films) in Broad Lane and the Woodvale Sector included an area from midway

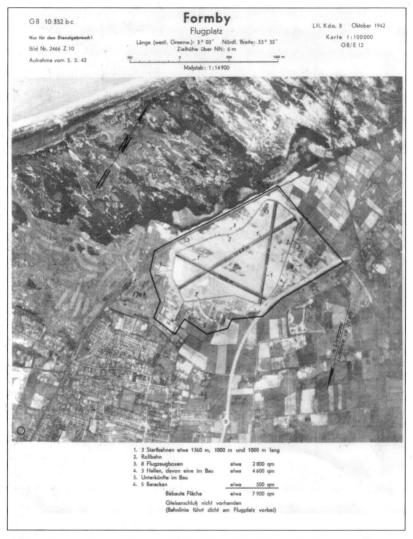

German Reconnaissance photograph, 5th May 1942. (Via Author)

between England and the Isle of Man, a line from Llandudno to Derby then north up the Pennines towards Carlisle and west to the northern tip of the Lake District. It included Liverpool, Manchester, Birkenhead, Preston, Bolton, Bury, Lancaster and Barrow-in-Furness. Any enemy aircraft in this area were the responsibility of Woodvale. The bordering

*315 Squadron, AVM Wjejski decorating Fg Off Stembrowicz on 14th August 1942.
(Gp Cpt J A McDonald)*

sectors were known as Andreas (Isle of Man) to the west, Atcham (Shropshire) to the south and Church Fenton (Yorks) to the east.

Number 308 Squadron was ordered to move south to Exeter on 31st March to be replaced by another Polish squadron, No 315, who arrived from Northolt on 2nd April 1942 also with Spitfires. They had been involved in constant battles with the Luftwaffe over south-east England, the Channel and Northern France. The CO Squadron Ldr Janus, was awarded a second bar to his Polish decoration for bravery 'Krzyz Walecznych' four days after arrival as they settled into the routine vacated by No 308 Squadron. On 3rd May, 315 were to score the first kill by a Woodvale-based aircraft when Plt Off Stembrowicz was vectored onto a Ju88 over the sea, intercepted and shot it down following it all the way until it hit the sea. The following day was Polish National day and was accordingly celebrated in style. Further scrambles took place on 30th May and 3rd, 5th, 19th, 24th and 27th June but no enemy aircraft were seen. It is interesting to note that a Luftwaffe vertical reconnaissance photograph was taken on 5th May 1942 and although aircraft were scrambled the enemy aircraft was never seen or intercepted.

Woodvale could now accommodate more units, so a detachment of No 285 Squadron arrived on 14th April from Wrexham with one

315 Squadron visit by Countess of Jersey, 14th August 1942. (Gp Cpt J A McDonald)

Oxford and two Defiants for army co-operation work. They would provide targets for AA calibration, prediction and practice firing. They did not have drogue targets to trail behind. Other detachments were at Squires Gate and Honiley in Warwickshire. This unit used a dispersal by the railway. An advance party of a detachment from No 776 Squadron (FAA) arrived from Speke on 16th May, followed a few days later by their aircraft, Rocs, Skuas and Chesapeakes. A Fleet Requirements Unit (FRU), 776 provided aircraft for similar purposes to those of No 285 Squadron, only for the Navy, including ships and shore establishments. HMS *Queen Charlotte* at nearby Ainsdale Lido kept this unit very busy and the detachment remained until the HQ move from Speke in April 1945.

There was now space for a second fighter squadron and No 256 Squadron moved across the Ribble from Squires Gate in June 1942 with a mixture of Defiants, Beaufighters and Blenheims for night fighter work.

On 14th August 315 scored another 'Damaged', which was quite a day for the squadron. The Countess of Jersey, Virginia Cherrill, was visiting and was being entertained by the squadron to a fly-past when Flt Lt Miksa and Sgt Malek were scrambled to intercept another Ju88 ten miles north of Anglesey heading towards Barrow-in-Furness. They gave chase at 22,000 ft diving with the enemy to 2,000 ft above the sea and each pilot scoring hits but unable to bring it down. Malek was hit and had to make a safe forced landing at Squires Gate and Miksa got back to Woodvale safely. The squadron was sending detachments to Valley in Anglesey to extend its area of operation and Fg Off Sawiak intercepted and shot down a Ju88 which crash landed in Ireland. Unfortunately he was also hit and crashed. He died from his injuries. Sawiak and two other 315 aircrew Plt Off T T Nawrocki and Fg Off F Fiedorczuk are all buried at Our Lady of Compassion Church, Formby. A few weeks earlier No 256 Squadron had also made contact with an enemy aircraft but it escaped into cloud. They had ten more scrambles in August with three in September but no contacts were made.

On 5th September 315 returned to Northolt to be replaced by a third Polish Spitfire squadron, No 317 also from Northolt. This squadron had suffered terrible losses whilst operating from Northolt and Exeter and although scrambled many times and constantly undertaking sector reconnaissance patrols they did not encounter the enemy whilst at Woodvale.

Number 256 squadron suffered a terrible accident on 31st October when one of their Beaufighters collided with a Wellington over Bangor in North Wales killing both Squadron Ldr R de W K Winlaw and Plt Off C T Ashton. Two more aircrew from 256 lost their lives in an aircraft accident on 7th November and another pilot from the squadron just managed to get into Woodvale on one engine after the other failed 50 miles out to sea.

By October 1942 the detachment of No 285 Squadron had grown to two Oxfords and six Defiants and a further detachment arrived, this one from No 116 (Calibration) Squadron whose HQ was at Heston in Middlesex. This unit had two Oxfords for calibrating AA guns and co-operating with Anti-Aircraft Command across the north of England. In February 1943 No 256 Squadron started to convert onto Mosquitoes. Number 317 managed 42 sorties in January and continued to send detachments to Valley looking for enemy aircraft flying up the Irish Sea, unfortunately without success. They were ordered to move to Kirton-in-Lindsay, Lincolnshire on 10th February and their seventeen aircraft flew east on 13th having been grounded by bad weather. On the same day No 195 Squadron arrived from Duxford with the new Hawker Typhoon aircraft having only reformed with this type the previous November. The Sabre engine, which powered the Typhoon, was plagued with problems, which continued at Woodvale. The sand

285 Squadron Defiant with ground crew, 1942. (John Hudson)

285 Squadron Flt Lt Reynolds and pilots by Oxford. (John Hudson)

still blowing around after all the construction made matters worse as the squadron tried to overcome the engine problems and become an efficient fighting force. Morale was boosted on 20th February when the USAAF brought in a P-38 Lightning for mock attack and performance matching with the Typhoon. The Typhoon excelled and totally out-manoeuvred the Lightning much to the squadron's joy. By the end of the month the squadron had 15 Typhoons, two Hurricanes and a Tiger Moth for liaison duty.

The engine problems continued for 195 Squadron. Sgt Jones crash landed a Typhoon on 9th March, writing it off and seriously injuring himself. The routine was formation flying, when they had enough serviceable aircraft; air-to-air firing with the squadron Hurricane towing a target; practice Rhubarbs; Sector recces and attacks, ground-controlled interceptions; dog fighting; cine gun practice; calibration; battle climbs and low flying. A scramble on 3rd April took two aircraft towards Anglesey with one suffering engine failure and force landing at RAF Mona, badly damaging the aircraft. A fatality occurred on 9th April when Sgt Walter A Dixon, a Canadian, crashed on take off, just cleared the Southport to Liverpool electric line and crashed on the golf course. The aircraft did not catch fire but Sgt Dixon died immediately and is buried at St Peter's Church graveyard in Freshfield. The Sabre engine was so unreliable that serviceability was very low so the two flights, A and B, flew alternate days utilizing any aircraft that was serviceable. Special air intake covers were manufactured on base to stop sand being ingested into the engines whilst the aircraft were parked on the ground. The squadron lost another Typhoon on 16th April when Plt Off Morgan crash landed at Warton just short of the runway. Fortunately he was uninjured and the aircraft was repaired eventually.

Ken Sharples was an airman with 195 and remembers his time at Woodvale very well. He wrote that A Flight operated out of new buildings and dispersals whilst B Flight operated out of the old railwayside farm house midway along the railway line. The aircraft were parked in blast protected revetments. Some of the blister hangars were also used for aircraft maintenance. He remembers that the pilots used the Scarisbrick Hotel on Lord Street, Southport as their local. He also remembered some of the dispersed living huts had false doors painted on the side of the building as camouflage but it also fooled many an airman when returning from a night out and a few drinks! He also wrote about a lady taxi driver at Freshfield Station who would run the airmen back to the camp but as he was an AC2 Flight Mechanic

256 Squadron in front of a Beaufighter, circa June 1942.
(Via HMS Nightjar)

Engineer earning about three shillings a day (15p) he normally walked back to camp, a long way from Freshfield station.

The Woodvale Sector was getting quieter but several scrambles are recorded. One on 11th May turned out to be a Hudson on return from Gibraltar, lost over the Irish Sea and brought in for a safe landing. The squadron was given short notice that it was to move to Ludham in Norfolk on 13th May and the main party left the next day. Ludham was much more active than Woodvale, as far as enemy aircraft were concerned, with the squadron recording its first kill, shooting down an Me109 over Southwold only the next day. Due to engine problems eight aircraft were left at Woodvale awaiting engines to get them to Ludham. They eventually flew out a few weeks later.

Number 285 Squadron was still operating an average of nine sorties a day but lost Sgt Duckworth when his Oxford crashed inland and hit an anti-invasion post, damaging the aircraft so badly that he died from his injuries. A more successful event took place on 10th July 1943 when a USAAF B-24 Liberator got lost en route to the UK from Gander, Newfoundland. The pilot contacted Woodvale Sector but the weather was very poor with bad visibility. A Beaufighter had tried to guide the aircraft into Woodvale but failed. Flt Sgt Bolland of 285 Squadron volunteered to try and lead the stricken aircraft in to Woodvale. Initially permission was refused but eventually the CO relented and Bolland took off. He found the American aircraft and guided it home aided by an impressive display of pyrotechnics from flying control. Flt Sgt Bolland was immediately awarded a Green Endorsement for his skill. Bolland had a lucky escape a few days later. He had just taken off in a Martinet when his engine cut and he had to make a forced landing by Harrington Barracks in Formby. He hit a barrack hut and his aircraft burst into flames but two soldiers managed to pull him clear and he did not have serious injuries.

Number 256 Squadron left Woodvale for Ford in April with their newly acquired Mosquitoes but the dispersals vacated by Nos 195 and 256 squadrons did not remain empty for long. On 15th May No 198 Squadron moved in from Manston in Kent and also had the unreliable Typhoon fighters. They had just re-equipped from Hurricanes and were to work up and become fully effective as ground attack fighters at Woodvale before returning to more hostile flying in the south. The squadron provided daylight fighter cover for the Woodvale Sector with 15 aircraft getting airborne on 20th May for a 'Ramrod' raid on Andreas on the Isle of Man. Scrambles were ordered on 19th and 26th May when they were ordered to patrol over Lancaster. No enemy

256 Squadron by Mosquito, 1943. (G A Peakman)

aircraft was seen but Plt Off Walters broke away and was observed by the Royal Observer Corps to hit the sea near St Anne's. His No 2, Plt Off Williams, abandoned the sortie due to bad weather and he also nearly crashed breaking cloud cover to find himself only just above the ground. Pilots from Canada, Australia and Britain made up 198, with a Czech CO, Squadron Ldr J Manek. They did not stay long at Woodvale, their Typhoons were much more reliable than those issued to No 195 Squadron and they were ordered to Martlesham Heath in Suffolk on 5th June.

Number 501 Squadron spent two weeks holding the readiness for the Woodvale Sector in May and June, equipped with Spitfire Vbs. They arrived from Martlesham Heath, Suffolk, only to move on to Westhampnett (a satellite of Tangmere) in Sussex two weeks later. The constant move of squadrons continued with No 322 (Dutch) Squadron reforming here on 12th June 1943 to continue the sector cover. The squadron was actually the personnel of No 167 (Gold Coast) Squadron, which disbanded at Westhampnett and immediately reformed at Woodvale on the same day with Spitfire Vb aircraft. Commanded by Squadron Ldr A C Stewart, 322 was to be manned totally by Dutch personnel with the first batch of Dutch pilots arriving on 16th June. A few scrambles kept the readiness section (two aircraft at a time) on its toes during June and July even with the rapidly

322 Squadron Spitfire and RAF Liberator by tower. (Van Eijk, 1944)

changing personnel. To expand the area of operations, a detachment of
six aircraft were sent to Llanbedr, on the Welsh coast, on 16th July for
temporary cover against enemy reconnaissance aircraft but after no
sightings for a week they returned to Woodvale. Members of 322
Squadron bought a parrot for the squadron and it was recorded on
27th July that it could not yet talk. It was adopted as the squadron
mascot but also recorded that it undertook a sector recce alone on 21st
August when someone left its cage door open. It flew around for a
while, did a good landing and returned to its hangar!

Three days later, 322 Squadron had to relocate to another dispersal
area to make room for No 256 Squadron returning from Ford with
fourteen Mosquitoes. They were not to stay for long as half the
squadron was sent on embarkation leave whilst the rest kitted up and
had vaccinations ready for departure to Malta on 25th September. Sten
guns were issued to 250 airmen and rifles to 56. The Operational
Record Book quotes that they hope there are no accidents as most of
them 'do not know their butt from the barrel'. The equipment was
shipped out to Middlesborough on 3rd September and the ground
party were ready to leave Woodvale on 10th September when they all
marched out to Woodvale station to join a special train to take them to
Glasgow for embarkation. In spite of the fact that the movement was
supposed to be secret, a large crowd of wives, sweethearts and
acquaintances were ready to bid them farewell. The air party, under

command of Wing Commander G R Park DFC, left Woodvale for Portreath in Cornwall on 25th September and then on to Malta.

The gaps at Woodvale were never left empty, nor did the Woodvale operations room slow down. Most scrambles were now of a humanitarian nature often using the Walrus aircraft of No 275 Squadron based at Andreas in the Isle of Man. 'A' Flight of 322 Squadron carried out Rhubarbs on RAF Wigtown on 22nd July and the next day Nos 306 and 308 squadrons operated out of Woodvale for practice escort duties with USAAF B-17 Fortress formations.

Number 9 Group HQ at Barton Hall near Preston had its own Communications Flight operating out of Samlesbury. The runways at Samlesbury required repairing in late summer 1943 so its mixture of aircraft relocated to Woodvale. The Flight operated Leopard Moths, Hurricanes, Masters, Oxfords, Vegas, Gulls and Mentors. After three weeks the runways were ready back at Samlesbury so the Flight returned there. No 322 received a new CO on 21st August when Captain K C Kuhlmann, DFC (SAAF) arrived and the squadron dispersed four Spitfires to Valley for convoy protection and again to try and stop German reconnaissance flights down the Irish Sea. Two further scrambles saw no action but two aircraft were written off in training accidents, fortunately without injury to their pilots.

The Command of RAF Woodvale and the Woodvale Sector changed on 26th August 1943 when Group Captain T B Prickman arrived from the RAF Staff College. His stay was very short and he was replaced by Gp Cpt C Walter OBE on 22nd September who was to remain for almost a year. At this date the station had the following personnel:

128	RAF Officers	10	WAAF Officers
138	WO & SNCOs	9	WAAF SNCOs
1,276	Airmen	462	Airwomen
1,542		**481**	

Number 776 Squadron continued to provide targets for the Royal Navy anywhere in the north-west but a Chesapeake crash landed on 23rd August after engine failure over HMS *Queen Charlotte* at Ainsdale, with the pilot just making it over the airfield boundary. Again on 30th another Chesapeake pilot touched the sea with his propeller and just made it back to base. In both cases the pilot was uninjured. On 11th September 322 Squadron sent 12 Spitfires to escort Princess Mary from Yeadon near Leeds to the Isle of Man and also for her return. On 30th

they managed to intercept three B-17 Flying Fortresses lost in bad weather, two landing at Woodvale and the third making it to Burtonwood. Woodvale Sector was keeping the Air Sea Rescue Walrus and Ansons of No 275 Squadron at Andreas busy with scrambles virtually every day. During November and December many lost aircraft were recovered to Woodvale for safe landings; three P-47 Thunderbolts on 18th October; three Fortresses on 30th; a Fortress on 4th November; two Wellingtons on 7th; a Beaufighter on 17th and a P-38 Lightning on 11th November. Really cold weather in December reduced flying by 322 Squadron for most of the month but on 19th December they were on a practice patrol when ordered to find eleven B-24 Liberators lost on the sector. They found them and escorted them back to make safe landings at Woodvale even though it was freezing weather. These eleven aircraft must been quite a sight to see on the ground at Woodvale.

The third Christmas at Woodvale saw a mix of nationalities, with Nos 322 and 295 Squadrons in residence with Spitfires, Defiant Target Tugs and Martinet, Oxford, Hurricane II and Beaufighter I aircraft plus the detachment of No 776 Squadron (FAA) with Rocs, Skuas, Martinets, Chesapeakes and Seafires – quite a mix of aircraft. A production entitled the *Woodvale Follies* ran for five nights in the gymnasium on the communal site. The officers served the Christmas dinner to the airmen and airwomen in the Airmen's Mess on Christmas day and there was a dance in the NAAFI in the evening. The only flying was a single sortie to wish the Operation Room crew a 'Happy Christmas' from 322 Squadron. An informal party was held in the Officers' Mess on Boxing Day, another evening dance at the NAAFI and a further party to wish farewell to 322 Squadron who were to move to Hawkinge in Kent on 30th December, before becoming operational on 4th January 1944 over France.

Again the fighter defence of the north-west was not neglected as 322's dispersals were immediately taken up by No 222 (Natal) Squadron who arrived from Hornchurch, Essex. They were just in time for a big New Year's Eve party with a US dance band and many famous musicians – quite a welcome. The January weather was bad and cold but being near the sea Woodvale is rarely closed by snow. Flying continued on 2nd January and No 315 (Czech) Squadron stopped overnight on 6th January en route from Ibsley, Hampshire to Ayr, Scotland but their refuelling stop was held up by bad weather so they stayed the night. Another 15 Spitfires parked on the airfield overnight.

Oblique aerial 200842 looking north-west. (RAF Museum)

January 1944 was to be a busy month as No 12 (P)AFU arrived from Grantham on 10th. This unit provided advanced twin-engine pilot training on Blenheim Vs and 16 arrived on this day on what was known as the 'W' (for Woodvale) Detachment. The unit's home base at Grantham, Lincolnshire had grass runways and the constant pounding of landings and take off over the winter had rendered them dangerous. It was decided to lay Sommerfeld tracking on the grass runways to provide a firmer base for aircraft and whilst this was done the airfield laws closed. The unit operated a satellite airfield at Harlaxton, Lincolnshire to where most of its aircraft were dispersed but it could not accommodate them all, hence the 'W' Detachment. In late 1944 the unit had 37 Oxfords, 57 Blenheims and 4 Ansons. Woodvale was a little quieter with very few Luftwaffe movements recorded in the Sector but still had two squadrons and a detachment occupying the base.

Being a training unit put great demand on instructors and flying control at Woodvale to provide space and time for the trainee pilots. Accidents were common on such units and the first did not take long to happen at Woodvale. Only two days after arrival a student forgot to lower his undercarriage on approach and belly-landed. With the operational units at Woodvale the senior training officers started to look for an alternative site and visited Poulton, Cheshire set in the grounds of Eton Hall, the home of the Duke of Westminster. This base was a satellite to No 57 OTU at Hawarden, Flints, flying Spitfires and 12 (P)AFU moved there for a short time thinking it would be better than Woodvale. However Flying Control was far from satisfactory and the proximity of trainee pilots in Spitfires from Hawarden made matters worse so the detachment reverted back to Woodvale on 21st March staying until 16th August 1944 when it could return to Grantham. A serious crash nearly killed a crew of two on 6th July when a Blenheim crashed on overshoot after an engine failure. The aircraft cart wheeled into the ground from about 100 feet and the injured crew was flown to the RAF Hospital at Cosford for treatment.

February was notable for the movement of squadrons. Number 219 Squadron reported on 11th February, on return from overseas and after a short leave started to re-equip with Mosquito NF.XVII aircraft. On the same day No 222 Squadron left for Acklington, Northumberland. On 14th the advanced party of No 316 (Polish) Squadron arrived from Acklington followed by the rest of the squadron and its Spitfires two days later. It was the third Polish squadron to be based at Woodvale and immediately took over the sector fighter-interceptor role from 222 Squadron. The squadron took part in army co-operation exercises on 22nd February plus another on 25th. On this day four Spitfires from 322 Squadron spent a night at Woodvale en route to the APC at Ayr unable to carry on due to bad weather. Next day they were replaced by aircraft from No 349 Squadron routing the other way and again stopped for refuelling but were unable to continue with more bad weather en route. On 2nd March a Halifax from Skipton-on-Swale, Yorks landed with one engine unserviceable.

Number 219 returned from leave to find its new Mosquitoes waiting for them. These were night fighters equipped with AI (Airborne Interception) radar and carried a crew of two, pilot and navigator. The navigator had to operate this new equipment and an AI equipped Wellington was detached to Woodvale to train the navigators on this equipment. Woodvale was deemed to be unsuitable for this work so the squadron moved to Honiley, Warwickshire in April. This was the end of night fighters based at Woodvale to provide night cover for the Woodvale sector. Business chasing Luftwaffe was at an all time low and it was considered safe to rely on units outside the sector for this cover. The day fighter squadron No 316 lost a pilot on 21st March when Flt Sgt Kowalski crashed in a Spitfire LFVb. He was buried at Formby but it is assumed he was exhumed and buried elsewhere as the whereabouts of the grave is not known.

Early 1944 saw Woodvale as busy as ever, a Skua for 776 Squadron crashed into the sea off Ainsdale but the pilot was uninjured. There were several scrambles for 316 but no sight of enemy aircraft. Number 341 Squadron was accommodated over night on 8th March and on 18th three squadrons, Nos 438, 439 and 440, landed for refuelling their Typhoons. On the same day a P-38 from BAD#2 at Warton crashed in the sand dunes immediately west of the airfield whilst attempting to land, killing the pilot, Lt H W Vallee. An FAA Hurricane was diverted to Woodvale in an emergency on 11th March followed by three Fireflies from Burscough on 31st.

On 13th April, 316 Squadron heard that they were to re-equip with Mustangs and by 23rd, sixteen Mustang Mk IIIs had arrived. They converted themselves to the new aircraft which gave them better range and performance over the Spitfire Vbs they had been operating up to then. They were kept operational for the sector defence on Spitfires until happy they could operate the Mustang satisfactorily. It was not uncommon to see ten Mustangs in formation over west Lancashire as they converted and got used to their new mounts. Their first scramble was to escort a lost Wellington in to land. Unfortunately for Woodvale they were moved to Coltishall, Norfolk on 29th April. Here they undertook shipping patrols, convoy escorts and scrambles, not dissimilar to their role at Woodvale. Their first action was on 2nd June on a 'Day Ranger' exercise over Holland.

As usual the fighter defence was retained and No 63 Squadron replaced 316. It arrived from Turnhouse on 27th April flying Hurricanes but actually converting to Spitfire Vbs at the time. They soon completed the conversion and provided two aircraft at dawn-to-dusk readiness with two others available at 30 minutes' availability. The rest of the time was spent converting, undertaking training and practising sweeps in the sector. With enemy activity low, the squadron improved their cover by sending a detachment to Ballyhalbert, Northern Ireland and another to Dundonald, Ayrshire so they could cover the whole of the northern part of the Irish Sea. Sorties were extended to include air-sea rescue searches, army co-operation and interception exercises. The two detachments were recalled on 28th May but not before the Squadron lost Fg Off G L Storey who spun in whilst in a steep turn and crashed into some houses in Ainsdale. His Spitfire burst into flames and he was killed and two civilians were badly burned attempting to rescue him.

The CO, Squadron Ldr M A Doniger, was given short notice that the squadron was to relocate to Lee-on-Solent, Hampshire on 28th May and the unit left that day leaving Woodvale devoid of any fighter cover for the first time. What no one realized was that the Invasion of France was about to begin and every available squadron was brought south ready to support D-Day. It is amazing how such an operation was kept so secret. The pilot of a Woodvale based No 285 Squadron Beaufighter, Warrant Officer S Craven, would not have realized the importance of his role when he carried the Orders of the Day from General Eisenhower, the Supreme Allied Commander, to Northern Ireland on that 6th June 1944! Nor would 63 Squadron have realised why they had to move south so quickly. They flew air cover sorties over the invasion beaches and with the beaches well secured in Allied hands they were allowed to return to Woodvale on 3rd July having gained nine Spitfires whilst at Lee. A detachment was again placed at Ballyhalbert, but their new role was to be tactical reconnaissance so their training was to concentrate on army co-operation but no suitable facilities existed near Woodvale. On 4th July they were scrambled to shoot down a barrage balloon which had broken free and on 14th two more were scrambled to try to locate a Dakota which had crashed into the sea but without success. The squadron sought co-operation with the Mustang OTU, No 41 at Hawarden but endured a rather inactive period at Woodvale and moved back to Lee-on-Solent on 30th August after recalling its three detachments at Eshott, Northumberland, Peterhead, Aberdeenshire and Ballyhalbert, Co Down.

Woodvale was now permanently without a fighter squadron and with the continued success in Europe and so little enemy air activity in the Lancashire area the Sector Control Room in Broad Lane was closed on 4th August 1944. The sector was enlarged and came under the control of Church Fenton, Yorkshire. As the status of Woodvale was reduced (not being a Sector station any more) the rank of the CO was downgraded and after a series of rapid changes finally settled when Wing Commander C R Sturwick arrived on 24th August.

HQ No 9 Group at Preston closed down on 15th September and was absorbed into No 12 group at Watnall, Nottinghamshire with no fighters based in north-west England but the Typhoons of No 3 Tactical Exercise Unit at Annan, Dumfriesshire, were tasked to provide cover if required.

With the Blenheims of the 'W' Detachment returning to Grantham in August and no day or night fighter squadron in residence, Woodvale still housed No 285 Squadron, No 776 Squadron detachment, No 116 Squadron detachment. It also had a detachment of No 650 Squadron

Aerial view of control tower, 1945 (Author)

which arrived on 18th June with two Hurricanes for Army co-operation. The HQ was at Cark and there was one other detachment at Netheravon, Wiltshire. So, although not housing a front line squadron the base was still very busy indeed and continued to receive a large number of visitors. One reason was the Palace Hotel in Birkdale, Southport. This huge Victorian hotel (now demolished but its pub, the Fisherman's Rest, remains, in Weld Road) was taken over by the American Red Cross for rest and rehabilitation of mostly USAAF personnel. The Palace Hotel was the first where both officers and enlisted men were allowed to use the same facilities, which greatly helped keeping a complete bomber crew together. Many were flown in and Woodvale was the nearest airfield to the hotel. In one week, ending 5th August 1944, for example, the following aircraft visited Woodvale: four Anson Is, one Tiger Moth, one Miles Master, three Martinet TTIs, two UC-78 Brasshats, four B-24 Liberators, two B-17 Flying Fortresses, a Spitfire VB, a Reliant CI and an A-20 Boston.

A Dakota air ambulance aircraft landed at Woodvale at 23.30 on 10th

August with 24 wounded on board. The aircraft had been flying around the west coast of England for four hours and was unable to land due to bad weather. The men on board were becoming very frightened as most had never even flown before and had little or no food for eight to nine hours. They were immediately admitted into the station sick quarters for the night as the nearest US hospital was over 40 miles away in Warrington. The 24 filled all the empty beds and the WAAF ward! But the Red Cross at the Palace Hotel were contacted and they provided many excellent comforts. A convoy of ambulances carried the men to the 168th US Hospital at Warrington the following day. A far worse disaster occurred on 25th October 1944 when a USAAF B-24 Liberator crashed on approach in very bad weather. The pilot was guided down by Flying Control with rudimentary equipment. They got him to the end of the runway in near zero visibility and as he saw the runway he had to turn to line up properly, he was so low that a wing caught the ground causing the aircraft to cartwheel and crash. Some of the men were thrown out on impact and survived but four were killed outright and three more died later in station sick quarters. The remaining thirteen were taken to hospital and survived. The aircraft was bringing US personnel to the Palace Hotel. The pilot lost his wristwatch in the accident but it was found at the site and returned to him still working!

The exodus of squadrons from Woodvale continued with No 285 Squadron moving out on 11th November to Andover, Hampshire. As often happened here the gap was partly filled by a detachment of No 577 Squadron which moved in from Sealand, Flint, on the same day. This unit had a monthly target of 400 flying hours of army co-operation with its Hurricanes and Oxfords. During the month all aircraft were moved to another dispersal and rendered immobile at night and were guarded because information had been received that German prisoners of war were planning an escape. However this did not materialise.

Christmas 1944 was quieter than the previous year but the station still managed to put on a pantomime and dances and parties took place as usual. In January 577 Squadron commenced co-operation duties with No 19 Initial Training Camp at Harrington Barracks in Formby, with the military College of Science at Bury, east Lancashire and also supplementing No 776 Squadron on RN co-operation. On 22nd March 650 Squadron withdrew its detachment, leaving only two detachments at Woodvale from 776 and 577 Squadrons. The threat from the Luftwaffe was now zero and there was plenty of space at Woodvale for other units. The living quarters were adequate and the men and women stationed there enjoyed their off-duty time in Southport or Liverpool. The permanent staff were naturally wondering what would become of the base. Their questions were answered when the RAF agreed to pass control of Woodvale to the Fleet Air Arm and Woodvale was to become a satellite (or tender in naval terms) to HMS *Ringtail* at Burscough, a few miles east. Number 577 Squadron was to remain as a lodger unit but 776 was an FAA squadron with its HQ at Speke which immediately relocated to Woodvale. A Navy party moved in to 'navalise' Woodvale. The records do not state exactly what they did but station HQ would be renamed the Quarterdeck, the messes would become wardrooms and the barracks would become cabins plus the toilets would become 'heads'.

The war in Europe was looking as if it would now be won but the war in the Pacific was far from over so the FAA was building up its ships, carriers and flying units ready to depart as a matter of urgency. Hence Woodvale was commissioned as HMS *Ringtail II* on 7th April 1945. The FAA was not slow in bringing in aircraft. All the Rocs, Chesapeakes, Skuas, Martinet and Seafires of 776 Squadron moved into Woodvale closely followed by No 889 Squadron which reformed here on 1st June. This squadron had disbanded in Ceylon (now Sri Lanka) and had received six Grumman Hellcats by 1st July. This was followed by B Flight of No 736 Squadron which was a fighter affiliation unit and arrived from Hal Far in Malta with Seafires, Beaufighters and a Dominie. The fourth Naval unit to arrive was No 816 squadron which arrived from Machrihanish, Argyll on 1st July with 12 Firefly FR.Is. Once fully worked up, this unit moved to Inskip on 11th August making room for No 822 Squadron which moved in from Belfast on 29th August also with Fireflies. Thus Woodvale now had three front line and two second line units stationed there with feverish flying as the units worked up ready to face the Japanese. Events on 15th August suddenly stalled all these efforts when the war in Japan dramatically ended as a result of the two atomic bombs dropped by the Americans. Suddenly there was no requirement for FAA units or Woodvale. One Squadron, 889, had already had a short embarkation on HMS *Ravager* off the Lancashire coast and was at Belfast during August working up with HMS *Trouncer* only to be recalled to Woodvale and disbanded on 10th September. B Flight of 736 Squadron disbanded on 26th September; followed on 4th October when 822 Squadron relocated back to Burscough and two days later the very last FAA aircraft departed as 776 Squadron also moved to Burscough. The RAF remained for two days before 577 Squadron moved to Barrow leaving

Woodvale devoid of any aircraft or life.

Woodvale, like many hundreds of 'temporary' Second World War airfields had been built in haste, rapidly became extremely busy and protected Merseyside against the Luftwaffe for four years. It appeared likely that it would close. The FAA would hand it back to the RAF who would place it under care and maintenance only to eventually dispose of it. However this was not to be the case. Formby Council was quick off the mark suggesting that Woodvale should become Southport airport. This was contested by Southport who did not want it but their arguments came to an end when the Air Ministry announced that the Auxiliary squadrons disbanded at the end of the Second World War would reform and 611 (West Lancashire) Squadron would reform at Woodvale with effect from 22nd July 1946. The squadron was originally to reform at its original pre-war base at Speke, then it was to be Hooton Park, Cheshire but it eventually reformed here where excellent facilities existed. Woodvale had been immediately reclaimed from the FAA and No 5 MT Company moved in from Sefton Park, Liverpool with a vast fleet of vehicles but their requirement had diminished and they disbanded in September 1946 leaving the airfield available for 611 Squadron and their Spitfire XIVs. These were upgraded to F.22s and eventually the squadron took on Meteor F4 jet fighters in 1951. For this the main runway was extended slightly northwards and a new Bellman hangar constructed on the main site to accommodate the higher tail of the Meteor. No sooner had this been completed than 611 were moved to Hooton Park and the units there moved to Woodvale. No 19 Reserve Flying School, University of Liverpool Air Squadron and the THUM Flight all arrived in July 1951 flying Chipmunks, Oxfords, Ansons and Tiger Moth; Chipmunk and Spitfire PR19 respectively.

THUM stood for Temperature and HUMidity and was a meteorological flight making daily flights to take readings at different altitudes for our national weather forecast. This unit gave up its Spitfires for Mosquitoes in 1957 and the three retiring Spitfires were the last to fly routine RAF sorties in the UK and formed the basis of the Battle of Britain Memorial Flight. Two of the original three were still flying with the Flight in 1994. The RFS closed in July 1954. Manchester University Air Squadron arrived with Chipmunks in 1953 and the THUM Flight disbanded in May 1959. Number 5 CAACU operated Meteors from Woodvale from January 1958 to June 1971. Number 10 AEF formed in December 1958 to provide Air Cadets with air experience in Chipmunks, being one of 13 formed around the country.

Most of the dispersed living sites were closed immediately after the Second World War with many becoming temporary homes for squatters displaced from their homes in Liverpool by enemy bombing. The final sites (Communal with Officers' and Sergeants' Messes) were vacated and all were demolished by the early 1960s.

Woodvale is still an active RAF station housing Manchester & Salford UAS, Liverpool USA and No 10 AEF, all flying Tutor aircraft. It also houses HQ Merseyside Wing ATC, the Merseyside Police Helicopter and various privately owned aircraft. The new Officers' Mess was built in the late 1990s and only one of the original three hangars remains. Most of the Second World War buildings have been replaced with more modern buildings, or substantially improved. Three runways remain available for aircraft, no dispersals are now to be seen but the original control tower still dominates the airfield. RAF Woodvale provides a perfect buffer to stop urban sprawl between Formby and Southport and long may it remain in RAF colours. Throughout the RAF, Woodvale is said to be 'known only to a few, but forgotten by none'!

ACKNOWLEDGEMENTS

I have been overwhelmed by the help and support I have received from my friends and fellow aviation enthusiasts and airfield historians in the North West of England. I have called for favours from specialists on specific airfields and every one has fallen over backwards to help. To you all I thank you most sincerely and am in your debt.

In no specific order I would like to thank the following: Russell Brown and Mark Gaskell (Lancashire Aircraft Investigation Team); Chris J Foulds; Ray Jones (Burscough), Mike Lewis (*Rapide* Magazine); David J Smith (Speke, Cark and others); John Mulliner (Hesketh Park); Lloyd Robinson; Harry Holmes (Warton); Roger Thomas (English Heritage); Barry Abraham (Airfield Research Group); Mr Williams from Ramsgate (Burscough); Euen P Jones (1820 Sqn Burscough); Glynn Griffiths (curator Haverigg (Millom) Museum); Brian Tomlinson and all at BAe Systems North West Heritage Group (Samlesbury); Jerry Shore (Fleet Air Arm Museum, Yeovilton); Chris Jones (BAe Systems); J W Appleby (Barrow); James C J Paul (Barrow); Peter Yuile (Barrow/Walney Island); R Alan Scholefield (Barton); Phil Butler (Speke); Lt Cdr Iain Wallace (Inskip); Lt Cdr Philip Furse RN (Retd) (Inskip); Richard Riding (former Editor of *Aeroplane Monthly*); Jim Buey (Chairman Manchester Branch FAA Association), George B Gosney deceased (BAD#2) plus fellow members of the BAD#1 and BAD#2 Associations, many of whom have generously loaned or gifted material on Burtonwood and Warton respectively.

I have taken extracts from dozens of sources including the web site of the Lancashire Aircraft Investigation Team; *Rapide*, the Magazine of the North West Vintage Aviation Enthusiast and its predecessor *Swift*; *FlyPast* when it was the Magazine of the Merseyside Aviation Society and the current *FlyPast* (same Editor – Ken Ellis); *Aviation News*; *Aircraft Illustrated*; *The Aeroplane*; *Air Pictorial* and many others.

Additionally I have used the records at the National Archive in Kew specifically the Air 27 and Air 28 documents for RAF station and unit histories; plus numerous personal memories and records and my own extensive archive on military aviation in the North West.

BIBLIOGRAPHY

Action Stations 3 Military Airfields of the North-West, by David J Smith. Patrick Stephens, 1981. ISBN 0-85059-485-5

Aircraft of the Royal Air Force since 1918, by Owen Thetford. Putnam & Company, London. ISBN 0 370 10056 5

Bombers over Merseyside, The Authoritive Record of the Blitz 1940-41, Liverpool Daily Post & Echo, 1943

Dizzy Heights, The Story of Lancashire's First Flying Men, by Chris Aspin. Helmshore Local History Society, 1988. ISBN 0 906881 04 8

Aircraft Factories, Origins, Development and Archaeology, by A D George. Manchester Polytechnic Occasional paper, November 1986.

An Illustrated History of Liverpool Airport, by Phil Butler. Merseyside Aviation Society, May 1983. ISBN 0 902420 40 2

Port at War, Mersey Docks and Harbour Board, 1946

Rapide, The Magazine for the North-West Vintage Aviation Enthusiast. (Various issues). Published by Coulton-Lewis Communications, 7 Lawn Drive, Upton, Chester CH2 1ER

Royal Air Force Flying Training and Support Units, by Ray Sturtivant, John Hamlin and James J Halley. Air-Britain (Historians) Ltd, 1997. ISBN 0 85130 252 1

20th Century Defences in Britain – An Introductory Guide. Handbook of The Defence of Great Britain Project. Council for British Archaeology, 1996. Reprinted 2001. ISBN 1 872414 74 5

Royal Air Force Woodvale, by Aldon P Ferguson. Airfield Publications, 1991. ISBN 0 9511113 2 9

Eighth Air Force Base Air Depot – RAF Burtonwood, by Aldon P Ferguson. Airfield Publications, 1986. ISBN 0 9511113 0 2

Royal Air Force Burtonwood – Fifty Years in Photographs, by Aldon P Ferguson. Airfield Publications, Wargrave, Berks, 2002. ISBN 0 9511113 1 0

Prisoner of War Camps (1939-1948) a Twentieth Century Military Recording Project, by Roger J C Thomas. English Heritage via

National Monuments Record Service, Swindon, 2003 Available on internet at www.English-Heritage.org.uk

Fields of Deception, Britain's Bombing Decoys of World War Two, by Colin Dobinson. Methuen Printing & English Heritage, 2000. ISBN 1 357 910864 2

English Electric Aircraft and their Predecessors, by Stephen Ransom and Robert Fairclough, 1987. Putnam. ISBN 0 85177 806 2

Flypast, journal of the Merseyside Aviation Society (now *Air-Britain* (Merseyside) Branch) particularly article on Samlesbury dated September 1985

RAF Squadrons, by Wing Commander C G Jefford. *Airlife*, Shrewsbury, 2001. ISBN 1 84037 141 2

Coastal, Support & Special Squadrons of the RAF and their Aircraft, by John D R Rawlings. Jane's London, 1982. ISBN 07106 0187 5

British Military Airfield Architecture, by Paul Francis. Patrick Stephens Ltd, Sparkford, 1996. ISBN 1 85260 462 X

Military Airfields in the British Isles 1939–1945 Parts 1, 2 & 3, by Steve Willis and Barry Holliss. Enthusiasts Publications, Newport Pagnell, 1981

Sun, Sand and Silver Wings (The story of Aviation on the Southport & South West Lancashire Coast from 1910 to 2003), by John Mulliner. Hobby Publications, 2004. ISBN 1 872839 09 6

Liverpool Airport – An Illustrated History, by Phil Butler. Tempus Publishing Ltd, The Mill, Brimscombe Port, Stroud, Glos GL5 2QG, 2004. ISBN 0 7524 3168 4

British Naval Aircraft since 1912, by Owen Thetford. Putman, London. ISBN 0370 30021 1

The Squadrons of the Fleet Air Arm, by Ray Sturtivant and Theo Ballance. Air-Britain, Tonbridge, Kent. ISBN 0 85130 223 8

The World's Greatest Air Depot, The US 8th Air Force at Warton 1942-45, by Harry Holmes. Airlife Publishing Ltd, Shrewsbury, 1998. ISBN 1 85310 969 X

Warton in Wartime, by Harry Holmes. Tempus Publishing Ltd, Stroud, Glos, 2001. ISBN 0 7524 2120 4

Magazines including *FlyPast, Aircraft Illustrated, Air Pictorial, RAF Flying Review, Airfield Review, RAF News*.

INDEX

283

RAF Units
Squadrons

Other Units